WEST-E

020

English Language, Literature, and Composition

Teacher Certification Exam

By: Sharon Wynne, M.S.
Southern Connecticut State University

"And, while there's no reason yet to panic, I think it's only prudent that we make preparations to panic."

XAMonline, INC.
Boston

To obtain permission(s) to use the material from this work for any purpose including workshops or seminars, please submit a written request to:

XAMonline, Inc.
25 First St. Suite 106
Cambridge MA 01141
Toll Free 1-800-509-4128
Email: info@xamonline.com
Web www.xamonline.com
Fax: 1-781-662-9268

Library of Congress Cataloging-in-Publication Data

Wynne, Sharon A.
      English Language, Literature, and Composition 10041: Teacher
      Certification / Sharon A. Wynne. -2nd ed. ISBN 978-1-60787-139-2
      1. English Language Literature and Composition 10041.
      2. Study Guides.   3.WEST_E
      4. Teachers' Certification & Licensure.   5. Careers

Disclaimer:
The opinions expressed in this publication are the sole works of XAMonline and were created independently from the National Education Association, Educational Testing Service, or any State Department of Education, National Evaluation Systems or other testing affiliates.

Between the time of publication and printing, state specific standards as well as testing formats and website information may change that is not included in part or in whole within this product. Sample test questions are developed by XAMonline and reflect similar content as on real tests; however, they are not former tests. XAMonline assembles content that aligns with state standards but makes no claims nor guarantees teacher candidates a passing score. Numerical scores are determined by testing companies such as NES or ETS and then are compared with individual state standards. A passing score varies from state to state.

Printed in the United States of America   œ-1

West-E: English Language, Literature, and Composition 0041
ISBN: 978-1-60787- 139-2

About the WEST-E/Praxis II Examination in English Language, Literature, and Composition

The Praxis Examination in English is broken down into four sections:

Content Knowledge
Up to 5 hours (examinees may take more than one test per session)

Categories
1.0 Reading Process and Comprehension
        25% of the exam
2.0 Literature and Language
        30% of the exam
3.0 Writing Process and Applications
        30% of the exam
4.0 Oral and Visual Communication
        15% of the exam

Essays
2 hours—4 Essay questions

Categories
4.0 Interpreting Literature: Poetry
        1 question—25% of the exam
5.0 Interpreting Literature: Prose
        1 question—25% of the exam
6.0 Issues in English: Understanding Literary Issues
        1 question—25% of the exam
7.0 Issues in English: Literary Issues and Literary Texts
        1 question—25% of the exam

Pedagogy
1 hour—2 Constructed Response questions

Categories
8.0 Teaching Literature
        1 question—50% of the exam
9.0 Responding to Student Writing
        1 question—50% of the exam

Essay Scoring

For **Competencies 4.0-7.0**, responses are graded holistically. The score range is 0 to 3.

A score of 3:
- Analyzes the specified literary element/central idea/literary issue in the selection accurately and with some depth.
- Paraphrases or summarizes the central idea fully and accurately.
- Shows a sound understanding of the selection.
- Supports points with appropriate examples from the selection and explains how the examples support those points.
- Is coherent and demonstrates control of language, including diction and syntax.
- Demonstrates facility with the conventions of standard written English.
- For the Literary Issues question: Develops a thesis according to the demands of the question and uses appropriate examples from two literary works to support the thesis.

A score of 2:
- Analyzes the specified literary elements/central idea/literary issue in the selection with overall accuracy but may overlook or misinterpret some elements.
- Demonstrates understanding of the selection but may contain some misreadings.
- Supports points with appropriate examples from the selection but may fail to explain how the examples support those points.
- Is coherent and demonstrates control of language, including diction and syntax.
- Displays control of the conventions of standard written English but may have some flaws.

A score of 1:
Demonstrates some ability to engage with the selection/issue statement but is flawed in one or more of the following ways:
- Incorrectly identifies literary elements in the selection or provides a superficial analysis of those elements.
- Inaccurately paraphrases or summarizes the central idea.
- Demonstrates an insufficient or inaccurate understanding of the selection.
- Fails to support points with appropriate examples from the selection.
- Lacks coherence or has serious problems with the control of language, including diction and syntax.
- Contains serious and persistent writing errors.

A score of 0:
>   A zero is given for blank papers, off-topic responses, responses containing severely inaccurate or incoherent observations, or responses that merely rephrase the question.

Pedagogy Scoring

Competency 8.0 Teaching Literature

The question consists of three parts. The score range is 0 to 6. Points are distributed as follows:

Part A—2 points
>   1 point for each appropriate literary feature central to the work of literature. Each literary feature must be specific to the work chosen and appropriate for the grade level.

Part B—2 points
>   1 point for each appropriate obstacle to understanding, including the explanation for why the obstacle is likely. Each obstacle must be specific to the work chosen and appropriate for the grade level.

Part C—2 points
>   1 point for the discussion of each appropriate instructional activity designed to help students understand the literary features and/or overcome obstacles to understanding. Each instructional activity must be specific to the work chosen and appropriate for the grade level.

If the response contains a significant number of errors in the conventions of standard written English, one point will be subtracted from the total points earned for the question. Responses on a literary work other than one chosen from the list provided in the question will receive a score of 0.

The criteria for evaluating whether a literary feature, obstacle, or instructional activity is "appropriate" are established through a "model answers" methodology. This methodology is described as follows.

The "Model Answers" Methodology

For each question, experienced English teachers are asked to write representative responses that, in their estimation, are consistent with the knowledge that prospective beginning English teachers should have. These teachers are carefully chosen to represent the diverse perspectives and situations relevant to the testing population.

The question writer uses these "model answers" to develop a question-specific scoring guide for the question, creating a list of specific examples that would receive full credit. This list is considered to contain *examples* of correct answers, not all the possible correct answers.

The question-specific scoring guides based on model answers provide the basis for choosing the papers that will serve as benchmark and sample papers for the purpose of training the scorers at the scoring session for the question.

During the scoring session while reading student papers, scorers can add new answers to the scoring guide as they see fit.

Training at the scoring session is aimed to ensure that scorers do not score papers on the basis of their opinions or their own preferences but rather make judgments based on the carefully established criteria in the scoring guide.

Competency 9.0 Responding to Student Writing

The question consists of four parts. The score range is 0 to 6. Points are distributed as follows.

Part A—1 point for the identification of one significant strength and explanation of how it contributes to the paper's effectiveness.

Part B—1 point for the identification of one significant weakness and explanation of how it interferes with the paper's effectiveness.

Part C—2 points: 1 point for the correct identification of each of the two specific errors.

Part D—2 points for the discussion of the follow-up assignment that is connected to the strengths or weaknesses of the student's paper and that contributes to the development of the student as a writer.

If the response contains a significant number of errors in the conventions of standard written English, one point will be subtracted from the total points earned for the question. Responses on a literary work other than one chosen from the list provided in the question will receive a score of 0.

The criteria for evaluating whether a strength, weakness, error, or follow-up assignment is awarded the point or points are established through the "Model Answers" methodology. See the above description.

TABLE OF CONTENTS

COMPETENCY 10 HISTORICAL, SOCIAL, AND CULTURAL ASPECTS OF LITERATURES FROM AROUND THE WORLD

Skill 10.1 Demonstrate knowledge of the common structural and stylistic elements of and shared themes in literary works from the oral tradition.

Skill 10.2 Analyze how social and cultural issues and issues relating to gender, sexual orientation, and ethnicity are explored in traditional and contemporary literature for adolescents and young adults.

Skill 10.3 Analyze how writers from diverse cultural backgrounds and various historical periods have commented on major historical events.

Skill 10.4 Analyze how writers from diverse cultural backgrounds and various historical periods have influenced public opinion about and understanding of social and cultural issues through their literary works.

Skill 10.4 Analyze the expression of specific cultural values, ideas, and attitudes in literary works.

COMPETENCY 11 THE SHAPING OF THE ENGLISH LANGUAGE BY HISTORICAL, SOCIAL, CULTURAL, AND TECHNOLOGICAL INFLUENCES

Skill 11.1 Recognize the significance of historical events that have influenced the development of the English language.

Skill 11.2 Recognize the effects of technological innovations on the English language.

Skill 11.3 Relate English derivatives and borrowings, including slang terms, to their origins in other languages.

Skill 11.4 Recognize regional and social variations in language in the United States.

COMPETENCY 12 THE WRITING PROCESS.

Skill 12.1 Demonstrate knowledge of ways to generate content for writing.

Skill 12.2 Demonstrate knowledge of ways to organize ideas before writing.

Skill 12.3 Determine the audience and purpose of writing.

Skill 12.4   Recognize methods of drafting text so that it shows consistent development of a central idea.

Skill 12.5   Recognize methods of revising text to eliminate wordiness, ambiguity, redundancy, and clichés.

Skill 12.6   Recognize methods of revising text to clarify meaning.

Skill 12.7   Recognize methods of editing text so that it conforms to the conventions of Standard American English.

Skill 12.8   Demonstrate familiarity with proofreading techniques and other tools used to finalize a text for publishing.

COMPETENCY 13 ELEMENTS OF EFFECTIVE COMPOSITION

Skill 13.1   Recognize effective ways to present original ideas or perspectives in a text clearly, concisely, and coherently.

Skill 13.2   Recognize the appropriate organizational structure/format, tone/voice, and word choice for various writing purposes and audiences.

Skill 13.3   Recognize methods of developing an introduction to a text that draws a reader's attention, specifies the topic or issue, or provides a thesis.

Skill 13.4   Recognize effective ways to organize ideas in a text.

Skill 13.5   Recognize effective ways to emphasize, link, and contrast important ideas in a text.

Skill 13.6   Recognize effective ways to incorporate graphic features in a text.

Skill 13.7   Recognize methods of developing a conclusion to a text that provides a restatement or summary of ideas, a resolution, or a suggested course of action.

COMPETENCY 14 CONVENTIONS OF STANDARD AMERICAN ENGLISH

Skill 14.1   Demonstrate knowledge of the conventions of capitalization.

Skill 14.2   Demonstrate knowledge of the conventions of punctuation.

Skill 14.3   Demonstrate knowledge of the conventions of spelling.

Skill 14.4   Demonstrate knowledge of the correct use of the parts of speech in sentences.

Skill 14.5   Recognize ways to form simple, compound, complex, and compound-complex sentences in which there is subject–verb and pronoun–antecedent agreement.

COMPETENCY 15 EXPOSITORY WRITING

Skill 15.1   Demonstrate knowledge of forms of writing that are appropriate for describing events, providing information, or answering questions.

Skill 15.2   Demonstrate the ability to select an appropriate subject or topic for writing and to formulate a fundamental question for addressing through writing.

Skill 15.3   Determine appropriate primary sources and secondary sources for locating and gathering information about a subject or topic.

Skill 15.4   Evaluate the relevance and reliability of information sources.

Skill 15.5   Recognize methods of developing a thesis statement that expresses the central idea of a piece of writing.

Skill 15.6   Demonstrate the ability to select an appropriate organizational structure or pattern for developing ideas in writing.

Skill 15.7   Demonstrate knowledge of methods of paraphrasing, summarizing, and quoting sources appropriately and of acknowledging and documenting sources to avoid plagiarism.

COMPETENCY 16 NARRATIVE WRITING

Skill 16.1   Demonstrate knowledge of forms of writing that are appropriate for expressing personal thoughts and feelings, exploring various points of view, or telling a story.

Skill 16.2   Recognize specific details that are important to include in narrative writing to achieve an effect or fulfill a purpose.

Skill 16.3   Apply strategies for composing narrative writing by presenting characters and actions.

Skill 16.4   Apply strategies for interpreting and evaluating the motives of characters and the causes of actions.

Skill 16.5 Apply strategies for composing narrative writing that makes effective and appropriate use of various literary elements.

Skill 16.6 Apply strategies for writing personal notes, letters, and stories that convey a message or point of view clearly and concisely and that engage and maintain the reader's interest.

COMPETENCY 17 PERSUASIVE WRITING

Skill 17.1 Demonstrate knowledge of forms of writing that are appropriate for influencing beliefs, arguing a point, or expressing an opinion.

Skill 17.2 Demonstrate the ability to assess the interests and knowledge of the intended audience for persuasive writing.

Skill 17.3 Demonstrate the ability to establish a clear position or controlling idea.

Skill 17.4 Demonstrate the ability to present an argument logically through the use of meaningful examples or details, sound reasoning, and effective transitions.

Skill 17.5 Demonstrate the ability to present an argument through the use of rhetorical appeals.

Skill 17.6 Demonstrate the ability to select relevant, complete, and accurate information or evidence from primary and secondary sources that can be used to support points expressed in persuasive writing.

Skill 17.7 Demonstrate the ability to anticipate questions, concerns, and counterarguments for points expressed in persuasive writing and to incorporate effective responses to them into the writing.

COMPETENCY 18 LISTENING AND SPEAKING.

Skill 18.1 Identify the characteristics and purposes of various types of listening, including critical, empathic, reflective, and deliberative.

Skill 18.2 Demonstrate knowledge of the barriers to listening effectively, including selective listening.

Skill 18.3 Apply strategies for listening actively.

Skill 18.4 Distinguish among types of speech delivery that are appropriate for various purposes, content, audiences, and occasions.

Skill 18.5   Distinguish among styles of language that are appropriate for various purposes, content, audiences, and occasions.

Skill 18.6   Demonstrate knowledge of rhetorical strategies used to enhance clarity and generate interest in speeches.

Skill 18.7   Recognize the different roles that voice and body language play in speech delivery.

COMPETENCY 19 PRESENTATIONS.

Skill 19.1   Recognize methods of establishing clear objectives for a presentation.

Skill 19.2   Recognize methods of organizing a presentation to achieve objectives and meet an audience's needs and expectations.

Skill 19.3   Recognize methods of modifying a presentation to better correspond to the specific characteristics of various audiences.

Skill 19.4   Recognize methods of incorporating appropriate and effective visual aids into a presentation to reinforce a message, clarify a point, or create excitement and interest.

Skill 19.5   Demonstrate knowledge of appropriate technologies and media to produce various types of communications and to convey specific messages.

COMPETENCY 20 USING VISUAL IMAGES IN VARIOUS MEDIA

Skill 20.1   Recognize messages, meanings, and themes conveyed through various visual images in various media.

Skill 20.2   Recognize how certain media combinations are used to emphasize and reinforce messages, meanings, and themes.

Skill 20.3   Analyze how the elements of visual images are manipulated to convey particular messages, meanings, and themes.

Skill 20.4   Analyze how visual images are used to change behavior and influence public opinion by appealing to reason, emotion, authority, and convention.

GREAT STUDY AND TESTING TIPS!

What to study in order to prepare for the subject assessments is the focus of this study guide but equally important is *how* you study.

You can increase your chances of truly mastering the information by taking some simple but effective steps.

Study Tips:

1. **Some foods aid the learning process.** Foods such as milk, nuts, seeds, rice, and oats help your study efforts by releasing natural memory enhancers called CCKs (*cholecystokinin*) composed of *tryptophan*, *choline*, and *phenylalanine*. All of these chemicals enhance the neurotransmitters associated with memory. Before studying, try a light, protein-rich meal of eggs, turkey, and fish. All of these foods release the memory-enhancing chemicals. The better the connections, the more you comprehend.

    Likewise, before you take a test, stick to a light snack of energy boosting and relaxing foods. A glass of milk, a piece of fruit, or some peanuts all release various memory-boosting chemicals and help you to relax and focus on the subject at hand.

2. **Learn to take great notes.** A by-product of our modern culture is that we have grown accustomed to getting our information in short doses (i.e. TV news sound bites or *USA Today*-style newspaper articles.)

    Consequently, we've subconsciously trained ourselves to assimilate information better in **neat little packages**. If you scrawl notes all over the paper, you fragment the flow of the information. Strive for clarity.

    Newspapers use a standard format to achieve clarity. Your notes can be much clearer through use of proper formatting. A very effective format is called the Cornell Method.

    *   Take a sheet of loose-leaf lined notebook paper and draw a line all the way down the paper about 1-2" from the left-hand edge.

    *   Draw another line across the width of the paper about 1-2" up from the bottom. Repeat this process on the reverse side of the page.

    Look at the highly effective result. You have ample room for notes, a left-hand margin for special emphasis items or inserting supplementary data from the textbook, a large area at the bottom for a brief summary, and a little rectangular space for just about anything you want.

3. **Get the concept, and then the details.** Too often we focus on the details and don't gather an understanding of the concept. However, if you simply memorize only dates, places, or names, you may well miss the whole point of the subject.

   A key way to understand things is to put them in your own words. If you are working from a textbook, automatically summarize each paragraph in your mind. If you are outlining text, don't simply copy the author's words.

   Rephrase them in your own words. You remember your own thoughts and words much better than someone else's, and you subconsciously tend to associate the important details to the core concepts.

4. **Ask Why.** Pull apart written material paragraph by paragraph and don't forget the captions under the illustrations.

   Example: If the heading is "Stream Erosion," flip it around to read "Why do streams erode?" Then answer the questions.

   If you train your mind to think in a series of questions and answers, not only will you learn more but you will also lessen the test anxiety because you are used to answering questions.

5. **Read for reinforcement and future needs.** Even if you only have 10 minutes, put your notes or a book in your hand. Your mind is similar to a computer; you have to input data in order to have it processed. *By reading, you are creating the neural connections for future retrieval.* The more times you read something, the more you reinforce the learning of ideas.

   Even if you don't fully understand something on the first pass, *your mind stores much of the material for later recall.*

6. **Relax to learn so go into exile.** Our bodies respond to an inner clock called biorhythms. Burning the midnight oil works well for some people, but not everyone.

   If possible, set aside a particular place to study that is free of distractions. Shut off the television, cell phone, and pager and exile your friends and family during your study period.

   If you really are bothered by silence, try background music. Light classical music at a low volume has been shown to aid in concentration.

   Music that evokes pleasant emotions without lyrics are highly suggested. Try just about anything by Mozart. It relaxes you.

7. **Use arrows, not highlighters.** At best, it's difficult to read a page full of yellow, pink, blue, and green streaks.

   Try staring at a neon sign for a while and you'll soon see my point; the horde of colors obscures the message.

   A quick note: a brief dash of color, an underline, and an arrow pointing to a particular passage are much clearer than a horde of highlighted words.

8. **Budget your study time.** Although you shouldn't ignore any of the material, *allocate your available study time in the same ratio that topics may appear on the test.*

Testing Tips:

1. **Get smart, play dumb. Don't read anything into the question.** Don't assume that the test writer is looking for something other than what is asked. Stick to the question as written and don't read extra things into it.

2. **Read the question and all the choices *twice* before answering the question.** You may miss something by not carefully reading and then rereading both the question and the answers.

   If you really don't have a clue as to the right answer, leave it blank on the first time through. Go on to the other questions as they may provide a clue on how to answer the skipped questions.

   If later on, you still can't answer the skipped ones . . . ***Guess.*** The only penalty for guessing is that you *might* get it wrong. Only one thing is certain; if you don't put anything down, you will get it wrong!

3. **Turn the question into a statement.** Look at the way the questions are worded. The syntax of the question usually provides a clue. Does it seem more familiar as a statement rather than as a question? Does it sound strange?

   By turning a question into a statement, you may be able to spot if an answer sounds right, and it may also trigger memories of material you have read.

4. **Look for hidden clues.** It's actually very difficult to compose multiple-foil (choice) questions without giving away part of the answer in the options presented.

In most multiple-choice questions you can often readily eliminate one or two of the potential answers. This leaves you with only two real possibilities and automatically your odds go to fifty-fifty for very little work.

5. **Trust your instincts.** For every fact that you have read, you subconsciously retain something of that knowledge. On questions that you aren't certain about, go with your basic instincts. *Your first impression on how to answer a question is usually correct.*

6. **Mark your answers directly on the test booklet.** Don't bother trying to fill in the optical scan sheet on the first pass through the test. *Just be very careful not to mismark your answers when you eventually transcribe them to the scan sheet.*

7. **Watch the clock!** You have a set amount of time to answer the questions. Don't get bogged down trying to answer a single question at the expense of 10 questions you can more readily answer.

COMPETENCY 1.0   READING PROCESS AND COMPREHENSION

Skill 1.1   Understand the role of phonological and phonemic awareness in the reading process and strategies for developing word identification skills and vocabulary knowledge.

Phonological Awareness

phoneme = sound

Phonological awareness means the ability of the reader to recognize the sounds or phonemes of spoken language. This recognition includes how these sounds can be blended together, segmented (divided up), and manipulated (switched around). This awareness eventually leads to phonics, a method for decoding language by unlocking letter-sound or grapheme-phoneme relationships.

Development of phonological skills for most children begins during the pre-K years. Indeed, by the age of 5, a child who has been exposed to fingerplays and poetry can recognize a rhyme. Such a child can demonstrate phonological awareness by filling in the missing rhyming word in a familiar rhyme or rhymed picture book. The procedure of filling in a missing word is called the cloze procedure. It can be used in oral or print literacy activities.

Children can be taught phonological awareness by directly pointing out the sounds made by letters singly (as in /b/) or in combination (as in /bl/) and by being taught to recognize individual sounds in words.

blended
segmented
manipulated

fill in rhyme = cloze
point out sound -bl

The Role of Phonological Awareness in Reading Development

Instructional methods to teach phonological awareness may include any or all of the following:

1. Auditory games during which children recognize and manipulate the sounds of words, separate or segment the sounds of words, take out sounds, blend sounds, add in new sounds, or take apart sounds to recombine them in new formations.
2. Snap game—the teacher says two words. The children snap their fingers if the two words share a sound, which might be at the beginning or end of the word. Children hear initial phonemes most easily, followed by final ones. Medial or middle sounds are most difficult for young children to discriminate. This can be observed in their oral responses as well as in their invented spelling. Silence occurs if the words share no sounds. Children love this simple game and it also helps with classroom management.
3. Language games model for children identification of rhyming words. These games help inspire children to create their own rhymes.
4. Read books that rhyme such as *Sheep in a Jeep* by Nancy Shaw or *The Fox on a Box* by Barbara Gregorich.
5. Share books that use alliteration (words that begin with the same sound) such as *Avalanche, A to Z*.

Phonemic Awareness

Phonemic awareness is a specific skill within the broader category of phonological awareness. Probably developing fairly late, it is the knowledge that words are comprised of individual phonemes that can be blended. "The two best predictors of early reading success are alphabetic recognition and phonemic awareness" (Marilyn Jaeger Adams).

"In order to benefit from formal reading instruction, children must have a certain level of phonemic awareness. . . . Phonemic awareness is both a prerequisite for and a consequence of learning to read" (Hallie Kay Yopp).

Theorist Marilyn Jager Adams, who researches early reading, has outlined five basic types of phonemic awareness tasks.

Task 1—Ability to hear rhymes and alliteration. For example, the children would listen to a poem, rhyming picture book, or song and identify the rhyming words heard, which the teacher might then record or list on a chart.

Task 2—Ability to do oddity tasks (recognize the member of a set that is different [odd] among the group). For example, the children would look at the pictures of grass, a garden, and a rose, answering this question: Which one starts with a different sound?

Task 3—The ability to orally blend words and split syllables. For example, the children can say the first sound of a word and then the rest of the word and put it together as a single word.

Task 4—The ability to orally segment words. For example, the ability to count sounds. The child would be asked to count or clap the sounds in "hamburger."

Task 5—The ability to do phonics manipulation tasks. For example, replace the "r" sound in rose with a "p" sound.

The Role of Phonemic Awareness in Reading Development

Children who have problems with phonics generally have not acquired or been exposed to phonemic awareness activities at home or in preschool. This includes extensive songs, rhymes, and read–alouds.

Instructional Methods

Since the ability to distinguish between individual sounds or phonemes within words is a prerequisite to the association of sounds with letters and manipulating sounds to blend words—a fancy way of saying "reading"—the teaching of phonemic awareness is crucial to emergent literacy (early childhood K-2 reading instruction). Children need a strong background in phonemic awareness in order for phonics instruction (sound-spelling relationship to printed materials) to be effective.

Instructional methods that may be effective for teaching phonemic awareness can include

1. clapping syllables in words;
2. distinguishing between a word and a sound;
3. using visual cues and movements to help children understand when the speaker goes from one sound to another;
4. incorporating oral segmentation activities that focus on easily-distinguished syllables rather than sounds;
5. singing familiar songs (e.g. Happy Birthday, Knick Knack Paddy Wack) and replacing key words with those of a different ending; and
6. dealing children a deck of picture cards and having them sound out the words for the pictures on their cards or calling for a picture by asking for its first and last sound.

Assessment of Phonemic Awareness

Throughout the year, teachers can maintain ongoing logs and rubrics for assessment of phonemic awareness for individual children. Such assessments would identify particular stated reading behaviors or performance standards, the date of observation of the child's behavior (in this context, phonemic activity or exercise), and comments.

The rubric or legend for assessing these behaviors might include the following descriptors:

1. Demonstrates or exhibits reading behavior consistently.
2. Makes progress/strides toward this reading behavior.
3. Has not yet demonstrated or exhibited this behavior.

Depending on the particular phonemic task the teacher models, the performance task might include:

1. Saying rhyming words in response to an oral prompt.
2. Segmenting a word spoken by the teacher into its beginning, middle, and ending sounds.
3. Counting correctly the number of syllables in a spoken word.

Phonological awareness involves the recognition that spoken words are composed of a set of smaller units such as onsets and rimes, syllables, and sounds. Phonemic awareness is a specific type of phonological awareness that focuses on the ability to distinguish, manipulate, and blend specific sounds or phonemes within an individual word. Think of phonological awareness as an umbrella and phonemic awareness as a specific spoke under this umbrella. Phonics deals with printed words and the learning of sound-spelling correlations, while phonemic awareness activities are oral. In reviewing reading research and theory, new distinctions and definitions appear often. The body of reading knowledge changes over time. The information and definitions in this guide are those accepted in the year of its publication and the time of its authoring and updating. As changes occur in accepted theories, they will be made in the guides and in the certification exams.

"If you believe that you learn to read by reading, you must learn to want to read. Reading to children, therefore, models both the 'how' and 'why' of reading" (Helen Depree and Sandra Iversen, *Early Literacy in the Classroom*).

"The long talk that parents have put off about the ways of the world might need to be an introduction to the facts about the English alphabet" (Terrence Moore, Ashbrook Center Fellow, and Principal of Ridgeview Classical Schools in Fort Collins, Colorado).

Skill 1.2 Demonstrate knowledge of the skills associated with phonological awareness.

Phonological awareness skills include but are not limited to the following:

1. Rhyming and syllabification.
2. Blending sounds into words—such as pic-tur-bo-k.
3. Identifying beginning or initial phonemes and ending or final phonemes in short, one-syllable words.
4. Breaking words down into sounds, which is also called "segmenting" words.

5. Removing initial sounds and substituting others. An example is /bat/ minus the /b/ with an /m/ substituted becomes /mat/.
6. Distinguishing spoken words and syllables.

Skill 1.3 Demonstrate knowledge of the alphabetic principle.

words → letters = sounds

The alphabetic principle is sometimes called graphophonemic awareness. This term means that written words are composed of letters (graphemes) that represent the sounds (phonemes) of written words.

Development of the Understanding that Print Carries Meaning

This understanding is demonstrated every day in the elementary classroom as the teacher holds up a selected book to read aloud to the class. The teacher explicitly and deliberately talks aloud about how to hold the book, focuses the class on looking at its cover, points to where to start reading, and sweeps her hands in the direction to begin, left to right.

When writing the morning message on the board, the teacher reminds the children that the message begins in the upper left hand corner at the top of the board to be followed by additional activities and a schedule for the rest of the day.

When the teacher invites children to make posters of a single letter such as *b* and list items in the classroom, their home, or outside that start with that letter, the children are concretely demonstrating that print carries meaning.

Strategies for Promoting Awareness of the Relationship Between Spoken and Written Language

1. Writing down or encoding what the children say on a language chart.
2. Highlighting the uses of print products found in the classroom such as labels, yellow sticky-pad notes, labels on shelves and lockers, calendars, signs, and directions.
3. Reading together big-print and oversized books to teach print conventions such as directionality.
4. Practicing how to handle a book: how to turn pages, to find the top and bottom of pages, and how to tell the difference between the front and back covers.
5. Discussing and comparing with children the length, appearance, and boundaries of specific words. For example, children can see that the names of Dan and Dora share certain letters and a similar shape.
6. Having children match oral words to printed words by forming an echo chorus as the teacher reads poetry or rhymes aloud and they echo the reading.
7. Having the children combine, manipulate, switch, and move letters to change words.
8. Working with letter cards to create messages and respond to the messages that they create.

Skill 1.4   Demonstrate knowledge of various word identification strategies.

To decode means to change communication signals into messages. Reading comprehension requires that the reader learn the code the message is written in and decode it to get the message.

Although effective reading comprehension requires identifying words automatically (Adams, 1990, Perfetti, 1985), children do not have to be able to identify every single word or know the exact meaning of every word in a text to understand it. Indeed, Nagy (1988) says that children can read a work with a high level of comprehension even if they do not fully know as many as 15 percent of the words within a given text. Children develop the ability to automatically decode and recognize words. They then can extend their ability to decode to multi-syllabic words.

J. David Cooper (2004) and other advocates of the Balanced Literacy Approach feel that children become literate, effective communicators and able to comprehend by learning phonics and other aspects of word identification through the use of engaging reading texts. Engaging text, as defined by the Balanced Literacy group, are those texts that contain highly predictable elements of rhyme, sound patterns, and plot. Researchers such as Jeanne Chall (1983) and Rudolf Flesch (1981) support a phonics-centered foundation before the use of engaging reading texts. This is at the crux of the phonics versus whole-language/balanced-literacy/integrated-language-arts teaching-of-reading controversy.

It is important for the new teacher to be informed about both sides of this controversy as well as the work of theorists who attempt to reconcile these two perspectives, such as Kenneth Goodman (1994). There are powerful arguments on both sides of this controversy, and each approach works well with some students and does not succeed with others.

As far as the examinations go, all that is asked of you is the ability to demonstrate that you are familiar with these varied perspectives. If asked on a constructed response question, you need to be able to show that you can talk about teaching some aspect of reading using strategies from one or the other or a combination of approaches. This guide is designed to provide you with numerous strategies representing both approaches.

The working teacher can, depending on the perspective of his /her school administration and the needs of the particular children he or she serves, choose from the strategies and approaches ones that work best for the children concerned.

Blending Letter Sounds

Prompts for graphophonic cues:
You said (the child's incorrect attempt). Does that match the letters you see?

If it were the word you just said, (the child's incorrect attempt), what would it have to start with?

If it were the word you just said (the child's incorrect attempt), what would it have to end with?

Look at the first letter/s . . . look at the middle letter/s

. . . the last letter. . What could it be?

If you were writing (the child's incorrect attempt) what letter would you write first?

What letters would go in the middle?

What letters would go last?

A good strategy to use in working with individual children is to have them explain how they finally correctly identified a word that was troubling them. If prompted and habituated through one-on-one teacher/tutoring conversations, they can be quite clear about what they did to "get" the word.

If the children are already writing their own stories, the teacher might say to them: "You know when you write your own stories, you would never write any story that did not make sense. You wouldn't and probably this writer didn't either. If you read something that does make sense, but doesn't match the letters, then it's probably not what the author wrote. This is the author's story, not yours, right now, so go back to the word and see if you can find out the author's story. Later on, you might write your own story."

Letter/Sound Correspondence and Beginning Decoding

Use this procedure for letter-sound investigations that support beginning decoding. First, focus on a particular letter/s which you want the child to investigate. It is good to choose one from a shared text that the children are familiar with. Make certain that the teacher's directions to the children are clear and either focuses them on looking for a specific letter or listening for sounds.

Next, begin a list of words that matches the task given to the children. Use chart paper to list the words that the children identify. This list can be continued into the next week as long as the children's focus is maintained on the list. This can be easily done by challenging the children with identifying a specific number of letters or sounds and "daring" them as a class team to go beyond those words or sounds.

Third, continue to add to the list. Focus the children at the beginning of the day on the goal of their individually adding to the list. Give them an adhesive note (sticky pad sheet) on which they can individually write down the words they find. Then they can attach their newly found words with their names on them to the chart. This provides the children with a sense of ownership and pride in their letter-sounding abilities. During shared reading, discuss the children's proposed additions and have the group decide if these fit in the directed category. If all the children agree that they do, include the words on the chart.

Fourth, do a word sort from all the words generated and have the children put the words into categories that demonstrate similarities and differences. They can be prompted to see if the letter appeared at the beginning of the word or at the end of the word. They might also be prompted to see that one sound could have two different letter representations. The children can then "box" the word differences and similarities by drawing colors established in a chart key.

Finally, before the children go off to read, ask them to look for new words in the texts that they can now recognize because of the letter/sound relationships on their chart. During shared reading, make certain that they have time to share these words they were able to decode because of their explorations.

Strategies for Helping Students Decode Single-Syllable Words that Follow Common Patterns and Multi-syllable Words

(This activity is presented in detail so it can actually be implemented with children in an intermediate classroom and also to provide detail for a potential constructed-response question on a certification examination.)

The CVC phonics card game developed by Jackie Montierth, a computer teacher in South San Diego for use with 5th and 6th grade students, is a good one to adapt to the needs of any group with appropriate modifications for age, grade level, and language needs.

The children use the vehicle of the card game to practice and enhance their use of consonants and vowels. Their fluency in this will increase their ability to decode words. Potential uses beyond whole-classroom instruction include use as part of the small-group word-work component of the reading workshop and as part of cooperative team learning. This particular strategy also is particularly helpful for grade four and beyond English Language learners who are in a regular English Language classroom setting.

The card game works well because the practice of the content is implicit for transfer as the children continue to improve their reading skills. In addition, the card game format allows "instructional punctuation" using a student-centered high-interest exploration.

Card Design: The teacher can use the computer or use 5"x 8" index cards or actual card-deck sized oaktag cards to create a deck. For repeated use and durability, it is recommended that the deck be laminated.

The deck should consist of the following:
1. 44 consonant cards (including the blends)
2. 15 vowel cards (including 3 of each vowel)
3. 5 wild cards (which can be used as any vowel)
4. 6 final e cards

The design of this project can also focus on particular CVC words that are part of a particular book, topic, or genre format. In advance of playing the game, children can also be directed to review the words on the word wall or other words on a word map.

Procedure: The game is best introduced first as part of a mini lesson with the teacher reading the rules and a pair of children demonstrating step by step when the game is played before the class for the first time. Have the children divide into pairs or small groups of no more than 4 per group. Each group needs one deck of CVC cards. Have each group choose a dealer. The dealer shuffles the cards and deals five cards to each player. The remaining cards are placed face down for drawing during the play. One card is turned over to form the discard pile. Players may not show their cards to the other players. The first player to the left of the dealer looks at his/her cards and, if possible, puts down three cards that make a consonant-vowel-consonant word. For more points, four cards forming a consonant-vowel-consonant word can be placed down. The player must then say the word and draw the number of cards he or she laid down. If he or she is unable to form a word, he/she draws either a card from either the draw or discard pile. The player then discards one card. All players must have five cards at all times. Play moves to the left. The game continues until one or more of the following happens:

- There are no more cards in the draw pile.
- All players run out of cards.
- No player can form a word.

The winner is the player who has laid down the most cards during the game. Players may only lay down words at the beginning of their turn. Proper names may not be counted as words.

Other ways the game may be played:

- The game can be played with teams of individuals in a small group of four or fewer competing against one another (excellent for special-needs or resource-room students).
- It can also be done as a whole class activity where all the students are divided into cooperative teams or small groups who compete against one another. This second approach will work well with a heterogeneous classroom that includes special needs and/or ELL children.
- Teachers of ELL learners can do this game in the native language first and then transition it into English, facilitating native-language reading skills and second-language acquisition. They can develop their own appropriate decks to meet the vocabulary needs of their children and to complement the curricula.

Using Phonics to Decode Words in Connected Text.

Identifying New Words

Some strategies to share with children during conferences or as part of shared reading include the following prompts:

- Look at the beginning letter/s. What sound do you hear?
- Stop to think about the text or story. What word with this beginning letter would make sense here?
- Look at the book's illustrations. Do they provide you with help in figuring out the new word?
- Think of what word would make sense, sound right, and match the letters that you see. Start the sentence over, making your mouth ready to say that word.
- Skip the word, read to the end of the sentence, and then come back to the word. How does what you've read help you with the word?
- Listen to whether what you are reading makes sense and matches the letters (asking the child to self-monitor). If it doesn't make sense, see if you can correct it on your own.
- Look for spelling patterns you know from the spelling pattern wall.
- Look for smaller words you might know within the larger word.
- Read on a little, and then return to the part that confused you.

Use of Semantic and Syntactic Cues to Help Decode Words

Semantic Cues

Students will need to use their base knowledge of word meanings, semantics, to help them decipher unknown words or text as well as to clarify reading when it does not seem to make sense. Some prompts the teacher can use that will alert the children to semantic cues include:

- Does that sentence make sense?
- Which word in that sentence does not seem to fit?
- Why doesn't it fit?
- What word might make sense in that sentence?

Syntactic Cues

The first strategy good readers use from their own knowledge base to help determine misreading is syntactic cues. Syntactic cues use the order of words and the student's knowledge of the oral English language to help determine if what was read could be accurate. Some prompts the teacher can use to encourage and develop syntactic cues in reading include:

- You read (child's incorrect attempt). Does that sound right?
- You read (child's incorrect attempt). When we talk, do we talk that way?
- How would we say it?

- Recheck that sentence. Does it sound right the way you read it?

Specific Terminology Associated With Phonics

It is important to have a clear understanding of the terms associated with phonics. Here are some definitions that are helpful for a clear understanding of phonic development in children.

Phoneme. A phoneme is the smallest unit of sound in the English language. In print, phonemes are represented by the letter and slashes. So /b/ represents the sound the letter b would make.

Morpheme. A morpheme is the smallest unit of grammar in the English language. In other words, it is the smallest unit of meaning, not just sounds.

Consonant Digraph. A consonant digraph are two consonants of the English language that when placed together in a word make a unique sound—a sound neither makes when alone. Examples: ch, th, sh, and wh.

Consonant Blend. A consonant blend is when two consonants are put together, but each retains its individual sound. The two sounds go together in a seamless manner to produce a blended sound. Examples: st, br, cl, etc.

Schwa sound. The schwa sound is a vowel sound that is neutral. It typically occurs in the unaccented syllable of a word. An example would be the sound of the /a/ at the end of the word sofa. It is represented in print by an upside down e.

Development of Phonics Skills with Individual Students

In *On Solid Ground* (2000), researcher and educator Sharon Taberski writes that it is much harder for children from ELL backgrounds and children from homes where other English dialects are spoken to use syntactic cues to attempt to self-correct. These children, through no fault of their own, do not have sufficient experience hearing Standard English spoken to use this cueing system as they read. The teacher should sensitively guide them through by modeling the use of syntactic and semantic cues.

Highly proficient readers can be paired as buddy tutors for ELL or special-needs classroom members or to assist the resource-room teacher during reading time. They can use the CVC Game developed by Jacki Montrieth to support their peers and can even modify the game to meet the needs of classroom peers. Of course, this also offers the highly proficient reader the opportunity to do a service-learning project while still in elementary school. It also introduces the learner to another dimension of reading, the role of the reader as trainer and recruiter of other peers into the circle of readers and writers!

If the highly proficient readers are so motivated or if their teachers so desire, the peer tutors can also maintain an ongoing reading progress journal for their tutees. This will be a wonderful way to realize the goals of the reading and writing workshop. There are many different strategies to help children who are struggling with their phonics skill development. A beginning step is to identify the area of difficulty within phonics. A simple assessment to help determine the exact area of difficulty is the

CORE Phonics Survey, which can be downloaded free. Once the area of deficit has been identified, small group instruction can be developed around these areas to increase specific skills.

When working on specific phonics skills, it is important to utilize decodable texts. There are numerous publishers who have available a variety of resources for different skills and texts for use within the classroom. If students continue to struggle, it may be necessary to utilize a more specific systematic and explicit phonics program. Some examples of these include: Wilson Reading, Early Intervention Reading, and Open Court.

"It is the good reader that makes the good book" (Ralph Waldo Emerson).

Skill 1.5   Demonstrate knowledge of the relationships between words such as homonyms, synonyms, and antonyms and the complexities related to word selection.

Students frequently encounter problems with homonyms—words that are spelled and pronounced the same as another but that have different meanings. Examples are *mean*, a verb, "to intend"; *mean*, an adjective, "unkind"; and *mean*, a noun or adjective, "average." These words are actually both homonyms and homographs (written the same way).

A similar phenomenon that causes trouble is heteronyms (also sometimes called heterophones), words that are spelled the same but have different pronunciations and meanings (in other words, they are homographs that differ in pronunciation or, technically, homographs that are not homophones). For example, the homographs *desert* (abandon) and *desert* (arid region) are heteronyms (pronounced differently); but *mean* (intend) and *mean* (average) are not. They are pronounced the same, or are homonyms.

Another similar occurrence in English is the capitonym, a word that is spelled the same but has different meanings when it is capitalized and may or may not have different pronunciations. Example: *polish* (to make shiny) and *Polish* (from Poland).

Some of the most troubling homonyms are those that are spelled differently but sound the same. Examples: *its* (3d person singular neuter pronoun) and *it's* ("it is"); *there* (an adverb), *their* (3d person plural pronoun) and *they're* ("they are").

Others: *to, too, two;*

Some homonyms/homographs are particularly complicated and troubling. Fluke, for instance is a fish, a flatworm, the end parts of an anchor, the fins on a whale's tail, and a stroke of luck.

Common homonyms that are troubling to student writers:

accept: tolerate; *except*: everything but.

add: put together with; *ad*: short for advertisement.

allowed: permitted; *aloud*: audibly.

allot: to distribute, allocate; *a lot* (often "*alot*"): much, many (a lot of).

allusion: indirect reference; *illusion*: a distortion of sensory perception.

bare: naked, exposed or very little (bare necessities); *bear*: as a noun, a large mammal and as a verb, to carry.

boy: a male adolescent or child; *buoy*: (noun) a floating marker in the sea.

bridal: pertaining to a bride (bridal gown, bridal suite); *bridle*: (noun) part of a horse's tack.

capital: punishable by death, with an upper-case letter, principal town or city, or wealth and money; *Capitol*: the home of the Congress of the United States and some other legislatures.

chord: group of musical notes; *cord*: rope, long electrical line.

compliment: a praising or flattering remark; *complement*: something that completes.

discreet: tactful or diplomatic; *discrete*: separate or distinct.

dyeing: artificially coloring; *dying*: passing away.

effect: outcome; *affect*: have an effect on.

gorilla: the largest of the great apes; *guerrilla*: a small combat group.

hair: an outgrowth of the epidermis in mammals; *hare*: rabbit.

hoard: to accumulate and store up; *horde*: large group of warriors, mob.

lam: US slang, "on the lam" means "on the run"; *lamb*: a young sheep.

lead: pronounced to rhyme with "seed", to guide or serve as the head of; *lead*: pronounced to rhyme with "head," a heavy metal; *led*: the past tense of "lead."

medal: an award to be strung around the neck; *meddle*: stick one's nose into others' affairs; *metal*: shiny, malleable element or alloy like silver or gold; *mettle*: toughness, guts.

morning: the time between midnight and midday; *mourning*: period of grieving after a death.

past: time before now (past, present and future); *passed*: past tense of "to pass."

piece: portion; *peace*: opposite of war.

peak: tip, height, to reach its highest point; *peek*: to take a brief look; *pique*: fit of anger; to incite (pique one's interest).

conduct

Strategies to help students conquer these demons: Practice using them in sentences. Context is useful in understanding the difference. Drill is necessary to overcome the misuses.

Following are various ways words are sometimes used to show relationships that can be puzzling to students.

Denotation: What a word literally means, as opposed to its connotative meaning.

For example, "Good night, sweet prince, and flights of angels sing thee to thy *rest"* refers to sleep.

Connotation: The ripple effect surrounding the implications and associations of a given word, distinct from the denotative, or literal meaning. For example, "Good night, sweet prince, and flights of angels sing thee to thy rest," refers to a burial.

Simile: Direct comparison between two things. "My love is like a red-red rose."

Metaphor: Indirect comparison between two things. The use of a word or phrase denoting one kind of object or action in place of another to suggest a comparison between them. While poets use them extensively, they are also integral to everyday speech. For example, chairs are said to have "legs" and "arms" although we know that it's humans and other animals that have these appendages.

Personification: Human characteristics are attributed to an inanimate object, an abstract quality, or animal. Examples: John Bunyan wrote characters named Death, Knowledge, Giant Despair, Sloth, and Piety in his *Pilgrim's Progress.* The metaphor of an arm of a chair is a form of personification.

Irony: Expressing something other than and particularly opposite the literal meaning such as words of praise when blame is intended. In poetry, it is often used as a sophisticated or resigned awareness of contrast between what is and what ought to be and expresses a controlled pathos without sentimentality. It is a form of indirection that avoids overt praise or censure. An early example: the Greek comic character Eiron, a clever underdog who by his wit repeatedly triumphs over the boastful character Alazon.

Skill 1.6 Apply strategies for building and extending readers' vocabulary knowledge.

The Relationship between Oral and Written Vocabulary Development and Reading Comprehension

Biemiller's (2003) research documents that those children entering 4th grade with significant vocabulary deficits demonstrate increasing reading comprehension problems. Evidence shows that these children do not catch up, but rather continue to fall behind.

Strategy One: Word Map Strategy

This strategy is useful for children grades 3-6 and beyond. The target group of children for this strategy includes those who need to improve their independent vocabulary acquisition abilities. Essentially teacher-directed learning, children are "walked through" the process. They are helped by the teacher to identify the type of information that makes a definition. They are also assisted in using context clues and background understanding to construct meaning

.

The word-map graphic organizer is the tool teachers use to complete this strategy with children. Word-map templates are available online from the Houghton Mifflin web site and from READWRITETHINK, the web site of the NCTE. The word map helps the children to visually represent the elements of a given concept.

The children's literal articulation of the concept can be prompted by three key questions: What is it? What is it like? What are some examples?

For instance, the word "oatmeal" might yield a word map with "What?" and in a rectangular box a hot cereal you eat in the morning, "What is it like?": hot, mushy, salty. "What are some examples?": instant oatmeal you make in a minute, apple-flavor oatmeal, Irish Oatmeal.

The procedure to be used in sharing this strategy with children is to select three concepts the children are familiar with. Then show them the template of a word map. Tell them that the three questions asked on the map and the boxes to fill in beneath them helps readers and writers to see what they need to know about a word. Next, help the children to complete at least two word maps for two of the three concepts that were pre-selected. Then have the children select a concept of their own to map either independently or in a small group. As the final task for this first part of the strategy, have the children, in teams or individually, write a definition for at least one of the concepts using the key things about it listed on the map. Have the children share these definitions aloud and talk about how they used the word maps to help them with the definitions.

For the next part of this strategy, the teacher should pick up an expository text or a textbook the children are already using to study mathematics, science, or social studies. The teacher should either locate a short excerpt where a particular concept is defined or use the content to write model passages of definition on his/her own. After the passages are selected or authored, the teacher should duplicate them. Then they should be distributed to the children along with blank word map templates. The children should be asked to read each passage and then to complete the word map for the concept in each passage. Finally, have the children share the word maps they have developed for each passage. Give them a chance to explain how they used the word in the passage to help them fill out their word map. End by telling them that the three components of the concept-class, description, and example are just three of the many components for any given concept.

This strategy has assessment potential because the teacher can literally see how the students understand specific concepts by looking at their maps and hearing their explanations. The maps the students develop on their own demonstrate whether they have really understood the concepts in the passages. This strategy serves to ready students for inferring word meanings on their own. By using the word-map strategy, children develop concepts of what they need to know to begin to figure out an unknown word on their own. It assists the children in grades 3 and beyond to connect prior knowledge with new knowledge.

This word map strategy can be adapted by the teacher to suit the specific needs and goals of instruction. Illustrations of the concept and the comparisons to other concepts can be included in the word mapping for children grades 5 and beyond. This particular strategy is also one that can be used with a research theme in other content areas.

Strategy Two: Preview in Context

This is a direct-teaching strategy that allows the teacher to guide the students as they examine words in context prior to reading a passage. Before beginning the strategy, the teacher selects only two or three key concept words. Then the teacher reads carefully to identify passages within the text that evidence strong context clues for the word.

Then the teacher presents the word and the context to the children. As the teacher reads aloud, the children follow along. Once the teacher has finished the read-aloud, the children re-read the material silently. After the silent re-reading, the children will be coached by the teacher to a definition of one of the key words selected for study. This is done through a child-centered discussion. As part of the discussion, the teacher asks questions that get the children to activate their prior knowledge and to use the contextual clues to figure out the correct meaning of the selected key words. Make certain that the definition of the key concept word is finally made by the children.

Next, help the children to begin to expand the word's meaning by having them consider the following for the given key concept word: synonyms, antonyms, other contexts or other kinds of stories/texts where the word might appear. This is the time to have the children check their responses to the challenge of identifying word synonyms and antonyms by having them go to the thesaurus or the dictionary to confirm their responses. In addition, have the children place the synonyms or antonyms they find in their word boxes or word journals. The recording of their findings will guarantee them ownership of the words and deepen their capacity to use contextual clues.

The main point to remember in using this strategy is that it should only be used when the context is strong. It will not work with struggling readers who have less prior knowledge. Through listening to the children's responses as the teacher helps them to define the word and its potential synonyms and antonyms, the teacher can assess their ability to successfully use context clues. The key to this simple strategy is that it allows the teacher to draw the child out and to grasp through the child's responses the individual child's thinking process. The more talk from the child the better.

Noncontextual Vocabulary Strategies

Hierarchical and Linear Arrays

The very complexity of the vocabulary used in this strategy description may be unnerving for the teacher. Yet this strategy, which is included in the Cooper (2004) literacy instruction, is really very simple once it is outlined directly for children.

By using the term "hierarchical and linear" arrays, Cooper really is talking about how some words are grouped based on associative meanings. The words may have a "hierarchical" relationship to one another. For instance, an undergraduate or a first grader is lower in the school hierarchy than the graduate student and second grader. Within an elementary school, the fifth grader is at the top of the hierarchy and the pre-K or kindergartener is at the bottom of the hierarchy. By the way, the term for this strategy obviously need not be explained in this detail to K-3 children but might be shared with some grade and age appropriate modifications with children in grades 3 and beyond. It will enrich their vocabulary development and ownership of arrays they create.

Words can have a linear relationship to one another in that they run a spectrum from bad to good—for example from K-3 experiences, pleased-happy-overjoyed. These relationships can be displayed in horizontal boxes connected with dashes. Below is another way to display hierarchical relationships.

Once you get past the seemingly daunting vocabulary words, the arrays turn out to be another neat, graphic organizer tool which can help children "see" how words relate to one another.

To use this graphic organizer, the teacher should pre-select a group of words from a read aloud or from the children's writing. Show the children how the array will look using arrows for the linear array and just straight lines for the hierarchy. In fact invite some children up to draw the straight hierarchy lines as it is presented, so they have a role in developing even the first hierarchical model.

Do one hierarchy array and one linear array with the pre selected word with the children. Talk them through filling out (or helping the teacher to fill out) the array. After the children have had their own successful experience with arrays, they can select the words from their independent texts or familiar, previously read favorites to study. They will also need to decide which type of array, hierarchical or linear, is appropriate. For 5th and 6th graders, this choice can and should be voiced using the now "owned" vocabulary words "hierarchical array" and "linear array."

This strategy is best used after reading, since it will help the children to expand their word banks.

Contextual Vocabulary Strategies

Vocabulary Self-Collection.

This strategy is one in which children, even on the emergent level from grade 2 and up, take responsibility for their learning. It is also by definition a student-centered strategy, which demonstrates student ownership of their chosen vocabulary.

This strategy is one that can be introduced by the teacher early in the year, perhaps even the first day or week. The format for self-collection can then be started by the children. It may take the form of a journal with photocopied template pages. It can be continued throughout the year.

To start, ask the children to read a required text or story. Invite them to select one word for the class to study from this text or story. The children can work individually, in teams, or in small groups. The teacher can also do the self-collecting so that this becomes the joint effort of the class community of literate readers. Tell the children that they should select words that particularly interest them or which are unique in some way.

After the children have had time to make their selections and to reflect on them, make certain that they have time to share them with their peers as a whole class. When all children have shown the words they have selected, have them provide a definition for their words. Each word that is given should be listed on a large experiential chart or even in a BIG BOOK format, if that is age- and grade-appropriate. The teacher should also share the word he or she selected and provide a definition. The teacher's definition and sharing should be somewhere in the middle of the children's recitations.

The dictionary should be used to verify the definitions. When all the definitions have been checked, a final list of child-selected (and single teacher-selected) words should be made.

Once this final list has been compiled, the children can record it in their word journals or they may opt to record only those words they find interesting in their individual journals. It is up to the teacher at the onset of the vocabulary self-collection activity to decide whether the children will be required to record all the words on the final list or whether they can eliminate some. The decision made at the beginning by the teacher must be adhered to throughout the year.

To further enhance this strategy, children, particularly those in grades 3 and beyond, can be encouraged to use their collected words as part of their writings or to record and clip the appearance of these words in newspaper stories or online. This type of additional recording demonstrates that the child has truly incorporated the word into his/her reading and writing. It also habituates children to be lifelong readers, writers, and researchers.

One of the nice things about this simple but versatile strategy is that it works equally well with either expository or narrative texts. It also provides children with an opportunity to use the dictionary.

Assessment is built into the strategy. As the children select the word for the list, they share how they used contextual clues and through the children's response to the definitions offered by their peers, their prior knowledge can be assessed.

What is most useful about this strategy is that it documents that children can learn to read and write by reading and writing. The children take ownership of the words in the self-collection journals and that can also be the beginning of writer-observation journals as they include their own writings. They also use the word lists as a start for writers' commonplace books. These books are filled with newspaper, magazine, and functional document clippings using the journal words.

This activity is a good one for demonstrating the balanced literacy belief that vocabulary study works best when the words studied are chosen by the child.

The Relationship between Oral Vocabulary and the Process of Identifying and Understanding Written Words

One way to explore the relationship between oral vocabulary and the comprehension of written words is through the use of Oral Records (which are discussed at length in the appendix). In *On Solid Ground: Strategies for Teaching Reading K-3,* Sharon Taberski (2000) discusses how oral reading records can be used by the K-3 teacher to assess how well children are using cueing systems. She notes that the running record format can also show visual depictions for the teacher of how the child "thinks" as the child reads. The notation of miscues in particular shows how a child "walks through" the reading process. They indicate if and in what ways the child may require "guided" support in understanding the words he or she reads aloud. Taberski notes that when children read, they need to think about several things at once. First, they must consider whether what they are reading makes sense (semantic or meaning cues). Next, they must know whether their reading "sounds right" in terms of Standard English (syntactic and structural cues). Third, they have to weigh whether their oral language actually and accurately matches the letters the words represent (visual or graphophonic cues).

In taking the running record and having the opportunity first-hand to listen to the children talk about the text, the teacher can analyze the relationship between the child's oral language and word comprehension. Information from the running record provides the teacher with a road map for differentiated cueing system instruction. For example, when a running record is taken, a child often makes a mistake but then self-corrects. The child may select from various cueing systems when he or she self-corrects. These include: "M" for meaning, "S" for syntax, and "V" for visual. The use of a visual cue means that the child is drawing on his or her knowledge of spelling patterns. Of course, Tabereski cautions, any relationship between oral language and comprehension that the teacher draws from an examination of the oral-reading records, must be drawn using a series of three or more of the child's oral reading records, taken over time, not just one.

A teacher can review children's running records over time to note their pattern of miscues and which cues they have the greatest tendency to use in their self-corrections. Whichever cueing system the children use to the greatest extent, it is necessary for the teacher to offer support in also using the other cueing systems to construct correct meaning. Taberski suggests that while assessing running records to determine the relationship between oral language and meaning, the children read from "just right" books.

Competency 2.0   READING COMPREHENSION AND FLUENCY

Skill 2.1   Demonstrate knowledge of factors that influence reading comprehension and fluency.

If there were two words synonymous with reading comprehension as far as the balanced literacy approach is concerned, they would be "constructing meaning." Cooper, Taberski, Strickland, and other key theorists and classroom teachers conceptualize the reader as interacting with the text and bringing his/her prior knowledge and experience to it. Writing is interlaced with reading and is a mutually integrative and supportive parallel process. Hence the division of literacy learning by the balanced literacy folks into reading workshop and writing workshop with the same anchor "readings" or books being used for both.

Consider the sentence, "The test booklet was white with black print, but very scary looking."

According to the idea of constructing meaning as the reader read this sentence, the schemata (generic information stored in the mind) of tests the reader had experienced was activated by the author's notion that tests are scary. Therefore, the ultimate meaning that the reader derives from the page is from the reader's own responses and experiences coupled with the ideas the author presents. The reader constructs a meaning that reflects the author's intent and also the reader's response to that intent.

It is also to be remembered that generally readings are fairly lengthy passages composed of paragraphs that in turn are composed of more than one sentence. With each successive sentence, and every new paragraph, the reader refocuses. The schemata are reconsidered, and a new meaning is

Five Key Strategies for Child Reading of Informational/Expository Texts.

1. Inferencing is a process that involves the reader's making a reasonable judgment based on the information given and engages children to literally construct meaning. In order to develop and enhance this key skill in children, a mini lesson might be used where the teacher demonstrates it by reading an expository book aloud (i.e. one on skyscrapers for young children) and then demonstrates for them the following reading habits: looking for clues, reflecting on what the reader already knows about the topic, and using the clues to figure out what the author means/intends.

2. Identifying main ideas in an expository text can be improved when the children have an explicit strategy for identifying important information. They can make this strategy part of their everyday reading style, "walking" through the following exercises during guided reading sessions. The child should read the passage so that the topic is readily identifiable to him or her. It will be what most of the information is about. Next the child should be asked to be on the lookout for a sentence within the expository passage that summarizes the key information in the paragraph. Then the child should read the rest of the passage or excerpt in light of this information and also note which information in the paragraph is less important. The important information the child has identified in the paragraph can be used to formulate the author's main idea. The child reader may even want to use some of the author's own language in stating that idea.

3. Monitoring means self-clarifying: The reader often realizes, in the course of reading a passage, that what he or she is reading is not making sense. The reader then has to have a plan for making sensible meaning out of the excerpt. Cooper and other balanced literacy advocates have a stop and think strategy they use with children. The child reflects, "Does this make sense to me?" When the child concludes that it does not, the child then either re-reads, reads ahead in the text, looks up unknown words or asks for help from the teacher. What is important about monitoring is that some readers ask these questions and try these approaches without ever being explicitly taught them in school by a teacher. However, these strategies need to be explicitly modeled and practiced under the guidance of the teacher by most if not all child readers.

4. Summarizing engages the reader in pulling together into a cohesive whole the essential bits of information within a longer passage or excerpt of text. Children can be taught to summarize informational or expository text by following these guidelines. First they should look at the topic sentence of the paragraph or the text and ignore the trivia. Then they should search for information that has been mentioned more than once and make sure it is included only once in their summary. Find related ideas or items and group them under a unifying heading. Search for and identify a main idea sentence. Finally, put the summary together using all these guidelines.

5. Generating questions can motivate and enhance children's comprehension of reading in that they are actively involved. The following guidelines will help children generate meaningful questions that will trigger constructive reading of expository texts.

   • First children should preview the text by reading the titles and subheadings. Then they should also look at the illustrations and the pictures. Finally they should read the first paragraph. These first previews should yield an impressive batch of specific questions.
   • Next, children should get into a Dr. Seuss mode and ask themselves a "THINK" question. Make certain that the children write down the

question. Then have them read to find important information to answer their "think" question. Ask that they write down the answer they found and copy the sentence or sentences where they found the answer. Also have the students consider whether, in light of their further reading through the text, their original question was a good one or not.

- Ask them to be prepared to explain why their original question was a good one or not. Once the children have answered their original "think" question, have them generate additional ones and then find their answers and judge whether these questions were "good" ones in light of the text.

Reading Fluency

At some point it is crucial that, just as the nervous, novice bike rider finally relaxes and speeds happily off; so too must the early reader integrate graphophonic cues with semantic and structural ones and move toward fluency. Before this is done, the oral quality of early readers has a stilted beat to it, which of course, does not promote reading engagement and enjoyment.

The teacher needs to be at his/her most theatrical to model for children the beauties of voice and nuance that are contained in the texts whose print they are tracking so anxiously. Children love nothing more than to mimic their teacher and can do so legitimately and without hesitation if the teacher takes time each day to theatrically recite a poem with them. The poem might be posted on chart paper and be up on the board for a week.

First the teacher can model the fluent and expressive reading of the poem. Then with a pointer, the teacher can lead the class in a recitation of it. As the week progresses, the class can recite it on their own.

Most teachers would immediately equate fluency with the amount of words read correctly per minute. However, reading fluency is more than reading speed. Students must also demonstrate good prosody. Prosody involves reading with expression, appropriate phrasing, and using good inflection.

Prosody is generally considered a part of fluency and is considered as such on all rubrics used to evaluate reading fluency. This is what takes robotic reading and makes it into something enjoyable to hear. Punctuation we provides the cues for reading with good prosody.

Modeling is one of the most effective strategies a teacher can use with students to increase their prosody skills. Teachers need to provide examples of good reading. In this way, students can hear how they should be reading by hearing the differences between good oral reading and poor oral reading.

Prosody can only be built by using oral reading, so any of the already mentioned strategies for improving fluency can also be used to increase this important aspect of reading. It is important for students to clearly understand that reading is not a race. It is not about the number of words they are able to read in a minute, but rather how well they are able to read a passage.

While the majority of reading will occur silently in the student's head, it is necessary to take the time to practice reading aloud sometimes to ensure that students develop the natural flow of language. Phrasing and expression will then transfer into their silent reading if the students are able to perform it orally. If they are unable to do the task orally, the reading in their head may be also be robotic or choppy, which can negatively impact comprehension.

Skill 2.2   Recognize the appropriate reading strategy to use for different texts and purposes.

Use of Reading Strategies for Different Texts

As children progress to the older grades (3-6), it is important for the teacher to model for them that in research on a social studies or science exploration, it may not be necessary to read every single word of a given expository information text. For instance, if the child is trying to find out about hieroglyphics, he or she might only read through those sections of a book on Egyptian or Sumerian civilization which dealt with picture writing.

The teacher, assisted by a child, should model how to go through the table of contents and the index of the book to identify only those pages that deal with picture writing. In addition, other children should come to the front of the room or to the center of the area where the reading group is meeting. They should then, with the support of the teacher, skim through the book for illustrations or diagrams of picture writing which is the focus of their need.

Children can practice the skills of skimming texts and scanning for particular topics that connect with their Social Studies, Science, and Mathematics content reading.

Skill 2.3   Demonstrate knowledge of strategies to use before, during, and after reading to enhance comprehension.

Cooper (2004), Taberski (2000), Cox (2005), and other researchers recommend a broad array of comprehension strategies before, during, and after reading.

Cooper (2004) suggests a broad range of classroom posters on the walls plus explicit instruction to give children prompts to monitor their own reading. An example follows:

Strategic Reading Guide

1. Do I infer/predict important information, use what I know, think about what may happen or what I want to learn?
2. Can I identify important information about the story elements?
3. Do I generate questions and search for the answers?
4. Does this make sense to me? Does this help me meet my purpose in reading?
5. If lost, do I remember fix-ups? Re-read, read further ahead, look at the illustrations, ask for help, think about the words, and evaluate what I have read.
6. Do I remember to think about how the parts of the stories that I was rereading came together? Storyboard panels, which are used by comic strip artists and by those artists who do advertising campaigns as well as television and film directors, are perfect for engaging children K-6 in a variety of comprehension strategies before, during, and after reading. They can storyboard the beginning of a story, read aloud, and then storyboard its predicted middle or end. Of course, after they experience or read the actual middle or ending of the story, they can compare and contrast what they produced with its actual structure. They can play familiar literature identification games with a buddy or as part of a center by storyboarding one key scene or characters from a book and challenging a partner or peer to identify the book and characters correctly.

Skill 2.4 Demonstrate knowledge of oral language activities that promote comprehension.

Taberski advocates using the "Stopping to Think About" strategy with expository texts as well as fictional ones.

This strategy is centered on the reader's using three "steps" as he or she goes through the expository text. These steps may be expressed as questions.

1. What do I, the reader, think is going to happen?
2. What clues in the text or illustrations or graphics lead me to think that this is going to happen?
3. How can I prove that I am right by going back to the text to demonstrate that this does happen or is suggested by actual clues in the text?

Taberski (2000) deliberately uses expository texts that relate to her grade's social studies and science lessons to model for children how to "stop and think" about the way an expository text is organized. She sometimes deliberately reads a section of a text or a non-fiction book aloud until the end of its chapter so that the children can consider what they have learned about the topic and how it is organized. Then together as a whole class or as a whole guided-reading group, they make predictions about what is coming next.

Skill 2.5 Demonstrate knowledge of literal comprehension skills.

Strategic reading occurs when students are reading to take in information. The purpose for reading is simply to learn. Typically, then, strategic reading occurs in nonfiction or expository texts. The students are generally given some guidance on what information they are to find.

In strategic reading, however, it is not a simple recall of facts. The students are required to read a great deal of information about a topic. Then they need to take all of that information and build their own foundation of knowledge. Constructing their own knowledge is what makes strategic reading different from simple literal recall. It is through this process that information is connected to prior knowledge.

These connections are key factors in comprehension. Strategic reading requires the reader to be able to tie new and old learning together to synthesize it into useful information. This process of thinking about reading and manipulating all learned is known as metacognition.

Metacognition is a complex set of variables for the reader. The reader needs to be aware of the reading process and be able to recognize when information does not make sense to them. During metacognition, students must stand back and think about their own thinking process. At this point, they need to adjust the things they are doing in order to clarify and make necessary connections. Throughout this process, the reader must continue to integrate the new and old.

Strategic readers call into play their metacognitive capacities as they analyze texts so that they are aware of the skills needed to construct meaning from the text structure. When reading strategically, students need to keep in mind several factors.

Self-Monitoring. When students self-monitor, they are, themselves, able to keep track of all the factors involved in the process. In this way, they are able to process the information in the manner that is best for them.

Setting the Purpose for Reading. In strategic reading, the child has a specific reason for reading the text. There is information they wish to gain and that should be clear to the student. If it is unclear, the student will not be successful.

Rereading. Rereading is probably one of the most-used methods for taking in overwhelming information. By revisiting the text more than once, the student is able to then take in smaller pieces of information that she missed after the first read.

Adjusting Reading Rates and Strategies. Similar to self-monitoring, the student must be able to understand that sometimes it will be necessary to read slower than at other times. Sometimes they will need to make adjustments to the way they are reading in order to be successful at gaining the information they want to gain.

Text Factors. Understanding the arrangement of nonfiction text with section titles and other unique organizational devices can provide the student with other tools to be successful. Knowing the structure of the text can save valuable time and decrease the necessity for rereading.

Skill 2.6   Demonstrate knowledge of inferential comprehension skills.

Inferencing is a process that involves the reader's making a reasonable judgment based on the information given and engages children to literally construct meaning. In order to develop and enhance this key skill in children, they might have a mini lesson where the teacher demonstrates this by reading an expository book aloud (i.e. one on skyscrapers for young children) and then demonstrates for them the following reading habits: looking for clues, reflecting on what the reader already knows about the topic, and using the clues to figure out what the author means/intends.

A theory or approach to the teaching of reading that gained currency in the late sixties and the early seventies was the importance of asking inferential and critical thinking questions of the reader that would challenge and engage the children in the text. This approach to reading went beyond the literal level of what was stated in the text to an inferential level of using text clues to make predictions and to a critical level of involving the child in evaluating the text. While asking engaging and thought-provoking questions is still viewed as part of the teaching of reading, it is only viewed currently as a component of the teaching of reading.

Taberski encourages the questioning strategy for promoting the use of inference in the comprehension of imaginative literary texts. She feels that if repeated sufficiently during the K-3 years and even if introduced as late as grade 4, these strategies will even serve the adult lifelong reader in good stead.

"Stopping to Think" is one of the strategies Taberski recommends for reflecting on the text as a whole. As part of this strategy, the reader is challenged to come up with the answer to these three questions: What do I think is going to happen? (Inferential); Why do I think this is going to happen? (evaluative and inferential); How can I prove that I am right by going back to the story? (inferential).

COMPETENCY 3   READING EXPOSITORY TEXTS

Skill 3.1   Identify the characteristics and purposes of various types of expository texts.

Expository text is non-fiction that provides information and facts. This text type is what newspapers, science, mathematics and history texts use. Currently there is much focus, even in elementary schools, on teaching children how to comprehend and author expository texts. They must produce brochures, guides, recipes, and procedural accounts on most elementary grade levels. The teaching of reading of expository texts requires working with a particular vocabulary and concept structure that is very different from that of the narrative text. Therefore, time must be taken to teach the reading of expository texts and contrast it with the reading of narrative texts. Simply put, expository text is written for the purpose of conveying information. It can be contrasted with narrative text, which tells a story; descriptive text, which recreates an experience for the purpose of reproducing it in one of the five senses, and persuasive text, whose purpose is to change minds or initiate actions.

News reporters generally become excellent writers because they get a lot of practice, which is a principle most writing teachers try to employ with their students. Also, news writing is instructive in skills for writing clearly and coherently. Reporters generally write in two modes: straight reporting and feature writing. In both modes, the writer must be concerned with accuracy and objectivity. The reporter does not write his opinions. He/she does not write persuasive discourse; his reporting is usually expository in nature—it intends only to convey information. The topic is typically assigned although some experienced reporters have the opportunity to seek out and develop their own stories.

Investigative reporting is sometimes seen as a distinct class although, technically, all reporters are "investigative." That is, they research the background of the story they're reporting, using as many means as are available. For example, the wife of a conservative, model minister murders him premeditatively and in cold blood. The reporter reports the murder and the arrest of the wife, but the story is far from complete until some questions are answered, the most obvious one being "why?" The reporter is obligated to try to answer that question and to do so will interview as many people as will talk to him about the lives of both minister and wife, their parents, members of the church, their neighbors, etc. The reporter will also look at newspaper archives in the town where the murder took place as well as in newspapers in any town the husband and/or wife has lived in previously. High-school yearbooks are a source that are often explored in these cases.

When Bob Woodward and Carl Bernstein, reporters for *The Washington Post,* began to break the Watergate story in 1972 and 1973, they set new standards for investigative reporting and had a strong influence on journalistic writing. Most reporters wanted to be Woodward and Bernstein and became more aggressive than reporters had been in the past. Even so, the basic techniques and principles still apply. The reporting of these two talented journalists demonstrated that while newspapers keep communities aware of what's going on, they also have the power to influence it.

A good news story is written as an "inverted pyramid." That is, the reasoning is deductive. The "thesis" or point is stated first and is supported with details. It reasons from general to specific. The lead sentence might be, "The body of John Smith was found in the street in front of his home with a bullet wound through his skull." The headline will be a trimmed-down version of that sentence and shaped to grab attention. It might read: "Murdered man found on Spruce Street." The news article might fill several columns, the first details having to do with the finding of the body, the next the role of the police; the third will spread out and include details about the victim's life, then the scope will broaden to details about his family, friends, neighbors, etc. If he held a position of prominence in the community, those details will broaden further and include information about his relationships to fellow-workers and his day-to-day contacts in the community. The successful reporter's skills include the ability to do thorough research, to maintain an objective stance (not to become involved personally in the story), and to write an effective "inverted pyramid."

Feature writing is more like an informative essay although it may also follow the inverted pyramid model. This form of reporting focuses on a topic designed to be interesting to at least one segment of the readership—possible sports enthusiasts, travelers, vacationers, families, women, food lovers, etc. The article will focus on one aspect of the area of interest such as a particular experience for the vacationing family. The first sentence might read something like this: "Lake Lure offers a close-to-home relaxing weekend getaway for families in East Tennessee." The development can be an ever-widening pyramid of details focused particularly on what the family can experience at Lake Lure but also directions for how to get there.

While the headline is intended to contain in capsule form the point that an article makes, it is rarely written by the reporter. This can sometimes result in a disconnection between headline and article. Well-written headlines will provide a guide for the reader as to what is in the article; they will also be attention-grabbers. This requires a special kind of writing, quite different from the inverted pyramid that distinguishes these writers from the investigative or feature reporter.

Business Letters

It may seem sometimes that the **business letter** is a thing of the past. Although much business-letter writing has been relegated to e-mail communications, letters are still a potentially valuable form of communication. A carefully-written letter can be powerful. It can alienate, convince, persuade, entice, motivate, and/or create good-will.

As with any other communication, it's worthwhile for the letter-writer to learn as much as possible about the receiver. This may be complicated if there will be more than one receiver of the message; in these cases, it's best to aim for the lowest common denominator if that can be achieved without "writing down" to any of those who will read and be affected or influenced by the letter. It may be better to send more than one form of the letter to the various receivers in some cases.

Purpose is the most powerful factor in writing a business letter. What is the letter expected to accomplish? Is it intended to get the receiver to act or to act in a specific manner? Are you hoping to see some action take place as the result of the letter? If so, you should clearly define for yourself what the purpose is before you craft the letter, and it's good to include a time deadline for the response.

Reasons for choosing the letter as the channel of communication include the following:

1. It's easy to keep a record of the transaction.
2. The message can be edited and perfected before it is transmitted.
3. It facilitates the handling of details.
4. It's ideal for communicating complex information.
5. It's a good way to disseminate mass messages at a relatively low cost.

The parts of a business letter are as follow: date line, inside address, salutation, subject line*, body, complimentary close, company name*, signature block, reference initials*, enclosure notation*, copy notation*, and postscript*.

Business letters typically use formal language. They should be straightforward and courteous. The writing should be concise, and special care should be taken to leave no important information out. Clarity is very important; otherwise, it may take more than one exchange of letters or phone calls to get the message across.

Most business letters are expository—that is, their purposes are to communicate information. However, some business letter may also be persuasive and be intended to change the recipient's mind or get him to act.

*optional

E-mail has revolutionized business communications. It has most of the advantages of business letters and the added ones of immediacy, lower costs, and convenience. Even very long reports can be attached to an e-mail. On the other hand, a two-line message can be sent and a response received immediately bringing together the features of a postal system and the telephone. Instant messaging goes even one step further. It can do all of the above—send messages, attach reports, etc.—and still have many of the advantages of a telephone conversation. E-mail has an unwritten code of behavior that includes restrictions on how informal the writing can be. The level of accepted business conversation is usually also acceptable in e-mails. Capital letters and bolding are considered shouting and are usually frowned on.

Personal Letters

When writing personal notes or letters, the writer needs to keep the following key matters in mind:

- Once the topic is determined, the writer must determine the appropriate tone to introduce and express it. Is humor appropriate? Seriousness? Bluntness or subtlety? Does the situation call for formal or informal language? The answers to these questions will depend, in good part, on the writer's relationship to the reader. Plan appropriately regarding situation and audience.
- Does the writer's introduction clearly explain the topic/situation to a reader who doesn't know or feel everything that the reader knows or feels? Don't assume that the writer and reader are "on the same page." Make a checklist to make sure that all key information is clearly and concisely expressed.
- If a note or letter involves a request, what type of response/result does the writer desire? Devise a strategy or strategies for achieving a desired outcome.
- If a note or letter involves a complaint about the reader, the writer will need to decide whether to ask for particular amends or to let the reader decide what, if anything, to do. If no amends are requested, the writer may wish to suggest ideas that would help to avoid similar conflicts in the future. Asking the reader for his or her opinions is also a possibility.
- If a timely response to any note or letter is needed, the writer must mention this.

Give students in-class opportunities to write a variety of personal notes and letters, whether involving "real life" or hypothetical situations. Invitations, thank-you notes, complaints, requests for favors, or personal updates are a few of the options available. Have students experiment with a variety of tones and strategies on a particular piece of personal correspondence, e.g., write a complaint letter in a blunt tone, then write the same complaint in a humorous tone; compare and contrast the drafts. Structure in-class activities to allow for peer feedback.

Textbooks are yet another type of expository writing that most of us are exposed to at one time or another. A textbook does not try to persuade or entertain; it only exists to give information—the purpose of expository writing. Other forms of exposition are directions. For example, if you buy a new cabinet, it may require that you put it together, so a set of instructions will come with it. The writer of those instructions does not need to persuade you to put the cabinet together nor does he need to stir you emotionally. He simply wants you to have the instructions in case you want the information required to assemble the cabinet—pure and simple exposition.

Skill 3.2   Demonstrate the ability to use effectively the organizational features of expository texts.

A textbook, a good example of expository writing, will have a table of contents, an important organizing device for the reader or user. Most expository writings of any length will likewise have tables of contents. Even those that do not have this feature more often than not will have an index, another important and useful organizing tool that makes the book much easier to use.

Generally, even a short expository writing will be broken into clearly identifiable parts by headings, usually in a different font style or numbered for the reader's convenience. In addition, footnotes and endnotes serve an important function for the reader. The writer is saying that there's more information here that the reader might want, but by putting the information such as the source for the material or background for the information in a note, the text goes uninterrupted. On the other hand, it's there if the reader wants it.

Indexes are very valuable for searching for a particular item in a piece of writing such as a textbook. The reader does not have to search through the table of contents and headings in order to find exactly the piece of information he is looking for. Indexes are very common nowadays and can be generated electronically.

Glossaries are very valuable if terms are being used that may not be understood by the reader. For example, many of us have a passing knowledge about software and hardware, but a writer of informative information about a piece of software that we might benefit from may want to include a glossary to help such readers understand what they are seeking to understand.

Skill 3.3   Recognize accurate summaries of expository texts.

An effective summary will first of all declare what *point* the writer made in this piece. The summary should then follow the steps the writer used to support and demonstrate the point. In most expository texts, each of those steps has its own paragraph and the point that paragraph makes will be one step in the analysis. There will probably also be an introduction that will lay out what the writing is about and sometimes how the writer will cover it. There may also be a conclusion where the writer recalls for you, the reader, the points that have been made. However, the conclusion may also make recommendations for further study of the topic, even going so far as to recommend other writings.

To gauge how accurate the summary is, you will need to follow the reasoning of the writing being summarized and measure whether or not the summary is true to the writer's intent and approach.

Skill 3.4 Distinguish between general statements and specific details presented in an expository text.

From general to specific is a continuum. In other words, a term or phrase may be more specific than another term or more general than another one. For example, car is about the middle of the continuum; however, if I mention John Smith's car, it has become more specific. The most specific is a unique item: John Smith's 2007 Lexus, serial #000000000. Cars is a general term that can be narrowed and narrowed and narrowed to suit whatever purposes the writer has for the term. For instance, it would be possible to make a statement about all the cars in the United States, which has been narrowed somewhat from the general term "cars." It is, however, still a very general concept. A thesis statement is typically a generality: All the cars in the United States run on gasoline. Then specifics would be needed to prove that generalization.

In developing a line of reasoning, the choice will be either inductive, going from the specific to the general, or deductive, going from the general to the specific. Inductive reasoning might be as follows: "I tasted a green apple from my grandfather's yard when I was five years old, and it was sour. I also tasted a green apple that my friend brought to school in his lunchbox when I was eight years old, and it was sour. I was in Browns' roadside market and bought some green Granny Smith apples last week, and they were sour." This is a series of specifics. From those specifics, I might draw a conclusion—a generalization—all apples are sour, and I would have reasoned inductively to arrive at that generalization.

The same simplistic argument developed deductively would begin with the generalization: *all green apples are sour*. Then specifics would be offered to support that generalization: the sour green apple I tasted in my grandfather's orchard, the sour green apple in my friend's lunchbox, the Granny Smith apples from the market.

When reasoning is this simple and straightforward, it's easy to follow, but it's also easy to see fallacies. For example, this person hasn't tasted all the green apples in the world; and, in fact, some green apples are not sour. However, it's rarely that easy to see the generalizations and the specifics. In determining whether a point has been proven, it's necessary to do that.

Sometimes generalizations are cited on the assumption that they are commonly accepted and do not need to be supported. An example: all men die sooner or later. Examples wouldn't be needed because that is commonly accepted. Now, some people might require that "die" be defined, but even the definition of "die" is assumed in this generalization.

Some current generalizations that may assume at least some common acceptance: Providing healthcare for all citizens is the responsibility of the government. All true patriots will support any war the government declares.

Flaws in argument, either intended or unintended, frequently have to do with generalizations and specifics. Are the specifics sufficient to prove the truth of the generality? Does a particular specific actually apply to this generalization? Many times it will depend on definitions. The question can always be asked: has the writer (or speaker) established the generalization?

Skill 3.5   Identify the main idea and purpose of an expository text, whether stated or implied, and details used to support the main idea.

The stated purpose of a piece of writing hinges on what the reader intends to accomplish. If his purpose is simply to convey information that may be useful or even critical to the reader, then the writing can be said to be expository. So how can the reader identify this purpose? The piece of writing must be unraveled so the various parts of it can be looked at separately. Are those parts simply evidence that supports the informational purpose of this writer? On the other hand, is this writer trying to change your mind or get you to do something? If this is the case, the writing is not expository but persuasive. Expository writing has no interest in persuading a person to change his mind or to go out and act on something the writer is recommending; however, that's exactly what persuasive writing intends to achieve.

In expository writing, the purpose is often set out in the beginning of the passage. However, if the purpose is never stated, then the reader must peruse the entire passage and ask *what was the writer trying to do*? Going back and looking at the details that have been given for support of the author's point will sometimes help untangle what the writer was about when he wrote this passage. An effective piece of writing is usually transparent and clear about the purpose of the writer as well as the supporting points.

An example of expository writing is a biography, David McCullough's *John Adams*, for instance. However, many biographies have been written on the life of this president, and each has its own focus. McCullough's was Adams' character and his relationship to his wife, Abigail. Another biography would have an entirely different take even though the events would coincide. It would be worthwhile to read more than one of these, but to make a report or talk about McCullough's, it would be necessary to focus on what this particular writer focused on and report just which incidents he chose to include in his biography.

Skill 3.6   Recognize primary and secondary source material and assess the credibility and objectivity of various sources of information used in an expository text.

Primary sources are works, records, and the like that were created during the period being studied or immediately after it. Secondary sources are works written significantly after the period being studied and based upon primary sources. Primary sources are the basic materials that provide raw data and information. Secondary sources are the works that contain the explications of, and judgments on, this primary material.

Primary sources include the following kinds of materials:

- Documents that reflect the immediate, everyday concerns of people: memoranda, bills, deeds, charters, newspaper reports, pamphlets, graffiti, popular writings, journals or diaries, records of decision-making bodies, letters, receipts, snapshots, and others.
- Theoretical writings that reflect care and consideration in composition and an attempt to convince or persuade. The topic will generally be deeper and have more pervasive values than is the case with "immediate" documents. These may include newspaper or magazine editorials, sermons, political speeches, or philosophical writings.
- Narrative accounts of events, ideas, and trends written with intentionality by someone contemporary with the events described.
- Statistical data, although statistics may be misleading.
- Literature and nonverbal materials, novels, stories, poetry and essays from the period, as well as coins, archaeological artifacts, and art produced during the period.

Secondary sources include the following kinds of materials:

- Books written on the basis of primary materials about the period of time.
- Books written on the basis of primary materials about persons who played a major role in the events under consideration.
- Books and articles written on the basis of primary materials about the culture, the social norms, the language, and the values of the period.
- Quotations from primary sources.
- Statistical data on the period.
- The conclusions and inferences of other historians.
- Multiple interpretations of the ethos of the time.

Questions for Analyzing Sources

To determine the authenticity or credibility of your sources, consider these questions:

> Learn more about **Assessing the Credibility of Online Sources**
> http://www.webcredible.co.uk/
> user-friendly-resources/web-
> credibility/assessing-credibility-online-
> sources.shtml

1. Who created the source and why? Was it created through a spur-of-the-moment act, a routine transaction, or a thoughtful, deliberate process?
2. Did the recorder have firsthand knowledge of the event? Or did the recorder report what others saw and heard?
3. Was the recorder a neutral party, or did the recorder have opinions or interests that might have influenced what was recorded?
4. Did the recorder produce the source for personal use, for one or more individuals, or for a large audience?
5. Was the source meant to be public or private?
6. Did the recorder wish to inform or persuade others? (Check the words in the source. The words may tell you whether the recorder was trying to be objective or persuasive.) Did the recorder have reasons to be honest or dishonest?
7. Was the information recorded during the event, immediately after the event, or after some lapse of time? How large a lapse of time?

Skill 3.7   Demonstrate the ability to make inferences and draw conclusions from information presented in an expository text.

We draw inferences all the time, just as in Skill 3.4, where the writer concluded that all green apples were sour based on her experience with green apples. We look around us and see things that "add up" and from those things we draw conclusions or inferences. These inferences are often wrong and can lead to very unfortunate outcomes. For example, the conclusion that young black men are dangerous has led to many unfortunate arrests and imprisonment of innocent, decent young men. We need to be very careful that what we are seeing is what we think we are seeing and that the conclusion we have come to can be defended on that basis.

In an expository text, you can expect that the writer will draw a conclusion. Keeping in mind that inductive reasoning is based on looking at many phenomena and deciding that a particular characteristic will always occur when other prior circumstances are present, we can use that reasoning to draw conclusions. But we must go to great lengths to test it out. Are other possible conclusions possible, given those circumstances? Is it going too far to conclude that any time that particular characteristic occurs, it has been caused by those precluding circumstances?

Skill 3.8   Recognize the organizational structures of expository texts that aid in comprehension.

Organizational Structures

Authors choose a particular organization to best present the concepts they are writing about. Teaching students to recognize organizational structures helps them to understand authors' literary intentions, and helps them decide which structure to use in their own writing.

Cause and Effect: When writing about *why* things happen, as well as *what* happens, authors commonly use the cause-and-effect structure. For example, when writing about how he became so successful, a CEO might talk about how he excelled in math in high school, moved to New York after college, and stuck to his goals even after multiple failures. These are all *causes* that led to the *effect*, or result, of his becoming a wealthy and powerful businessman.

Compare and Contrast: When examining the merits of multiple concepts or products, compare and contrast lends itself easily to organization of ideas. For example, a person writing about foreign policy in different countries will put them against each other to point out differences and similarities, easily highlighting the concepts the author wishes to emphasize.

Problem and Solution: This structure is used in a lot of handbooks and manuals. Anything organized around procedure-oriented tasks, such as a computer repair manual, gravitates toward a problem-and-solution format because it offers such clear, sequential text organization.

Introductions and Conclusions

Introductions:

It's important to remember that in the writing process, the introduction should be written last. Until the body of the paper has been determined—thesis development—it's difficult to make strategic decisions regarding the introduction. The Greek rhetoricians called this part of a discourse *exordium*, a "leading into." The basic purpose of the introduction, then, is to lead the audience into the discourse. It can let the reader know what the purpose of the discourse is and it can condition the audience to be receptive to what the writer wants to say. It can be very brief or it can take up a large percentage of the total word count. Aristotle said that the introduction could be compared to the flourishes that flute players make before their performance—an overture in which the musicians display what they can play best in order to gain the favor and attention of the audience for the main performance.

In order to do this, we must first of all know what we are going to say; who the readership is likely to be; what the social, political, economic, etc., climate is; what preconceived notions the audience is likely to have regarding the subject; and how long the discourse is going to be.

There are many ways to do this:
- Show that the subject is important.
- Show that although the points we are presenting may seem improbable, they are true.
- Show that the subject has been neglected, misunderstood, or misrepresented.
- Explain an unusual mode of development.
- Forestall any misconception of the purpose.
- Apologize for a deficiency.
- Arouse interest in the subject with an anecdotal lead-in.
- Ingratiate oneself with the readership.
- Establish one's own credibility.

The introduction often ends with the thesis, the point or purpose of the paper. However, this is not set in stone. The thesis may open the body of the discussion, or it may conclude the discourse. The most important thing to remember is that the purpose and structure of the introduction should be deliberate if it is to serve the purpose of "leading the reader into the discussion."

Conclusions:

It's easier to write a conclusion after the decisions regarding the introduction have been made. Aristotle taught that the conclusion should strive to do five things:

1. Inspire the reader with a favorable opinion of the writer.
2. Amplify the force of the points made in the body of the paper.
3. Reinforce the points made in the body.
4. Rouse appropriate emotions in the reader.
5. Restate in a summary way what has been said.

The conclusion may be short or it may be long depending on its purpose in the paper. Recapitulation, a brief restatement of the main points or certainly of the thesis is the most common form of effective conclusions. A good example is the closing argument in a court trial.

Skill 3.9   Interpret graphic features in expository texts.

Tables that simply store descriptive information in a form available for general use are called repository tables. They usually contain primary data and simply summarize raw data. They are not intended to analyze the data, so any analysis is left to the reader or user of the table. A good example of a repository table would be a report of birth statistics by the federal Health and Human Services Department. An analytical table, on the other hand, is constructed from some sort of analysis of primary or secondary data, possibly from a repository table or from the raw data itself. An example of an analytical table would be one that compares birth statistics in 1980 to birth statistics in 2005 for the country at large. It might also break the data down into comparisons by state.

Graphs also present data in visual form. Whereas tables are useful for showing large numbers of specific, related facts or statistics in a brief space, trends, movements, distributions, and cycles are more readily apparent in a graph. However, although graphs can present statistics in a more interesting and comprehensible form than tables, they are less accurate. For this reason, the two will often be shown together.

While the most obvious use for **maps** is to locate places geographically, they can also show specific geographic features such as roads, mountains, rivers, etc. The can also show information according to geographic distribution such as population, housing, manufacturing centers, etc.

A wide range of **illustrations** may be used to illuminate the text in a document. They may also be a part of a graphic layout designed to make the page more attractive.

Some possibilities for the analysis of data whether presented in tables, charts, graphs, maps, or other illustrations are as follow:
Qualitative descriptions—drawing conclusions about the quality of a particular treatment or course of action as revealed by the illustration.
Quantitative descriptions—how much do the results of one particular treatment or course of action differ from another one, and is that variation significant?
Classification—worthwhile information derived from breaking the information down into classifications.
Estimations—estimating future performance on the basis of the information in the illustration.
Comparisons—is it useful to make comparisons based on the data?
Relationships—are relationships between components revealed by the scrutiny of the data?
Cause-and-effect relationships—is it suggested by the data that there were cause-and-effect relationships that were not previously apparent?
Mapping and modeling—if the data were mapped and a model drawn up, would the point of the document be demonstrated or refuted?

Questions to ask regarding an illustration: Why is it in this document? What was the writer's purpose in putting it in the document and why at this particular place? Does it make a point clearer? What implications are inherent in a table that shows birth statistics in all states or even in some selected states? What does that have to do with the point and purpose of this piece of writing? Is there adequate preparation in the text for the inclusion of the illustration? Does the illustration underscore or clarify any of the points made in the text? Is there a clear connection between the illustration and the subject matter of the text?

COMPETENCY 4   READING PERSUASIVE TEXTS

Skill 4.1   Identify the characteristics and purposes of various types of persuasive texts.

News stories are always assumed to be unbiased. It can be argued, of course, that no one can be entirely unbiased and that it's the nature of the written word that those biases may creep into the reporting of news. Even so, the professional reporter and/or editor will exercise the strength necessary to keep his or her own biases out of the reporting as much as possible.

Editorializing is an entirely different thing. Most newspapers, for instance, have an editorial position, which will often correspond to political parties. A newspaper may, for instance, declare itself to be Republican. This does not mean that the newspaper will favor the party of choice in news reporting. It does, however, mean that editorial materials will probably be slanted in that direction. In a time of election, a newspaper will often come out for one candidate over another and try to influence its readership to follow suit. A newspaper will often take a side when an issue is on the docket at time of election or even at other times. An editorial will frequently state an opinion about a matter that concerns the newspaper's readership.

Petitions represent an effort to bring about some change. They are more often than not aimed at a government official or public entity. Perhaps the most commonly-recognized form of petition is prayer, where an individual is asking a deity to bring about a change or grant some request. Petitions (except prayer, of course) are signed by a large number of persons although it may be oral rather than written. Nowadays, the Internet is sometimes used for purposes of petitioning an official or a governmental body. A petition may also be a legal document in a lawsuit. For example, a parent may petition the court for custody of his or her child.

The place where we see most marketing efforts by companies that have something to sell is the Internet. However, we do occasionally see a marketing brochure that will tout the excellence, value, and usefulness of a certain product. These brochures, like television commercials, will probably use some of the devices listed in Skill 4.5 under "Rhetorical Techniques Used to Achieve Certain Effects."

The reading of newspapers has declined in response to the development of television as the medium of choice for information. Some long-published newspapers are even going out of business. However, many businesses still use newspaper ads to get the word out about their products and to build confidence in themselves. These are less expensive than television and, especially in smaller towns, may be the only way to reach potential buyers. Just as with television ads, the cost is considerable, but newspaper ads may be more cost-effective in terms of cost vs. yield.

Skill 4.2   Distinguish between fact and opinion in a persuasive text.

Facts and Opinions

Facts are statements that are verifiable. **Opinions** are statements that must be supported in order to be accepted. Facts are used to support opinions. For example, "Jane is a bad girl" is an opinion. However, "Jane hit her sister with a baseball bat" is a *fact* upon which the opinion is based. Judgments are opinions—decisions or declarations based on observation or reasoning that express approval or disapproval. Facts report what has happened or exists and come from observation, measurement, or calculation. Facts can be tested and verified whereas opinions and judgments cannot. They can only be supported with facts.

Most statements cannot be so clearly distinguished. "I believe that Jane is a bad girl" is a *fact*. The speaker knows what he/she believes. However, it obviously includes a judgment that could be disputed by another person who might believe otherwise. Judgments are not usually so firm. They are, rather, plausible opinions that provoke thought or lead to factual development.

Skill 4.3   Evaluate the relevance, importance, and sufficiency of facts offered in support of an argument presented in a persuasive text.

An argument is a generalization that is proven or supported with facts. If the facts are not accurate, the generalization remains unproven. Using inaccurate "facts" to support an argument is called a *fallacy in* reasoning. Some factors to consider in judging whether the facts used to support an argument are accurate are as follow:

1. Are the facts current or are they out of date? For example, if the proposition "birth defects in babies born to drug-using mothers are increasing," then the data must include the latest that is available.
2. Another important factor to consider in judging the accuracy of a fact is its source. Where was the data obtained, and is that source reliable?
3. The calculations on which the facts are based may be unreliable. It's a good idea to run one's own calculations before using a piece of derived information.

Even facts that are true and have a sharp impact on the argument may not be relevant to the case at hand.

1. Health statistics from an entire state may have no relevance, or little relevance, to a particular county or zip code. Statistics from an entire country cannot be used to prove very much about a particular state or county. To say that Italians have volatile personalities may not be relevant to all Italians.
2. An analogy can be useful in making a point, but the comparison must match up in all characteristics or it will not be relevant. Analogy should be used very carefully. It is often just as likely to destroy an argument as it is to strengthen it.

The importance or significance of a fact may not be sufficient to strengthen an argument. For example, of the millions of immigrants in the U.S., using the experience of a single family to support a solution to the immigration problem will not make much difference overall even though those single-example arguments are often used to support one approach or another. They may achieve a positive reaction, but they will not prove that one solution is better than another. If enough cases were cited from a variety of geographical locations, the information might be significant.

How much is enough? Generally speaking, three strong supporting facts are sufficient to establish the thesis of an argument. For example:

Thesis: All green apples are sour.
- When I was a child, I bit into a green apple from my grandfather's orchard, and it was sour.
- I once bought green apples from a roadside vendor, and when I bit into one, it was sour.
- My grocery store had a sale on green Granny Smith apples last week, and I bought several only to find that they were sour when I bit into one.

The fallacy in the above argument is that the sample was insufficient. A more exhaustive search of literature, etc., will probably turn up some green apples that are not sour.

Sometimes more than three arguments are too many. On the other hand, it's not unusual to hear public speakers, particularly politicians, who will cite a long litany of facts to support their positions.

Fact vs. Opinion

Use the chart below to identify both facts and opinions in a text and be sure to explain how you know whether the details you write down are either facts or opinions.

	Text Details & Direct Quotes From the Text	Explain How You Know the Details are Facts or Opinions

Facts		
Opinions		

http://www.greece.k12.ny.us/instruction/ela/6-12/Tools/factvsopinion.pdf

Skill 4.4 Assess the credibility and objectivity of various sources of information used in a persuasive text.

Students enjoy sharing their opinions. Some of them may be voicing what they have heard from others, while some are discovering their own voices. All are trying to make sense of their worlds. Helping them distinguish between fact and opinion, realize conclusions, and make inferences develops critical reasoning.

Bias

Everyone is biased in some way because everyone has a perspective—a way of perceiving or preferring. While objectivity is a goal, we often fall short with our subjective perceptions and attitudes. What we want to avoid, however, is to be so slanted that we are unfairly biased. This weakens are credibility and undercuts the force of our argument.

What we need to do then is to avoid conscious bias and be sensitive to unconscious bias because preconceptions can compromise integrity of research. Conscious (deliberate) bias is unethical. Unconscious bias can be difficult to detect and/or control. It reflects the mentality of the reader or writer. You should be mentally alert to detect bias. Avoid racial, sexist, ageist, ethnic, and religious bias whenever possible. Sometimes the bias is more subtle and thus harder to detect.

Personal bias—For example, a researcher with an on-the-job injury may be partial in job safety studies.

Cultural bias—For example, a person with a strong work ethic may be partial in a study of the chronically unemployed.

Professional bias—For example, a teacher with a set work pattern may not be receptive to an alternative method.

Persuasive

Some questions to ask:

A • Title (How relevant is it to your topic?)
B • Date (How current is the source?)
C • Organization (What institution is this source coming from?)
D • Length (How in depth does it go?)

Check for signs of bias:

- Does the author or publisher have political ties or religious views that could affect objectivity?
- Is the author or publisher associated with any special-interest groups that might only see one side of an issue, such as Greenpeace or the National Rifle Association?
- How fairly does the author treat opposing views?
- Does the language of the piece show signs of bias?

Keep an open mind while reading, and don't let opposing viewpoints prevent you from absorbing the text. Remember that you are not judging the author's work; you are examining its assumptions, assessing its evidence, and weighing its conclusions.

Skill 4.5   Analyze how tone, style, and rhetorical techniques are used to achieve certain effects in a persuasive text.

Style and Tone

Often writers have an emotional stake in a subject; and their purpose, either explicitly or implicitly, is to convey those feelings to the reader. In such cases, the writing is generally subjective: that is, it stems from opinions, judgments, values, ideas, and feelings.

In literature, style means a distinctive manner of expression and applies to all levels of language, beginning at the phonemic level with word choices, alliteration, assonance, and others, moving to the syntactic level, characterized by length of sentences, choice of structure and phraseology (diction), and patterns, and even extending beyond the sentence to paragraphs and chapters. Critical readers determine what is distinctive about the writer's use of these elements. All of these are instrumental in creating style.

The tone of a written passage is the author's attitude toward the subject matter. The tone (mood, feeling) is revealed through the qualities of the writing itself and is a direct product of such stylistic elements as language and sentence structure. The tone of the written passage is much like a speaker's voice; instead of being spoken, however, it is the product of words on a page.

Tone may be thought of generally as positive, negative, or neutral. Below is a statement about snakes that demonstrates this.

> Many species of snakes live in Florida. Some of those species, both poisonous and non-poisonous, have habitats that coincide with those of human residents of the state.

The voice of the writer in this statement is neutral. The sentences are declarative (not exclamations or fragments or questions). The adjectives are few and nondescript—*many, some, poisonous* (balanced with *non-poisonous*). Nothing much in this brief paragraph would alert the reader to the feelings of the writer about snakes. The paragraph has a neutral, objective, detached, impartial tone.

Then again, if the writer's attitude toward snakes involves admiration, or even affection, the tone would generally be positive:

> Florida's snakes are a tenacious bunch. When they find their habitats invaded by humans, they cling to their home territories as long as they can, as if vainly attempting to fight off the onslaught of the human hordes.

An additional message emerges in this paragraph: the writer quite clearly favors snakes over people. The writer uses adjectives like *tenacious* to describe feelings about snakes. The writer also humanizes the reptiles, making them brave, beleaguered creatures. Obviously, the writer is more sympathetic to snakes than to people in this paragraph.

If the writer's attitude toward snakes involves active dislike and fear, then the tone would also reflect that attitude by being negative:

> Countless species of snakes, some more dangerous than others, still lurk on the urban fringes of Florida's towns and cities. They will often invade domestic spaces, terrorizing people and their pets.

Here, obviously, the snakes are the villains. They *lurk,* they *invade,* and they *terrorize.* The tone of this paragraph might be said to be distressed about snakes.

In the same manner, a writer can use language to portray characters as good or bad. A writer uses positive and negative adjectives, as seen above, to convey the manner of a character.

Rhetorical Techniques Used to Achieve Certain Effects
(Most easily seen in advertising)

Beauty Appeal: Beauty attracts us; we are drawn to beautiful people, places, and things.

Celebrity Endorsement: This technique associates product use with a well-known person. By purchasing this product we are led to believe that we will attain characteristics similar to the celebrity.

Compliment the Consumer: Advertisers flatter the consumer who is willing to purchase their product. By purchasing the product the consumer is recognized by the advertisers for making a good decision with the selection.

Escape: Getting away from it all is very appealing; you can imagine adventures you cannot have; the idea of escape is pleasurable.

Independence/Individuality: This technique associates product with people who can think and act for themselves. Products are linked to individual decision making.

Intelligence: This technique associates product with smart people who can't be fooled.

Lifestyle: This technique associates product with a particular style of living/way of doing things.

Nurture: Every time you see an animal or a child, the appeal is to your paternal or maternal instincts, so this technique associates products with taking care of someone.

Peer Approval: This technique associates product use with friendship /acceptance. Advertisers can also use this negatively to make you worry that you'll lose friends if you don't use a certain product.

Rebel: This technique associates products with behaviors or lifestyles that oppose society's norms.

Rhetorical Question: This technique poses a question to the consumer that demands a response. A question is asked and the consumer is supposed to answer in such a way that affirms the product's goodness.

Scientific/Statistical Claim: This provides some sort of scientific proof or experiment, very specific numbers, or an impressive sounding mystery ingredient.

Unfinished Comparison/Claim: This technique uses phrases such as "Works better in poor driving conditions!" Works better than what?

Skill 4.6   Recognize incomplete, inaccurate, extraneous, or unclear information and faulty reasoning in persuasive texts.

A fallacy is, essentially, an error in reasoning. In persuasive speech, logical fallacies are instances of reasoning flaws that make an argument invalid. For example, a premature generalization occurs when you form a general rule based on only one or a few specific cases, which do not represent all possible cases. An illustration of this is the statement, "Bob Marley was a Rastafarian singer. Therefore, all Rastafarians sing."

A common fallacy in reasoning is the *post hoc ergo propter hoc* ("after this, therefore because of this") or the false-cause fallacy. These occur in cause/effect reasoning, which may either go from cause to effect or effect to cause.

They happen when an inadequate cause is offered for a particular effect; when the possibility of more than one cause is ignored; and when a connection between a particular cause and a particular effect is not made.

> Learn more about
> **Post Hoc Fallacy**
> http://www.sjsu.edu/depts/itl/graphics/adhom/posthoc.html

An example of a *post hoc*: Our sales shot up thirty-five percent after we ran that television campaign; therefore the campaign caused the increase in sales.

It might have been a cause, of course, but more evidence is needed to prove it.

An example of an **inadequate cause for a particular effect**: An Iraqi truck driver reported that Saddam Hussein had nuclear weapons; therefore, Saddam Hussein is a threat to world security.

More causes are needed to prove the conclusion.

An example of **ignoring the possibility of more than one possible cause**: John Brown was caught out in a thunderstorm and his clothes were wet before he was rescued; therefore, he developed influenza the next day was because he got wet.

Being chilled may have played a role in the illness, but Brown would have had to contract the influenza virus before he would come down with it whether or not he had gotten wet.

> An example of **failing to make a connection between a particular cause and an effect** assigned to it. Anna fell into a putrid pond on Saturday; on Monday she came down with polio; therefore, the pond caused the polio.

This, of course, is not acceptable unless the polio virus is found in a sample of water from the pond. A connection must be proven.

COMPETENCY 5   READING FUNCTIONAL AND TECHNICAL TEXTS

Skill 5.1   Identify the characteristics and purposes of various types of functional texts and technical texts.

Remember that there are multiple ways to get information. Read an encyclopedia article about a topic to get a general overview, and then focus from there. Note important names of people associated with a subject, time periods, and geographic areas. And finally, don't forget about articles in magazines and newspapers, or even personal interviews with experts related to your field of interest! To be life-long learners, students should learn to conduct their own research, and they need to know what resources are available to them and how to use them.

Dictionaries are useful for spelling, writing, and reading. Students looking up a word in a dictionary should be an expected behavior, not a punishment or busy work that has no reference to their current reading assignment. Model the correct way to use the dictionary for some have never been taught proper dictionary skills. As the teacher, you need to demonstrate that as an adult reader and writer, you routinely and happily use the dictionary.

Encyclopedias in print or online are the beginning point for many research projects. While these entries may sometimes lack timeliness, they do provide students with general background.

Thesauruses. Whereas dictionaries contain definitions and pronunciations, thesauruses contain synonyms (some also contain antonyms). Used by most writers, they provide quick hints for words with the same or approximately the same meaning as another. Most writers turn to the thesaurus when they want to avoid repetition of a word. There are even specialized thesauruses for various fields. A number of thesauruses are available; the most commonly used one is Roget's.

Atlases contain maps of a particular region although an atlas of the entire Earth can be found. Also, there are atlases of other planets. Atlases typically show geographic features and political boundaries, but they may be more specialized and even show geopolitical or social statistics. They can be found in libraries bound into books; however, the information sought may very well be available online.

Databases hold billions of records so students should be taught effective search techniques such as using key words and Boolean operators. Learning that "and" and "or" will increase the number of hits while "not" or "and not" will decrease the number of hits can save researchers time and effort.

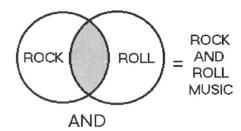

Learn more about **Boolean Operators** at http://www.bgsu.edu/colleges/library/info srv/lue/boolean.html

The **Internet** is a multi-faceted goldmine of information, but you must be careful to discriminate between reliable and unreliable sources. Use sites that are associated with an academic institution, such as a university or a scholarly organization. Typical domain names will end in "edu" or "org." Students (and everyone) should evaluate any piece of information gleaned from the Internet. For example, if you google "etymology" you can find a multitude of sources. Don't trust a single one. The information should be validated by at least three sources. Wikipedia is very useful, but it can be changed by anyone who chooses; so any information on it should be backed up by other sources.

Timetables and schedules make our lives better in many ways and knowing how to read them can be useful. For example, airlines publish timetables that show arrival and departure times of their flights. These may be for a week or even longer. However, these schedules sometimes change, so it's best to call before planning to take a flight. Teaching students to use schedules is another way to equip them for the real world.

Instruction manuals come with most pieces of equipment. Going through a simple one with students will raise their awareness to the kinds of written materials available. Sometimes people ignore the instruction manuals and proceed on their own to use a piece of equipment to their grief. Reading the manual is always important even though some of them may not be very useful.

Product warranties represent an obligation on the part of the seller that an article purchased from him is what it was represented to be. It will usually guarantee repair or replacement within a certain period of time and under certain conditions. These come with many pieces of equipment, especially those that cost a lot. It's a wise consumer who pays attention to those warranties.

Disclaimers are statements relieving the posting party of certain liabilities. Just as a product may come with a warranty, it may also come with a disclaimer relieving it of any responsibility or obligation in certain cases.

Safety regulations apply to many aspects of our lives, most particularly to transportation. For example, anyone who drives a car must abide by certain safety regulations. To be certain that all drivers are aware of those regulations, before a license is granted, the driver must pass a test. Anyone who operates a boat is also subject to certain regulations.

Policies pervade our lives. We have life insurance policies that stipulate payment in a certain amount under certain conditions. Many companies have employee policies that guide the way employees function within that company. These are usually spelled out in a manual and provided to all employees. The federal government probably has the most policies of any other entity in the country.

A Contract is an exchange of promises between at least two parties stipulating that each party will do a certain thing or things. Contracts properly executed may be enforced by law—in other words, they are legally binding.

A Law is an enforceable set of rules. These may be enacted by any governmental agency with the legal authority to write them and enforce them. For research purposes, most laws can be read at governmental sites online.

Skill 5.2 Demonstrate the ability to use information presented in functional texts to perform tasks.

The dictionary will be the source you'll most often turn to for information about the meaning of a word or its definition. Many companies are publishing dictionaries nowadays, so it's good to know that the most reliable general-use American dictionary is the one published by Merriam-Webster because of the amount of research that supports its choices. This dictionary comes in many versions, the most commonly-used one being the collegiate version, which is updated more frequently than the unabridged version, which may be found in most libraries. If the information regarding a word is not in the collegiate version, you may go to the unabridged one, where you will probably find it. On the other hand, if you want the history of the word, the Oxford English Dictionary of English is the most reliable. It can also be found in most libraries although electronic editions are also available nowadays.

For locating people and places, you will no doubt begin with the local phone book if that person lives in your town. If not, you can sometimes find a person by going to yellowbook.com or other online references that contain the information typically found in a phone book. If you are trying to find a location, an atlas that includes the area being researched may solve your problem. There are, however, many online sites that also have search functions for places and locations such as Google.

If you are planning a trip, you will want to investigate which mode of transportation best meets your needs. Most people travel longer distances nowadays by airplane. In order to get the information you need about times and prices, you may call the airline, call a travel agent, or go online to the airline's site. If you are making your trip by automobile, you will need maps that cover the entire trip. For example, if you're traveling from Texas to Florida, you'll want maps that include the highways in all the states you'll be traveling through and an atlas, perhaps, so you can see all those states and their locations with regard to one another.

Newspapers are very good sources for finding whatever goods and services you need; however, the yellow pages in a phone book also provide good guides. Some online sites offer lists of the best service agencies in your area. For example, if you are having a new bathroom put in, that site will let you know the construction companies with the best reputation for doing quality work for a reasonable price.

If you are searching for a job, the newspaper want-ads may be the best primary source for finding what's available in your area. However, there may be employment agencies in your town or area either run by companies or governmental agencies. You'll want to find out who will pay for that service before you sign anything. There are many online employment service agencies nowadays. Make certain the agency you choose is legitimate. The employer should pay the fees. One very large jobsite is Monster.com. You will need an effective resumé, of course.

Skill 5.3   Demonstrate the ability to use information presented in technical texts to develop skills and gain knowledge.

You can probably teach yourself to use computer software you've never used before. Typically, a manual will come with the software; however, there are also many guides available at book stores for many of the commonly-used programs. For example, if you want to learn to use Quark Xpress, the manual that comes with it is very useful. However, you can also go out and buy a book that may add to the information in the manual in very helpful ways, especially for a new user. To learn in this way requires patience and perseverance.

If you have a new washing machine, you'll want to read the manual that comes with it. It will tell you what each of the features will do and how to access those functions. For example, how do you get the gentlest agitation? How do you adjust water temperature? How high do you fill it with clothes to be washed, etc. The same is true with any unfamiliar equipment. Many people just jump in and use a piece of equipment they are not familiar with on the assumption that they know how to navigate the various devices and functions. This is not a good idea. If there is a manual, it should be read before using the equipment.

Consumers have rights that are guaranteed by the federal government, but most of us do not know what they are. The federal government spells them out at http://www.fdic.gov/consumers/consumer/rights/index.html. The rights have to do with many aspects of our lives such as mortgages, leases, credit, charge cards, and many others. State, county, and city governments have their own set of consumer rights that may add to those of the federal government. To find out what those rights are, you can call court houses and state, county, and city offices to get a list of these or you can go directly to the site and ask to see them.

To be responsible citizens of our neighborhoods, our cities, and our country, we need to show concern and sensitivity for others, including those of other cultures. We need to participate actively in our communities, both local, national, and global. We should seek an understanding of and be concerned about our governments both local and national. We need to have an interest in history and current events. We need to take an active role in preserving our environment. A responsible citizen takes responsibility for understanding the issues appearing on a ballot for passage either up or down or the people who are running for election. A responsible citizen votes regularly and votes his conscience. Many citizens act out their commitment to responsible citizenship by getting involved in their elections either locally or nationally.

Skill 5.4 Interpret graphic features in functional and technical texts.

Answers.com calls a diagram "a plan, sketch, drawing, or outline designed to demonstrate or explain how something works or to clarify the relationship between the parts of a whole. *Mathematics.* A graphic representation of an algebraic or geometric relationship. A chart or a graph." Functional and technical texts are more likely to use diagrams to make their points clear than are other kinds of communications, so we need to be able to understand how they work. They are especially effective at showing actions, processes, events, and ideas. For visually-inclined people, they are particularly helpful.

Maps use a variety of tools to convey and organize their information. For example, there will be a key/legend that includes a ruler to help the reader of the map measure the distance from one place to another. Certain symbols will be used to point out features such as roadside parks, railroad tracks, or bodies of water such as streams. Roads may be depicted as to 4-lane, 2-lane, or unpaved. It's important to make oneself aware of the key/legend before trying to use a map.

Flowcharts are special kinds of charts that show an algorithm or process. There will be boxes of various shapes and, possibly, colors that will be connected by arrows that show directional movement. These are used for various kinds of analysis, design, or documentation of a process. They are frequently seen in explanations of a computer program or process. Many Internet sites go into detail about the use of flowcharts. Just google flowchart.

Schematic Drawings are structural or procedural diagrams, usually of an electrical or mechanical system or a graphical representation of any system. For example, if there is a sound system in an auditorium that can be used from the projection booth behind the auditorium, from the podium at the front of the auditorium, or from the rear-projection booth behind the podium, a schematic diagram of the sound circuits would be very useful for a person who wanted to make a presentation in that auditorium.

Blueprints are reproductions of an architecture or an engineering design on paper. The term is sometimes used more generally in a metaphoric sense of any detailed plan. They are called "blue" prints because they were originally made by exposing the diagram outlines on photosensitive "blue" paper. If you are going to have a new house built, the architect will furnish you with a blueprint of the plan for the house. In other words, you can see on paper the footprint of your not-yet-built house.

Competency 6   READING VARIOUS GENRES OF FICTION AND DRAMA.

Skill 6.1   Recognize the characteristics of various types of fictional narratives.

The major literary genres include allegory, ballad, drama, epic, epistle, essay, fable, novel, poem, romance, and the short story.

Allegory: A story in verse or prose with characters representing virtues and vices. There are two meanings, symbolic and literal. John Bunyan's *The Pilgrim's Progress* is the most renowned of this genre.

Ballad: An *in medias res* story told or sung, usually in verse and accompanied by music. Literary devices found in ballads include the refrain, or repeated section, and incremental repetition, or anaphora, for effect. Earliest forms were anonymous folk ballads. Later forms include Coleridge's Romantic masterpiece, "The Rime of the Ancient Mariner."

Drama: Plays—comedy, modern, or tragedy—typically in five acts. Traditionalists and neoclassicists adhere to Aristotle's unities of time, place, and action. Plot development is advanced via dialogue. Literary devices include asides, soliloquies, and the chorus representing public opinion. Greatest of all dramatists/playwrights is William Shakespeare. Other dramaturges include Ibsen, Williams, Miller, Shaw, Stoppard, Racine, Moliére, Sophocles, Aeschylus, Euripides, and Aristophanes.

Epic: Long poem usually of book length reflecting values inherent in the generative society. Epic devices include an invocation to a Muse for inspiration, purpose for writing, universal setting, protagonist and antagonist who possess supernatural strength and acumen, and interventions of a God or the gods. Understandably, there are very few epics: Homer's *Iliad* and *Odyssey*, Virgil's *Aeneid*, Milton's *Paradise Lost*, Spenser's *The Fairie Queene*, Barrett Browning's *Aurora Leigh*, and Pope's mock-epic, *The Rape of the Lock*.

Epistle: A letter that is not always originally intended for public distribution, but due to the fame of the sender and/or recipient, becomes public domain. Paul wrote epistles that were later placed in the *Bible*.

Essay: Typically a limited length prose work focusing on a topic and propounding a definite point of view and authoritative tone. Great essayists include Carlyle, Lamb, DeQuincy, Emerson, and Montaigne, who is credited with defining this genre.

Fable: Terse tale offering up a moral or exemplum. Chaucer's "The Nun's Priest's Tale" is a fine example of a *bete fabliau* or beast fable in which animals speak and act characteristically human, illustrating human foibles. *Aesop*

Legend: A traditional narrative or collection of related narratives, popularly regarded as historically factual but actually a mixture of fact and fiction.

Myth: Stories that are more or less universally shared within a culture to explain its history and traditions.

Novel: The longest form of fictional prose containing a variety of characterizations, settings, local color, and regionalism. Most have complex plots, expanded description, and attention to detail. Some of the great novelists include Austen, the Brontes, Twain, Tolstoy, Hugo, Hardy, Dickens, Hawthorne, Forster, and Flaubert.

Poem: The only requirement is rhythm. Sub-genres include fixed types of literature such as the sonnet, elegy, ode, pastoral, and villanelle. Unfixed types of literature include blank verse and dramatic monologue. *1a line poetic line w/s tercet + 1 quatrain*

Romance: A highly imaginative tale set in a fantastical realm dealing with the conflicts between heroes, villains and/or monsters. "The Knight's Tale" from Chaucer's *Canterbury Tales*, *Sir Gawain and the Green Knight*, and Keats' "The Eve of St. Agnes" are prime representatives.

Short Story: Typically a terse narrative, with less developmental background about characters than a novel. May use description, author's point of view, and tone. Poe emphasized that a successful short story should create one focused impact. Considered to be great short story writers are Hemingway, Faulkner, Twain, Joyce, Shirley Jackson, Flannery O'Connor, de Maupassant, Saki, Edgar Allen Poe, and Pushkin.

Skill 6.2 Analyze the elements of fiction in works of fiction and drama.

It's no accident that **plot** is sometimes called action. If the plot does not *move*, the story quickly dies. Therefore, the successful writer of stories uses a wide variety of active verbs in creative and unusual ways. If a reader is kept on his/her toes by the movement of the story, the experience of reading it will be pleasurable. The reader will probably want to read more of this author's work. Careful, unique, and unusual choices of active verbs will bring about that effect. William Faulkner is a good example of a successful writer whose stories are lively and memorable because of his use of unusual active verbs. In analyzing the development of plot, it's wise to look at the verbs. However, the development of believable conflicts is also vital. If there is no conflict, there is no story. What devices does a writer use to develop the conflicts, and are they real and believable?

Character is portrayed in many ways: description of physical characteristics, dialogue, interior monologue, the thoughts of the character, the attitudes of other characters toward this one, etc. Descriptive language depends on the ability to recreate a sensory experience for the reader. If the description of the character's appearance is a visual one, then the reader must be able to *see* the character. What's the shape of the nose? What color are the eyes? How tall or how short is this character? Thin or chubby? How does the character move? How does the character walk? Terms must be chosen that will create a picture for the reader. It's not enough to say the eyes are blue, for example. What blue? Often the color of eyes is compared to something else to enhance the readers' ability to visualize the character. A good test of characterization is the level of emotional involvement of the reader in the character. If the reader is to become involved, the description must provide an actual experience—seeing, smelling, hearing, tasting, or feeling.

Dialogue will reflect characteristics. Is it clipped? Is it highly dialectal? Does a character use a lot of colloquialisms? The ability to portray the speech of a character can make or break a story. The kind of person the character is in the mind of the reader is dependent on impressions created by description and dialogue. How do other characters feel about this one as revealed by their treatment of him/her, their discussions of him/her with each other, or their overt descriptions of the character? For example, "John, of course, can't be trusted with another person's possessions." In analyzing a story, it's useful to discuss the devices used to produce character, called characterization.

Setting may be visual, temporal, psychological, or social. Descriptive words are often used here also. In Edgar Allan Poe's description of the house in "The Fall of the House of Usher" as the protagonist/narrator approaches it, the air of dread and gloom that pervades the story is caught in the setting and sets the stage for the story. A setting may also be symbolic, as it is in Poe's story, where the house is a symbol of the family that lives in it. As the house disintegrates, so does the family.

The language used in all of these aspects of a story—plot, character, and setting—work together to create the **mood** of a story. Poe's first sentence establishes the mood of the story: "During the whole of a dull, dark, and soundless day in the autumn of the year, when the clouds hung oppressively low in the heavens, I had been passing alone, on horseback, through a singularly dreary tract of country; and at length found myself, as the shades of the evening drew on, within view of the melancholy House of Usher."

The **theme** of a poem or story is the point it makes—similar to the thesis in nonfiction. The theme is rarely stated outright. The burden falls on the reader to determine what point this work makes by taking a step back after carefully reading it and putting all the pieces together. "Good always prevails over evil," for example might be a theme of many stories.

Voice or **Point of view** refers to the eyes through which the story is viewed—or who is telling the story. *First person narrator*, where the only thoughts of a character are those of the one telling the story, is a common one. "The Fall of the House of Usher" is a good example of artistic use of first-person narrator point of view to achieve the purpose of the story. All the details and all of the actions are viewed through the eyes of the narrator. The horror of the events he records escalate until at the end, the narrator, himself, has become unbalanced. As the house disintegrates and the family with it, the narrator, himself also disintegrates. This would not be nearly as forceful a story with a different point of view. Other points of view are *omniscient*, where the person telling the story knows what more than one of the characters is thinking. A story told from a *limited omniscient* point of view will reveal the thoughts of only one character—typically the protagonist but not always.

Skill 6.3   Analyzing the use of common literary and rhetorical devices in works of fiction and drama.

Imagery can be described as a word or sequence of words that refers to any sensory experience—that is, anything that can be seen, tasted, smelled, heard, or felt on the skin or fingers. While writers of prose may also use these devices, it is most distinctive of poetry. The novelist or playwright intends to make an experience available to the reader. In order to do that, he/she must appeal to one of the senses. The most-often-used one, of course, is the visual sense. The poet will deliberately paint a scene in such a way that the reader can see it. However, the purpose is not simply to stir the visceral feeling but also to stir the emotions. Imagery might be defined as speaking of the abstract in concrete terms, a powerful device in the hands of a skillful writer.

A **symbol** is an object or action that can be observed with the senses in addition to its suggesting many other things. The lion is a symbol of courage; the cross a symbol of Christianity; the color green a symbol of envy. These can almost be defined as metaphors because society pretty much agrees on the one-to-one meaning of them. Symbols used in literature are usually of a different sort. They tend to be private and personal; their significance is only evident in the context of the work where they are used. A good example is the huge pair of spectacles on a sign board in Fitzgerald's *The Great Gatsby*. They are interesting as a part of the landscape, but they also symbolize divine myopia. A symbol can certainly have more than one meaning, and the meaning may be as personal as the memories and experiences of the particular reader. In analyzing a poem or a story, it's important to identify the symbols and their possible meanings.

Looking for symbols is often challenging, especially for novice readers. However, these suggestions may be useful: first, pick out all the references to concrete objects such as a newspaper, black cats, etc. Note any that the writer emphasizes by describing in detail, by repeating, or by placing at the very beginning or ending of a poem. Ask yourself, what is this story about? What does it add up to? Paraphrase the plot and determine whether or not the meaning depends upon certain concrete objects. Then ponder what the concrete object symbolizes in this particular work. Look for a character with the name of a prophet who does little but utter prophecy or a trio of women who resemble the Three Fates. A symbol may be a part of a person's body such as the eye of the murder victim in Poe's story *The Tell-Tale Heart* or a look, a voice, or a mannerism.

Some things a symbol is not: an abstraction such as truth, death, and love; in narrative, a well-developed character who is not at all mysterious; the second term in a metaphor.

An **allusion** is very much like a symbol, and the two sometimes tend to run together. An allusion is defined by Merriam Webster's *Encyclopedia of Literature* as "an implied reference to a person, event, thing, or a part of another text." Allusions are based on the assumption that there is a common body of knowledge shared by author and reader and that a reference to that body of knowledge will be immediately understood. Allusions to the Bible and classical mythology are common in western literature on the assumption that they will be immediately understood. This is not always the case, of course. T. S. Eliot's *The Wasteland* requires research and annotation for understanding. He assumed more background on the part of the average reader than actually exists. However, when Michael Moore on his web page headlines an article on the war in Iraq: "Déjà Fallouja: Ramadi surrounded, thousands of families trapped, no electricity or water, onslaught impending," we understand immediately that he is referring first of all to a repeat of the human disaster in New Orleans although the "onslaught" is not a storm but an invasion by American and Iraqi troops.

The use of allusion is a sort of shortcut. The writer can use an economy of words and count on meaning to come from the reader's own experience.

Figurative language is also called figures of speech. If all figures of speech that have ever been identified were listed, it would be a very long list. However, for purposes of analyzing poetry, a few are sufficient.

1. **Simile**: Direct comparison between two things. "My love is like a red-red rose."
2. **Metaphor**: Indirect comparison between two things. The use of a word or phrase denoting one kind of object or action in place of another to suggest a comparison between them. While poets and novelists use them extensively, they are also integral to everyday speech. For example, chairs are said to have "legs" and "arms" although we know that it's humans and other animals that have these appendages.
3. **Parallelism**: The arrangement of ideas in phrases, sentences, and paragraphs that balance one element with another of equal importance and similar wording. An example from Francis Bacon's *Of Studies*: "Reading maketh a full man, conference a ready man, and writing an exact man."
4. **Personification**: Human characteristics are attributed to an inanimate object, an abstract quality, or animal. Examples: John Bunyan wrote characters named Death, Knowledge, Giant Despair, Sloth, and Piety in his *Pilgrim's Progress*. The metaphor of an arm of a chair is a form of personification.
5. **Euphemism**: The substitution of an agreeable or inoffensive term for one that might offend or suggest something unpleasant. Many euphemisms are used to refer to death to avoid using the real word such as "passed away," "crossed over," or nowadays "passed."
6. **Hyperbole**: Deliberate exaggeration for effect or comic effect. An example from Shakespeare's *The Merchant of Venice*:
    > Why, if two gods should play some heavenly match
    > And on the wager lay two earthly women,
    > And Portia one, there must be something else
    > Pawned with the other, for the poor rude world
    > Hath not her fellow.
7. **Climax**: A number of phrases or sentences are arranged in ascending order of rhetorical forcefulness. Example from Melville's *Moby Dick*:
    > All that most maddens and torments; all that stirs up the lees of things; all truth with malice in it; all that cracks the sinews and

cakes the brain; all the subtle demonisms of life and thought; all evil, to crazy Ahab, were visibly personified and made practically assailable in Moby Dick.

8. **Bathos**: A ludicrous attempt to portray pathos—that is, to evoke pity, sympathy, or sorrow. It may result from inappropriately dignifying the commonplace, elevated language to describe something trivial, or greatly exaggerated pathos.

9. **Oxymoron**: A contradiction in terms deliberately employed for effect. It is usually seen in a qualifying adjective whose meaning is contrary to that of the noun it modifies such as wise folly.

10. **Irony**: Expressing something other than and particularly opposite the literal meaning such as words of praise when blame is intended. It is often used as a sophisticated or resigned awareness of contrast between what is and what ought to be and expresses a controlled pathos without sentimentality. It is a form of indirection that avoids overt praise or censure. An early example: the Greek comic character Eiron, a clever underdog who by his wit repeatedly triumphs over the boastful character Alazon.

11. **Alliteration**: The repetition of consonant sounds in two or more neighboring words or syllables. In its simplest form, it reinforces one or two consonant sounds. Example: Shakespeare's Sonnet #12:
    When I do **c**ount the **c**lock that **t**ells the **t**ime.
    While alliteration is most common to poetry, many prose writers also use it effectively to create a mood or underscore a theme.

Onomatopoeia: The naming of a thing or action by a vocal imitation of the sound associated with it such as buzz or hiss or the use of words whose sound suggests the sense. This device is often seen in comic books and strips such as *Batman*, but the accomplished novelist often relies on this device for effect.

12. **Malapropism**: A verbal blunder in which one word is replaced by another similar in sound but different in meaning. Comes from Sheridan's Mrs. Malaprop in *The Rivals* (1775). Thinking of the geography of contiguous countries, she spoke of the "geometry" of "contagious countries."

Figurative language allows for the statement of truths that more literal language cannot. Skillfully used, a figure of speech will help the reader see more clearly and to focus upon particulars. Figures of speech add many dimensions of richness to our reading and understanding of a work of prose; they also allow many opportunities for worthwhile analysis. The approach to take in analyzing a piece of writing on the basis of its figures of speech is to ask the question: What does it do for the work? Does it underscore meaning? Does it intensify understanding? Does it increase the intensity of our response?

Skill 6.4   Analyzing how narrative point of view affects the interpretation of a work of fiction or drama.

Voice and Point of View

There are at least thirteen possible choices for point of view (voice) in literature as demonstrated and explained by Wallace Hildick in his *13 Types of Narrative*. However, for purposes of helping students write essays about literature, three, or possibly four, are adequate.

The importance of teaching students to use this aspect of a piece of literature to write about it is not just as an analytic exercise but also should help them think about how a writer's choices impact the overall effect of the work.

Point of view or voice is essentially through whose eyes the reader sees the action. The most common is the **third-person objective**. If the story is seen from this point of view, the reader watches the action, hears the dialogue, reads

> Learn more about
> **Writing Fiction**
> http://crofsblogs.typepad.com/fiction/
> 2003/07/narrative_voice.html

descriptions and from all of those must deduce characterization—what sort of person a character is. In this point of view, an unseen narrator tells the reader what is happening, using the third person: he, she, it, they. The effect of this point of view is usually a feeling of distance from the plot. More responsibility is on the reader to make judgments than in other points of view. However, the author may intrude and evaluate or comment on the characters or the action.

The voice of the **first-person** narrator is often used also. The reader sees the action through the eyes of an actor in the story who is also telling the story. In writing about a story that uses this voice, the narrator must be analyzed as a character. What sort of person is this? What is this character's position in the story—observer, commentator, and actor? Can the narrator be believed, or is he/she biased? The value of this voice is that, while the reader is able to follow the narrator around and see what is happening through that character's eyes, the reader is also able to feel what the narrator feels. For this reason, the writer can involve the reader more intensely in the story itself and move the reader by invoking feelings—pity, sorrow, anger, hate, confusion, disgust. Many of the most memorable novels, such as Jane Austen's *Jane Eyre*, are written in this point of view.

Another voice often used may best be titled **omniscient** because the reader is able to get into the mind of more than one character or sometimes all the characters. This point of view can also bring greater involvement of the reader in the story. By knowing what a character is thinking and feeling, the reader is able to empathize when a character feels great pain and sorrow, which tends to make a work memorable, such as Leo Tolstoy's *War and Peace*. On the other hand, knowing what a character is thinking makes it possible to get into the mind of a pathological murderer and may elicit horror or disgust.

Omniscient can be broken down into **third-person omniscient** or **first-person omniscient**. In third-person omniscient, the narrator is not seen or known or acting in the story but is able to watch and record not only what is happening or being said but also what characters are thinking. In first-person omniscient on the other hand, the narrator plays a role in the story but can also record what other characters are thinking.

It is possible, of course, that the narrator is the pathological murderer, which creates an effect quite different from a story where the thoughts of the murderer are known but the narrator is standing back and reporting his behavior, thoughts, and intents.

Point of view or voice is a powerful tool in the hands of a skillful writer. The questions to be answered in writing an essay about a literary work are: What point of view has this author used? What effect does it have on the story? If it had been written in a different voice, how would the story be different?

Most credible literary works are consistent in point of view but not always, so consistency is another aspect that should be analyzed. Does the point of view change? Where does it vary? Does it help or hurt the effect of the story?

Skill 6.5   Analyze how word choice is used to create or reveal a particular mood, tone/voice, or style in a work of fiction or drama.

In analyzing fiction, poetry, or drama from the standpoint of the language used, it's helpful to understand the possibilities. For example, a novel writer who uses language peculiar to the American south will express a different tone and style than a writer whose prose is very formal. On the other hand, in analyzing characterization, the language the writer chooses to put in the mouth of a particular character is very useful in understanding who the character is and what role he or she is playing in the plot. Grasping what the relationship is between two characters is highly dependent on the language they use to communicate with each other. For some analysts, the language of a particular novelist is so distinctive, they can recognize something written by him or her even when it may not be identified as such.

Informal and formal language are distinctions made on the basis of the occasion as well as the audience. At a formal occasion, for example, a meeting of executives or of government officials, even conversational exchanges are likely to be more formal. Cocktail parties or golf games are examples where the language is likely to be informal. Formal language uses fewer or no contractions, less slang, longer sentences, and more organization in longer segments.

Slang comes about for many reasons: Amelioration is an important one that results often in euphemisms. Examples are "passed away" for dying or "senior citizens" for old people. Some usages have become so

Check out this link:
Do You Speak American?
http://www.pbs.org/speak/seatosea/st andardamerican/hamlet/

embedded in the language that their sources are long forgotten. For example, "fame" originally meant rumor. Some words originally intended as euphemisms, such as "mentally retarded" and "moron" to avoid using "idiot," have themselves become pejorative.

Slang is lower in prestige than Standard English and tends to first appear in the language of groups with low status. It is often taboo, and unlikely to be used by people of high status. It tends to displace conventional terms, either as shorthand or as a defense against perceptions associated with the conventional term.

Jargon is a specialized vocabulary. It may be the vocabulary peculiar to a particular industry such as computers ("firewall") or of a field such as religion ("vocation"). It may also be the vocabulary of a social group.

Black English is a good example. A Hardee's ad has two young men on the streets of Philadelphia discussing the merits of one of their sandwiches, and captions are required so others may understand what they're saying.

A whole vocabulary that has even developed its own dictionaries is the jargon of bloggers. The speaker must be knowledgeable about and sensitive to the jargon peculiar to the particular audience. That may require some research and some vocabulary development on the speaker's part.

Technical language is a form of jargon. It is usually specific to an industry, profession, or field of study. Sensitivity to the language familiar to the particular audience is important.

Regionalisms are those usages that are peculiar to a particular part of the country. A good example is the second person plural pronoun: you. Because the plural is the same as the singular, various parts of the country have developed their own solutions to be sure that they are understood when they are speaking to more than one "you." In the South, "you-all" or "y'all" is common. In the Northeast, one often hears "youse." In some areas of the Middle West, "you'ns" can be heard. *P. Htsburg*

Vocabulary also varies from region to region. A small stream is a "creek" in some regions but "crick" in some. In Boston, soft drinks are generically called "tonic," *pop* but it becomes "soda" in other parts of the northeast. It is "liqueur" in Canada, and "pop" when you get very far west of New York.

Euphemism and Doublespeak

Both euphemism and doublespeak substitute an agreeable or inoffensive term for one that might offend or suggest something unpleasant. It is the reason for the substitution that differentiates the terms.

Often euphemisms are used to maintain a more positive tone or to prevent offense. For example, *death* might be referred to as *passed away*, *crossed over*, or nowadays *passed*. The word *death* might be too hard for people to speak. On the other hand, doublespeak connotes a deliberate obfuscation or confusion of the meaning. For example, the killing of innocent civilians in time of war is called *collateral damage*. Here *death* is so minimized that it disappears.

In fact, *euphemism* could be a euphemism for *doublespeak*.

Semantic Connotations

To teach language effectively, we need to understand that as human beings acquire language they realize that words have **denotative** and **connotative** meanings. Generally, denotative words point to things and connotative words deal with mental suggestions that the words convey.

The word *skunk* has a denotative meaning if the speaker can point to the actual animal as he speaks the word and intends the word to identify the animal. *Skunk* has connotative meaning depending upon the tone of delivery, the socially acceptable attitudes about the animal, and the speaker's personal feelings about the animal.

Informative Connotations

Informative connotations are definitions agreed upon by the society in which the learner operates. A *skunk* is "a black and white mammal of the weasel family with a pair of perineal glands which secrete a pungent odor." The *Merriam Webster Collegiate Dictionary* adds "...and offensive" odor. Identification of the color, species, and glandular characteristics are informative. The interpretation of the odor as *offensive* is affective.

Affective Connotations

Affective connotations are the personal feelings a word arouses. A child who has no personal experience with a skunk and its odor or has had a pet skunk will feel different about the word *skunk* than a child who has smelled the spray or been conditioned vicariously to associate offensiveness with the animal denoted *skunk*.

> Learn more about **Connotation and Denotation** in "Elements of Poetry"
> http://bcs.bedfordstmartins.com/
> Virtualit/poetry/denotate_def.html

The very fact that our society views a skunk as an animal to be avoided will affect the child's interpretation of the word. In fact, you don't actually have to have seen a skunk (that is, have a denotative understanding) to use the word in either connotative expression. For example, one child might call another child a skunk, connoting an unpleasant reaction (affective use) or, seeing another small black and white animal, call it a skunk based on the definition (informative use).

Using Connotations

In everyday language, we attach affective meanings to words unconsciously; we exercise more conscious control of informative connotations. In the process of language development, the learner must come not only to grasp the definitions of words but also to become more conscious of the affective connotations and how his listeners process these connotations. Gaining this conscious control over language makes it possible to use language appropriately in various situations and to evaluate its uses in literature and other forms of communication.

ie "affect" of the wd

The manipulation of language for a variety of purposes is the goal of language instruction. Advertisers and satirists are especially conscious of the effect word choice has on their audiences. By evoking the proper responses from readers/listeners, we can prompt them to take action.

Choice of the medium through which the message is delivered to the receiver is a significant factor in controlling language. Spoken language relies as much on the gestures, facial expression, and tone of voice of the speaker as on the words that are spoken. Slapstick comics can evoke laughter without speaking a word. Young children use body language overtly and older children more subtly to convey messages. These refinements of body language are paralleled by an ability to recognize and apply the nuances of spoken language. To work strictly with the written work, the writer must use words to imply the body language.

Ambiguity

Ambiguity is any writing whose meaning cannot be determined by its context. Ambiguity may be introduced accidentally, confusing the readers and disrupting the flow of reading. If a sentence or paragraph jars upon reading, there is lurking ambiguity. It is particularly difficult to spot your own ambiguities, since authors tend to see what they mean rather than what they say.

For example, when Robert Frost writes "Good fences make good neighbors" in the poem "Mending Wall," students can spend much time discussing what that means in the context of the poem as well as in the context of their own lives.

> Read
> **"Mending Wall" by Robert Frost**
> http://www. writing.upenn.edu/~afilreis/88
> /frost-mending.html

Skill 6.6   Recognize the characteristics of major types of dramatic works.

Since the days of the Greeks, drama has undergone many permutations. Definitions which were once rigid have softened as theater has become a more accurate picture of the lives it depicts.

Tragedy: The classic definition dating back to Aristotle is that tragedy is a work of drama written in either prose or poetry, telling the story of a brave, noble hero who, because of some tragic character flaw (*hamartia*), brings ruin upon himself. It is characterized by serious, poetic language that evokes pity and fear.

In modern times, dramatists have tried to update drama's image by drawing its main characters from the middle class and showing their nobility through their nature instead of their standing. Sophocles' *Oedipus Rex* is the classic example of tragedy, while works of Henrik Ibsen and Arthur Miller epitomize modern tragedy.

Read more about
Greek Tragedy
http://depthome.brooklyn.cuny.
edu/classics/dunkle/studyguide/
tragedy.htm

Comedy: The comedic form of dramatic literature is meant to amuse and often ends happily. It uses techniques such as satire or parody, and can take many forms, from farce to burlesque. Examples include Dante Alighieri's *The Divine Comedy*, Noel Coward's play *Private Lives*, some of Geoffrey Chaucer's *Canterbury Tales*, and some of William Shakespeare's plays, such as *A Midsummer's Night Dream*.

Comic Drama: As the name suggests, this form of theater is a combination of serious and light elements. It originated in the Middle Ages under the auspices of the Catholic Church when it tried to reach the common people matters of faith in mystery and morality plans. The modern equivalent would be the television's "dramedies" that present a serious plot with comic elements.

Melodrama: This is a form of extreme drama that has a somewhat formulaic structure. The hero saves the day from the dastardly villain and wins the heart of the wholesome heroine. The word is a combination of *melody* and *drama* because music is often used to heighten the emotions. Although the term is sometimes used as a critical pejorative, it is a true art form with stereotyped characters and plot manipulations. Oftentimes, operas are melodramatic so it should be no surprise that soap operas are considered part of this genre.

Farce: This is an extreme form of comedy marked by physical humor, unlikely situations, and stereotyped characters. It is often considered a form of low comedy and is represented in movies by the Three Stooges, Charlie Chaplin, Harold Lloyd, and Buster Keaton. Today's students might easily recognize farce with movies like *Dumb and Dumber, There's Something About Mary, Talladega Nights,* and *Monty Python's Spamalot.*

Skill 6.7   Demonstrate knowledge of dramatic structure.

Dramatic Monologue: A dramatic monologue is a speech given by an actor as if talking to himself or herself, but actually intended for the audience. It reveals key aspects of the character's psyche and sheds insight on the situation at hand. The audience takes the part of the silent listener, passing judgment and giving sympathy at the same time. This form was invented and used predominantly by Victorian poet Robert Browning.

Tempo: Interpretation of dialogue must be connected to motivation and detail. During this time, the director is also concerned with pace and seeks a variation of tempo. If the overall pace is too slow, then the action becomes dull and dragging. If the overall pace is too fast, then the audience will not be able to understand what is going on, for they are being hit with too much information to process.

Dramatic Arc: Good drama is built on conflict of some kind—an opposition of forces or desires that must be resolved by the end of the story. The conflict can be internal, involving emotional and psychological pressures, or it can be external, drawing the characters into tumultuous events. These themes are presented to the audience in a narrative arc that looks roughly like this:

Following the Arc: Although any performance may have a series of rising and falling levels of intensity, in general the opening should set in motion the events that will generate an emotional high toward the middle or end of the story. Then, regardless of whether the ending is happy, sad, bittersweet, or despairing, the resolution eases the audience down from those heights and establishes some sense of closure.

Reaching the climax too soon undermines the dramatic impact of the remaining portion of the performance whereas reaching it too late rushes the ending and creates a jarringly abrupt end to events.

Skill 6.8   Analyze the use of common dramatic devices in dramatic works.

Traditionalists and neoclassicists adhere to Aristotle's unities of time, place, and action. Plot development is advanced via dialogue. Literary devices include asides, soliloquies, and the chorus representing public opinion. Greatest of all dramatists/playwrights is William Shakespeare. Other dramaturges include Ibsen, Williams, Miller, Shaw, Stoppard, Racine, Moliére, Sophocles, Aeschylus, Euripides, and Aristophanes.

Irony: An unexpected disparity between what is written or stated and what is really meant or implied by the author. Verbal, situational, and dramatic are the three literary ironies. Verbal irony is when an actor says one thing and means something else. Dramatic irony is when an audience perceives something that a character in the play does not know. Irony of situation is a discrepancy between the expected result and actual results. Shakespeare's plays contain numerous and highly effective use of irony.

Exposition: Fill-in or background information about characters meant to clarify and add to the narrative; the initial plot element which precedes the buildup of conflict.

Epiphany: The moment when the proverbial light bulb goes off in an actor's head and comprehension sets in.

Apostrophe: Literary device of addressing an absent or dead person, an abstract idea, or an inanimate object. For example, in William Shakespeare's *Julius Caesar*, Mark Antony addresses the corpse of Caesar in the speech that begins: O, pardon me, thou bleeding piece of earth, That I am meek and gentle with these butchers! Thou art the ruins of the noblest man that ever lived in the tide of times. Woe to the hand that shed this costly blood!

Connotation: The ripple effect surrounding the implications and associations of a given word, distinct from the denotative, or literal meaning. For example, Good night, sweet prince, and flights of angels sing thee to thy *rest* refers to a burial.

Consonance: The repeated usage of similar consonant sounds, most often used in poetry.

Hyperbole: Exaggeration for a specific effect.

Motif: A key, oft-repeated phrase, name, or idea in a literary work. Shakespeare's *Romeo and Juliet* represents the ill-fated-young-lovers motif.

Onomatopoeia: Word used to evoke the sound in its meaning. The early Batman series used *pow, zap, whop, zonk* and *eek* in an onomatopoetic way.

Oxymoron: A contradictory form of speech, such as jumbo shrimp, unkindly kind, or Mellencamp's "It hurts so good."

Soliloquy: A highlighted speech, in drama, usually delivered by a major character expounding on the author's philosophy or expressing, at times, universal truths. This is done with the character alone on the stage.

Stream of Consciousness: A style of acting that reflects the mental processes of the characters expressing, at times, jumbled memories, feelings, and dreams.

Tone: The discernible attitude inherent in an author's work regarding the subject, audience, or characters.

Wit: Keenness, and sagacity expressed through clever use of language.

COMPETENCY 7   GENRES OF LITERARY NONFICTION

Skill 7.1   Recognize the characteristics of various types of literary nonfiction.

Biography: A form of nonfictional literature, the subject of which is the life of an individual. The earliest biographical writings were probably funeral speeches and inscriptions, usually praising the life and example of the deceased. Early biographies evolved from this and were almost invariably uncritical, even distorted, and always laudatory. Beginning in the 18th century, this form of literature saw major development; an eminent example is James Boswell's *Life of Johnson*, which is very detailed and even records conversations. Eventually, the antithesis of the grossly exaggerated tomes praising an individual, usually a person of circumstance, developed. This form is denunciatory, debunking, and often inflammatory. A famous modern example is Lytton Strachey's *Eminent Victorians* (1918).

Autobiography: A form of biography, but it is written by the subject himself or herself. Autobiographies can range from the very formal to intimate writings made during one's life that were not intended for publication. These include letters, diaries, journals, memoirs, and reminiscences. Autobiography, generally speaking, began in the 15th century; one of the first examples is one written in England by Margery Kempe. There are four kinds of autobiography: thematic, religious, intellectual, and fictionalized. Some "novels" may be thinly disguised autobiography, such as the novels of Thomas Wolfe.

Informational books and articles: These make up much of the reading of modern Americans. Magazines began to be popular in the 19th century in this country, and while many of the contributors to those publications intended to influence the political/social/religious convictions of their readers, many also simply intended to pass on information. A book or article whose purpose is simply to be informative, that is, not to persuade, is called exposition (adjectival form: expository). An example of an expository book is the *MLA Style Manual*. The writers do not intend to persuade their readers to use the recommended stylistic features in their writing; they are simply making them available in case a reader needs such a guide. Articles in magazines such as *Time* may be persuasive in purpose, such as Joe Klein's regular column, but for the most part they are expository, giving information that television coverage of a news story might not have time to include.

Newspaper accounts of events: Expository in nature, of course, a reporting of a happening. That happening might be a school board meeting, an automobile accident that sent several people to a hospital and accounted for the death of a passenger, or the election of the mayor. They are not intended to be persuasive although the bias of a reporter or of an editor must be factored in. A newspapers' editorial stance is often openly declared, and it may be reflected in such things as news reports. Reporters are expected to be unbiased in their coverage and most of them will defend their disinterest fiercely, but what a writer *sees* in an event is inevitably shaped to some extent by the writer's beliefs and experiences.

Skill 7.2   Analyze how the narrative point of view, tone/voice, and style of a work of literary nonfiction affect the interpretation of the work

Narrative point of view is defined in Skill 6.4, and most of the things that can be said about point of view in a fictional work can also be said about that topic in nonfiction. For example, a reporter might speak in the first person: "As I approached the police car, two shots rang out." Or third person: "Many residents of the Fifth Ward appeared at City Hall yesterday to register a complaint about the streets in their neighborhood." Point of view is as powerful in nonfictional literature as it is in fictional.

Two characteristics that determine language style are **degree of formality** and **word choice**. The most formal language does not use contractions or slang while the most informal language will probably feature a more casual use of common sayings and anecdotes. Formal language will use longer sentences and will not sound like a conversation. The most informal language will use shorter sentences (not necessarily simple sentences—but shorter constructions) and may sound like a conversation.

In both formal and informal writing, there exists a **tone**, the writer's attitude toward the material and/or readers. Tone may be playful, formal, intimate, angry, serious, ironic, outraged, baffled, tender, serene, depressed, and so on. The overall tone of a piece of writing is dictated by both the subject matter and the audience. Tone is also related to the actual word choice which make up the document, as we attach affective meanings to words, called their **connotations**. Gaining this conscious control over language makes it possible to use language appropriately in various situations and to evaluate its uses in literature and other forms of communication. By evoking the proper responses from readers or listeners, we can prompt them to take action.

Reporters in both print and electronic media are pledged to be impartial in their reporting, and most of them abide by that commitment to a large extent. They tend to guard their objectivity very carefully. For example, they reject offers to promote a product even though they might earn considerably more monetary rewards than if they only worked as reporters. Given all of this, it still needs to be said that total objectivity may not be attainable. Even in a nonfiction work, the biases of the writer are very likely to play a role and in any analysis they should be taken into account. There are, of course, occasions when fact is blended with fiction as is often true with historical novels. In these cases, however, we are told at the outset that some of the information may be imagined rather than lived.

We don't expect that standard literary and creative devices peculiar to fiction will be used in non-fiction. However, we do sometimes see them, particularly in older works of nonfiction. A good measure for the organizational structure of nonfiction is whether or not it is simple, clear, and direct. Audience is particularly important in nonfiction, so in analyzing a work of nonfiction, it's useful to evaluate whether there is consistency in the surmised audience—that is, is it very technical in some places and very simple in others. A good measure for a work of nonfiction is how understandable it is for the potential reader, and whether it's presented in a balanced, coherent, and informed way.

Historically, cave paintings would be the first attempts at nonfiction unless, of course, the paintings represent what the painter hoped to catch rather than what he actually did catch. Keeping this in mind helps us distinguish between fiction and nonfiction and also makes it easier to think about the organization of the latter. It should be presented in a simple way without a lot of deliberate device or flourish. The introduction should be straightforward and lead the reader into the topic. The supporting paragraphs, likewise, should be straightforward and without ambiguity. A conclusion should restate in an easily understandable way the points that were made in the body.

Skill 7.3   Analyze how the organizational structure of a work of literary nonfiction is used to help develop the central idea or theme of the work.

When we read a work of fiction, we know we're not reading fact. We don't measure such a work by the same parameters as we do nonfiction, which we expect to be factual. If there are elements of a work of nonfiction that turn out not to be true, we feel that dishonesty and betrayal have occurred. In evaluating a work of nonfiction, then, the first question is whether it is factual and whether the writer can be trusted. We typically give the writer the benefit of the doubt and accept that what they are presenting can be relied upon to be true.

There are, of course, works that deliberately mix fiction and nonfiction, such as historical novels. The basis of such novels is a true historical event, and much of the action in the novel is taken from history. However, the author's imagination plays a role in many of the details since history probably didn't record them and the story is not very interesting without them.

The first nonfiction was cave paintings, assuming, of course, that the painter recorded what he caught rather than what he hoped to catch. Most of the nonfiction that has been produced in the past tends to be pretty mundane without a lot of thought for organization or structure. At any point in history there's a body of nonfiction that contains the currently-accepted truths of that period, such as scientific works. The material they contain is, of course, constantly being upgraded.

As to organization of nonfiction, it should be simple, straightforward, and understandable since the purpose is to convey information. Depending on the purpose for a particular writing, an introduction will clearly indicate what the topic is along with the purposes for writing such a piece. The supporting points in the body of the piece should likewise be clear and easy to follow. A conclusion is almost obligatory in a work of nonfiction for the purpose of touching again on the main points in the work itself. A scientific work, will, of course, be organized differently from a memoir. A blueprint will be organized differently from an almanac. However, all will be measured by whether or not the organization of the particular piece works to inform or persuade and whether its message can be clearly understood.

Skill 7.4   Analyze the use of common literary and rhetorical devices in works of literary nonfiction.

- **Simile**: This is a natural device for a nonfictional work, especially if its purpose is to explain something. Comparing something not clearly understood to something clearly understood by the reader is an important part of description and explanation.
- **Euphemism**: The substitution of an agreeable or inoffensive term for one that might offend or suggest something unpleasant is often used by writers or speakers, especially if they are attempting to persuade.
- **Hyperbole**: Deliberate exaggeration for effect or comic effect is as useful to the nonfiction writer as it is for the fiction-writer as long as he/she can be sure that the reader understands that overstatement is occurring.
- **Meiosis/understatement:** The opposite of hyperbole, meiosis grossly understates deliberately. This is often used in nonfiction for effect.

- **Analogy**: This is an extended comparison and, just as similes are effective and useful, especially in making a cloudy definition or point clear, so is the use of analogy. Analogy only works if all aspects of the comparison match up.
- **Anecdote**: Stories told for the purpose of exemplifying a point or making a point clear appear often in nonfictional works.
- **Examples**: Remembering that most works of nonfiction are making a point or explaining, examples are extremely helpful in clarifying a point or a definition.
- **Appeals to Emotion**: We would like to think that most people do not make decisions on this basis, but they do. We may require that what we are accepting as truth and reason are, in fact, based on logic and intelligence, but the truth is that we generally only change our minds or make a decision to take action when we have been moved emotionally.
- **Appeals to Authority**: Human beings also tend to trust a person because of who he is or what he is. It's only natural to believe a speaker on the topic of astronauts if that person is, in fact, an astronaut.

COMPETENCY 8   READING VARIOUS FORMS OF POETRY

Skill 8.1   Demonstrate knowledge of the formal characteristics of various types of poetry.

The **sonnet** is a fixed-verse form of Italian origin, which consists of 14 lines that are typically five-foot iambics rhyming according to a prescribed scheme. Popular since its creation in the thirteenth century in Sicily, it spread at first to Tuscany, where it was adopted by Petrarch. The Petrarchan sonnet generally has a two-part theme. The first eight lines, the octave, state a problem, ask a question, or express an emotional tension. The last six lines, the sestet, resolve the problem, answer the question, or relieve the tension. The rhyme scheme of the octave is abbaabba; that of the sestet varies.

Sir Thomas Wyatt and Henry Howard, Earl of Surrey, introduced this form into England in the sixteenth century. It played an important role in the development of Elizabethan lyric poetry, and a distinctive English sonnet developed, which was composed of three quatrains, each with an independent rhyme-scheme, and it ended with a rhymed couplet. A form of the English sonnet created by Edmond Spenser combines the English form and the Italian. The Spenserian sonnet follows the English quatrain and couplet pattern but resembles the Italian in its rhyme scheme, which is linked: abab bcbc cdcd ee. Many poets wrote sonnet sequences, where several sonnets were linked together, usually to tell a story. Considered to be the greatest of all sonnet sequences is one of Shakespeare's, which are addressed to a young man and a "dark lady" wherein the love story is overshadowed by the underlying reflections on time and art, growth and decay, and fame and fortune.

The sonnet continued to develop, more in topics than in form. When John Donne in the seventeenth century used the form for religious themes, some of which are almost sermons, or on personal reflections ("When I consider how my light is spent"), there were no longer any boundaries on the themes it could take.

That it is a flexible form is demonstrated in the wide range of themes and purposes it has been used for—all the way from more frivolous concerns to statements about time and death. Wordsworth, Keats, and Elizabeth Barrett Browning used the Petrarchan form of the sonnet. A well-known example is Wordsworth's "The World Is Too Much with Us." Rainer Maria Rilke's *Sonnette an Orpheus* (1922) is a well-known twentieth-century sonnet.

Analysis of a sonnet should focus on the form—does it fit a traditional pattern or does it break from tradition? If so, why did the poet choose to make that break? Does it reflect the purpose of the poem? What is the theme? What is the purpose? Is it narrative? If so, what story does it tell and is there an underlying meaning? Is the sonnet appropriate for the subject matter?

The **limerick** probably originated in County Limerick, Ireland, in the 18th century. It is a form of short, humorous verse, often nonsensical, and often ribald. Its five lines rhyme aabbaa with three feet in all lines except the third and fourth, which have only two. Rarely presented as serious poetry, this form is popular because almost anyone can write it.

Analysis of a limerick should focus on its form. Does it conform to a traditional pattern or does it break from the tradition? If so, what impact does that have on the meaning? Is the poem serious or frivolous? Is it funny? Does it try to be funny but does not achieve its purpose? Is there a serious meaning underlying the frivolity?

A **cinquain** is a poem with a five-line stanza. Adelaide Crapsey (1878-1914) called a five-line verse form a cinquain and invented a particular meter for it. Similar to the haiku, there are two syllables in the first and last lines and four, six, and eight in the middle three lines. It has a mostly iambic cadence. Her poem, "November Night," is an example:

> Listen…
> With faint dry sound
> Like steps of passing ghosts,
> the leaves, frost-crisp'd, break from the trees
> And fall.

Haiku is a very popular unrhymed form that is limited to seventeen syllables arranged in three lines thus: five, seven, and five syllables. This verse form originated in Japan in the seventeenth century where it is accepted as serious poetry and is Japan's most popular form. Originally, it was to deal with the season, the time of day, and the landscape although as it has come into more common use, the subjects have become less restricted. The imagist poets a other English writers used the form or imitated it. It's a form much used in classrooms to introduce students to the writing of poetry.

Analysis of a cinquain and a haiku poem should focus on form first. Does the haiku poem conform to the seventeen-syllables requirement and are they arranged in a five, seven, and five pattern? For a cinquain, does it have only five lines? Does the poem distill the words so as much meaning as possible can be conveyed? Does it treat a serious subject? Is the theme discernable? Short forms like these seem simple to dash off; however, they are not effective unless the words are chosen and pared so the meaning intended is conveyed. The impact should be forceful, and that often takes more effort, skill, and creativity than longer forms. This should be taken into account in their analysis.

Skill 8.2   Demonstrate knowledge of metrical and stanzaic structures.

Rhythm is a *pattern of recurrence* and in poetry is made up of stressed and relatively unstressed syllables. The poet can manipulate the rhythm by making the intervals between his stresses regular or varied, by making his lines short or long, by end-stopping his lines or running them over, by choosing words that are easier or less easy to say, by choosing polysyllabic words or monosyllables. The most important thing to remember about rhythm is that it conveys meaning.

The basic unit of rhythm is called a foot and is usually one stressed syllable with one or two unstressed ones or two stressed syllables with one unstressed one. A foot made up of one unstressed syllable and one stressed one is called an iamb. If a line is made of five iambs, it is iambic pentameter. A rhymed poem typically establishes a pattern such as iambic pentameter, and even though there will be syllables that don't fit the pattern, the poem, nevertheless, will be said to be in iambic pentameter. In fact, a poem may be considered weak if the rhythm is too monotonous.

The most common kinds of feet in English poetry:

iamb: -'
anapest: --'
trochee: '-
dactyl: '--
Monosyllabic: '
Spondee: "
Pyrrhic foot: --

Iambic and anapestic are said to be rising because the movement is from slack to stressed syllables. Trochaic and dactylic are said to be falling.

Meters are named as follows:
Monometer: a line of one foot
Dimeter: a line of two feet
Trimeter: a line of three feet
Tetrameter: a line of four feet
Pentameter: a line of five feet
Hexameter: a line of six feet
Heptameter: a line of seven feet
Octameter: a line of eight feet

Longer lines are possible, but a reader will tend to break them up into shorter lengths.

Some typical patterns of English poetry:
Blank verse: unrhymed iambic pentameter.
Couplet: two-line stanza, usually rhymed and typically not separated by white space.
Heroic couplet or closed couplet: two rhymed lines of iambic pentameter, the first ending in a light pause, the second more heavily end-stopped.
Tercet: a three-line stanza, which, if rhymed, usually keeps to one rhyme sound.
Terza rima: the middle line of the tercet rhymes with the first and third lines of the next tercet.
The quatrain: four-line stanza, the most popular in English.
The ballad stanza: four iambic feet in lines 1 and 3, three in lines 2 and 4, rhyming is abcb.
The refrain: a line or lines repeated in a ballad as a chorus.
Terminal refrain: follows a stanza in a ballad.
Five-line stanzas occur, but not frequently.
Six-line stanzas, more frequent than five-line ones.
The sestina: six six-line stanzas and a tercet. Repeats in each stanza the same six end-words in a different order.
Rime royal: seven-line stanza in iambic pentameter with rhyme ababbcc.
Ottava rima: eight-line stanza of iambic pentameter rhyming abababcc.
Spenserian stanza: nine lines, rhyming ababbcbcc for eight lines then concludes with an Alexandrine.
The Alexandrine: a line of iambic hexameter.
Free verse: no conventional patterns of rhyme, stanza, or meter.
Sonnet: a fourteen-line poem in iambic pentameter.
1) English sonnet: sometimes called a Shakespearean sonnet. Rhymes cohere in four clusters: abab cdcd efef gg
2) Italian or Petrarchan sonnet: first eight lines (the octave), abbaabba; then the sestet, the last six lines add new rhyme sounds in almost any variation; does not end in a couplet.

Skill 8.3   Analyze the use of formal rhyme schemes and other sound devices in works of poetry.

A poet chooses the form of his poetry deliberately, based upon the emotional response he hopes to evoke and the meaning he wishes to convey. Robert Frost, a twentieth-century poet who chose to use conventional rhyming verse to make his point is a memorable and often-quoted modern poet. Who can forget his closing lines in "Stopping by Woods"?

> And miles to go before I sleep,
> And miles to go before I sleep.

Would they be as memorable if the poem had been written in free verse?

Slant Rhyme: Occurs when the final consonant sounds are the same, but the vowels are different. Occurs frequently in Irish, Welsh, and Icelandic verse. Examples include: green and gone, that and hit, ill and shell.

Alliteration: Alliteration occurs when the initial sounds of a word, beginning either with a consonant or a vowel, are repeated in close succession. Examples include: Athena and Apollo, Nate never knows, People who pen poetry.

Note that the words only have to be close to one another: Alliteration that repeats and attempts to connect a number of words is little more than a tongue-twister.

The function of alliteration, like rhyme, might be to accentuate the beauty of language in a given context, or to unite words or concepts through a kind of repetition. Alliteration, like rhyme, can follow specific patterns. Sometimes the consonants aren't always the initial ones, but they are generally the stressed syllables. Alliteration is less common than rhyme, but because it is less common, it can call our attention to a word or line in a poem that might not have the same emphasis otherwise.

Assonance: If alliteration occurs at the beginning of a word and rhyme at the end, assonance takes the middle territory. Assonance occurs when the vowel sound within a word matches the same sound in a nearby word, but the surrounding consonant sounds are different. "Tune" and "June" are rhymes; "tune" and "food" are assonant. The function of assonance is frequently the same as end rhyme or alliteration; all serve to give a sense of continuity or fluidity to the verse. Assonance might be especially effective when rhyme is absent: It gives the poet more flexibility, and it is not typically used as part of a predetermined pattern. Like alliteration, it does not so much determine the structure or form of a poem; rather, it is more ornamental.

Onomatopoeia: Word used to evoke the sound in its meaning. The early Batman series used *pow, zap, whop, zonk* and *eek* in an onomatopoetic way.

Skill 8.4   Analyze the use of common poetic devices in works of poetry.

Novelists and effective prose writers use many of the same devices as poets; in fact, many successful novelists started out as poets. What follows repeats some of the same ideas and material as presented in Skill 6.3 as it applied to drama and fiction.

Imagery can be described as a word or sequence of words that refers to any sensory experience—that is, anything that can be seen, tasted, smelled, heard, or felt on the skin or fingers. While writers of prose may also use these devices, it is most distinctive of poetry. The poet intends to make an experience available to the reader. In order to do that, he/she must appeal to one of the senses. The most-often-used one, of course, is the visual sense. The poet will deliberately paint a scene in such a way that the reader can see it. However, the purpose is not simply to stir the visceral feeling but also to stir the emotions. A good example is "The Piercing Chill" by Taniguchi Buson (1715-1783):

> The piercing chill I feel:
> My dead wife's comb, in our bedroom,
>   Under my heel . . .

In only a few short words, the reader can feel many things: the shock that might come from touching the corpse, a literal sense of death, the contrast between her death and the memories he has of her when she was alive. Imagery might be defined as speaking of the abstract in concrete terms, a powerful device in the hands of a skillful poet.

A **symbol** is an object or action that can be observed with the senses in addition to its suggesting many other things. The lion is a symbol of courage; the cross a symbol of Christianity; the color green a symbol of envy. These can almost be defined as metaphors because society pretty much agrees on the one-to-one meaning of them. Symbols used in literature are usually of a different sort. They tend to be private and personal; their significance is only evident in the context of the work where they are used. A symbol can certainly have more than one meaning, and the meaning may be as personal as the memories and experiences of the particular reader. In analyzing a poem, it's important to identify the symbols and their possible meanings.

Looking for symbols is often challenging, especially for novice poetry readers. However, these suggestions may be useful: First, pick out all the references to concrete objects such as a newspaper, black cats, etc. Note any that the poet emphasizes by describing in detail, by repeating, or by placing at the very beginning or ending of a poem. Ask yourself, what is the poem about? What does it add up to? Paraphrase the poem and determine whether or not the meaning depends upon certain concrete objects. Then ponder what the concrete object symbolizes in this particular poem. Look for a character with the name of a prophet who does little but utter prophecy or a trio of women who resemble the Three Fates. A symbol may be a part of a person's body such as the eye of the murder victim in Poe's story *The Tell-Tale Heart* or a look, a voice, or a mannerism.

Some things a symbol is not: an abstraction such as truth, death, and love; in narrative, a well-developed character who is not at all mysterious; the second term in a metaphor. In Emily Dickenson's *The Lightning is a yellow Fork*, the symbol is the lightning, not the fork.

An **allusion** is very much like a symbol, and the two sometimes tend to run together. An allusion is defined by Merriam Webster's *Encyclopedia of Literature* as "an implied reference to a person, event, thing, or a part of another text." Allusions are based on the assumption that there is a common body of knowledge shared by poet and reader and that a reference to that body of knowledge will be immediately understood. Allusions to the Bible and classical mythology are common in western literature on the assumption that they will be immediately understood. This is not always the case, of course. T. S. Eliot's *The Wasteland* requires research and annotation for understanding. He assumed more background on the part of the average reader than actually exists. However, when Michael Moore on his web page headlines an article on the war in Iraq: "Déjà Fallouja: Ramadi surrounded, thousands of families trapped, no electricity or water, onslaught impending," we understand immediately that he is referring first of all to a repeat of the human disaster in New Orleans although the "onslaught" is not a storm but an invasion by American and Iraqi troops.

The use of allusion is a sort of shortcut for poets. They can use an economy of words and count on meaning to come from the reader's own experience.

Figurative language is also called figures of speech. If all figures of speech that have ever been identified were listed, it would be a very long list. However, for purposes of analyzing poetry, a few are sufficient.

1. **Simile**: Direct comparison between two things. "My love is like a red-red rose."
2. **Metaphor**: Indirect comparison between two things. The use of a word or phrase denoting one kind of object or action in place of another to suggest a comparison between them. While poets use them extensively, they are also integral to everyday speech. For example, chairs are said to have "legs" and "arms" although we know that it's humans and other animals that have these appendages.
3. **Parallelism**: The arrangement of ideas in phrases, sentences, and paragraphs that balance one element with another of equal importance and similar wording. An example from Francis Bacon's *Of Studies*: "Reading maketh a full man, conference a ready man, and writing an exact man."
4. **Personification**: Human characteristics are attributed to an inanimate object, an abstract quality, or animal. Examples: John Bunyan wrote

characters named Death, Knowledge, Giant Despair, Sloth, and Piety in his *Pilgrim's Progress.* The metaphor of an arm of a chair is a form of personification.

5. **Euphemism**: The substitution of an agreeable or inoffensive term for one that might offend or suggest something unpleasant. Many euphemisms are used to refer to death to avoid using the real word such as "passed away," "crossed over," or nowadays "passed."

6. **Hyperbole**: Deliberate exaggeration for effect or comic effect. An example from Shakespeare's *The Merchant of Venice*:

> Why, if two gods should play some heavenly match
> And on the wager lay two earthly women,
> And Portia one, there must be something else
> Pawned with the other, for the poor rude world
> Hath not her fellow.

7. **Climax**: A number of phrases or sentences are arranged in ascending order of rhetorical forcefulness. Example from Melville's *Moby Dick*:

> All that most maddens and torments; all that stirs up the lees of things; all truth with malice in it; all that cracks the sinews and cakes the brain; all the subtle demonisms of life and thought; all evil, to crazy Ahab, were visibly personified and made practically assailable in Moby Dick.

8. **Bathos**: A ludicrous attempt to portray pathos—that is, to evoke pity, sympathy, or sorrow. It may result from inappropriately dignifying the commonplace, elevated language to describe something trivial, or greatly exaggerated pathos.

9. **Oxymoron**: A contradiction in terms deliberately employed for effect. It is usually seen in a qualifying adjective whose meaning is contrary to that of the noun it modifies such as wise folly.

10. **Irony**: Expressing something other than and particularly opposite the literal meaning such as words of praise when blame is intended. In poetry, it is often used as a sophisticated or resigned awareness of contrast between what is and what ought to be and expresses a controlled pathos without sentimentality. It is a form of indirection that avoids overt praise or censure. An early example: the Greek comic character Eiron, a clever underdog who by his wit repeatedly triumphs over the boastful character Alazon.

11. **Alliteration**: The repetition of consonant sounds in two or more neighboring words or syllables. In its simplest form, it reinforces one or two consonant sounds. Example: Shakespeare's Sonnet #12:

> When I do count the clock that tells the time.

Some poets have used more complex patterns of alliteration by creating consonants both at the beginning of words and at the beginning of stressed syllables within words. Example: Shelley's "Stanzas Written in Dejection Near Naples"

> The City's voice itself is soft like Solitude's

12. **Onomatopoeia**: The naming of a thing or action by a vocal imitation of the sound associated with it such as buzz or hiss or the use of words whose sound suggests the sense. A good example: from "The Brook" by Tennyson:

> I chatter over stony ways,
> In little sharps and trebles,
> I bubble into eddying bays,
> I babble on the pebbles.

Skill 8.5   Analyze how the formal characteristics of a work of poetry relate to the tone, mood, or theme of the work.

Analysis of a sonnet should focus on the form—does it fit a traditional pattern or does it break from tradition? If so, why did the poet choose to make that break? Does it reflect the purpose of the poem? What is the theme? What is the purpose? Is it narrative? If so, what story does it tell and is there an underlying meaning? Is the sonnet appropriate for the subject matter?

The limerick probably originated in County Limerick, Ireland, in the 18th century. It is a form of short, humorous verse, often nonsensical, and often ribald. Its five lines rhyme aabbaa with three feet in all lines except the third and fourth, which have only two. Rarely presented as serious poetry, this form is popular because almost anyone can write it.

Analysis of a limerick should focus on its form. Does it conform to a traditional pattern or does it break from the tradition? If so, what impact does that have on the meaning? Is the poem serious or frivolous? Is it funny? Does it try to be funny but does not achieve its purpose? Is there a serious meaning underlying the frivolity?

A cinquain is a poem with a five-line stanza. Adelaide Crapsey (1878-1914) called a five-line verse form a cinquain and invented a particular meter for it. Similar to the haiku, there are two syllables in the first and last lines and four, six, and eight in the middle three lines. It has a mostly iambic cadence. Her poem, "November Night," is an example:

> Listen…
> With faint dry sound
> Like steps of passing ghosts,
> the leaves, frost-crisp'd, break from the trees
> And fall.

Haiku is a very popular unrhymed form that is limited to seventeen syllables arranged in three lines thus: five, seven, and five syllables. This verse form originated in Japan in the seventeenth century where it is accepted as serious poetry and is Japan's most popular form. Originally, it was to deal with the season, the time of day, and the landscape although as it has come into more common use, the subjects have become less restricted. The imagist poets and other English writers used the form or imitated it. It's a form much used in classrooms to introduce students to the writing of poetry.

Analysis of a cinquain and a haiku poem should focus on form first. Does the haiku poem conform to the seventeen-syllables requirement and are they arranged in a five, seven, and five pattern? For a cinquain, does it have only five lines? Does the poem distill the words so as much meaning as possible can be conveyed? Does it treat a serious subject? Is the theme discernable? Short forms like these seem simple to dash off; however, they are not effective unless the words are chosen and pared so the meaning intended is conveyed. The impact should be forceful, and that often takes more effort, skill, and creativity than longer forms. This should be taken into account in their analysis.

COMPETENCY 9   MAJOR THEMES, CHARACTERISTICS, TRENDS, WRITERS, AND WORKS IN LITERATURES FROM AROUND THE WORLD

Skill 9.1   Demonstrate knowledge of the significance of major writers in literatures from around the world.

Germany

German poet and playwright, Friedrich von Schiller, is best known for his history plays, *William Tell* and *The Maid of Orleans*. He is a leading literary figure in Germany's Golden Age of Literature. Also from Germany, Rainer Maria Rilke, the great lyric poet, is one of the poets of the unconscious, or stream of consciousness. Germany also has given the world Herman Hesse, (*Siddartha*), Gunter Grass (*The Tin Drum*), and the greatest of all German writers, Goethe.

Scandinavia

Scandinavia has encouraged the work of Hans Christian Andersen in Denmark, who advanced the fairy tale genre with such wistful tales as "The Little Mermaid" and "Thumbelina." The social commentary of Henrik Ibsen in Norway startled the world of drama with such issues as feminism (*The Doll's House* and *Hedda Gabler*) and the effects of sexually transmitted diseases (*The Wild Duck* and *Ghosts)*. Sweden's Selma Lagerlof is the first woman ever to win the Nobel Prize for literature. Her novels include *Gosta Berling's Saga* and the world-renowned *The Wonderful Adventures of Nils*, a children's work.

Russia

Russian literature is vast and monumental. Who has not heard of Fyodor Dostoyevski's *Crime and Punishment*, or *The Brothers Karamazov*, or Count Leo

Tolstoy's *War and Peace*? These are examples of psychological realism. Dostoyevski's influence on modern writers cannot be overly stressed. Tolstoy's *War and Peace* is the sweeping account of the invasion of Russia and Napoleon's taking of Moscow, abandoned by the Russians. This novel is called the national novel of Russia. Further advancing Tolstoy's greatness is his ability to create believable, unforgettable female characters, especially Natasha in *War and Peace* and the heroine of *Anna Karenina*. Pushkin is famous for great short stories; Anton Chekhov for drama, (*Uncle Vanya*, *The Three Sisters*, *The Cherry Orchard*); Yevteshenko for poetry (*Babi Yar*).

France

France has a multifaceted canon of great literature that is universal in scope, almost always championing some social cause: the poignant short stories of Guy de Maupassant; the fantastic poetry of Charles Baudelaire (*Fleurs du Mal*); and the groundbreaking lyrical poetry of Rimbaud and Verlaine. Drama in France is best represented by Rostand's *Cyrano de Bergerac*, and the neo-classical dramas of Racine and Corneille (*El Cid*). The great French novelists include Andre Gide, Honore de Balzac (*Cousin Bette*), Stendel (*The Red and the Black*), the father/son duo of Alexandre Dumas (*The Three Musketeers* and *The Man in the Iron Mask*. Victor Hugo is the Charles Dickens of French literature, having penned the masterpieces, *The Hunchback of Notre Dame* and the French national novel, *Les Miserables*. The stream of consciousness of Proust's *Remembrance of Things Past*, and the Absurdist theatre of Samuel Beckett and Eugene Ionesco (*The Rhinoceros*) attest to the groundbreaking genius of the French writers.

Spain

Spain's great writers include Miguel de Cervantes (*Don Quixote*) and Juan Ramon Jimenez. The anonymous national epic, *El Cid*, has been translated into many languages.

Italy

Italy's greatest writers include Virgil, who wrote the great epic, *The Aeneid*; Giovanni Boccaccio (*The Decameron*); and Dante Alighieri (*The Divine Comedy*).

Ancient Greece

Greece will always be foremost in literary assessments due to Homer's epics, *The Iliad* and *The Odyssey*. No one, except Shakespeare, is more often cited. Add to these the works of Plato and Aristotle for philosophy; the dramatists Aeschylus, Euripides, and Sophocles for tragedy, and Aristophanes for comedy. Greece is the cradle not only of democracy, but of literature as well.

Far East

The classical Age of Japanese literary achievement includes the father Kiyotsugu Kanami and the son Motokkiyo Zeami who developed the theatrical experience known as Noh drama to its highest aesthetic degree. The son is said to have authored over 200 plays, of which 100 still are extant.

Katai Tayama (*The Quilt*) is touted as the father of the genre known as the Japanese confessional novel. He also wrote in the "ism" of naturalism. His works are definitely not for the squeamish.

The "slice of life" psychological writings of Ryunosuke Akutagawa gained him acclaim in the western world. His short stories, especially "Rashamon" and "In a Grove," are greatly praised for style as well as content.

China, too, has made contributions to the literary world. Li Po, the T'ang dynasty poet from the Chinese Golden Age, revealed his interest in folklore by preserving the folk songs and mythology of China. Po further allows his reader to enter into the Chinese philosophy of Taoism and to experience the feelings against expansionism during the T'ang dynastic rule. Back to the T'ang dynasty, which was one of great diversity in the arts, the Chinese version of a short story was created with the help of Jiang Fang. His themes often express love between a man and a woman.

North American Literature

When compared to other countries, America has had a relatively brief history and thus a comparatively smaller canon of literature. Nevertheless, its fiction and nonfiction have the depth and breadth to tell the story of its people. To study American literature is to study also American history. Students will discover the interconnectedness of writing as a reflection of the historical, social, ethnic, political and economic environment of the time.

American Literature is defined by a number of clearly identifiable periods.

Native American Works from Various Tribes

These were originally part of a vast oral tradition that spanned most of continental America from as far back as before the 15th century.

Characteristics of native Indian literature include
- Reverence for and awe of nature.
- The interconnectedness of the elements in the life cycle.

Themes of Indian literature often reflect
- The hardiness of the native body and soul.

- Remorse for the destruction of their way of life.
- The genocide of many tribes by the encroaching settlement and Manifest Destiny policies of the U. S. government.

The Colonial Period

Stylistically, early colonists' writings were neo-classical, emphasizing order, balance, clarity, and reason. Because the people had been schooled in England, their writing and speaking was still decidedly British even as their thinking became entirely American.

Early American literature reveals the lives and experiences of the New England expatriates who left England to find religious freedom.

William Bradford's excerpts from *The Mayflower Compact* relate vividly the hardships of crossing the Atlantic in such a tiny vessel, the misery and suffering of the first winter, the approaches of the American Indians, the decimation of their ranks, and the establishment of the Bay Colony of Massachusetts.

Anne Bradstreet's poetry relates colonial New England life. From her journals, modern readers learn of the everyday life of the early settlers, the hardships of travel, and the responsibilities of different groups and individuals in the community, Early American

> *"If ever two were one, then surely we.*
> *If ever man were loved by wife, then thee."*
> Read more about
> **Anne Bradstreet**
> http://www.annebradstreet.com/Default.htm

literature also reveals the commercial and political adventures of the Cavaliers who came to the New World with King George's blessing.

William Byrd's journal, *A History of the Dividing Line,* concerning his trek into the Dismal Swamp separating the Carolinian territories from Virginia and Maryland makes quite lively reading. A privileged insider to the English Royal Court, Byrd, like other Southern Cavaliers, was given grants to pursue business ventures.

The Revolutionary Period

The Revolutionary Period contains non-fiction genres: essay, pamphlet, speech, famous document, and epistle. Major writers and works of the Revolutionary Period include the following:

Thomas Paine's pamphlet, *Common Sense*, though written by a recently transplanted Englishman, spoke to the American patriots' common sense in dealing with the issues in the cause of freedom.

Other contributions are Benjamin Franklin's essays from *Poor Richard's Almanac* and satires such as "How to Reduce a Great Empire to a Small One" and "A Letter to Madame Gout."

There were great orations such as Patrick Henry's *Speech to the Virginia House of Burgesses* (the "Give me liberty or give me death" speech) and George Washington's *Farewell to the Army of the Potomac*. Less memorable are Washington's inaugural addresses, which strike modern readers as lacking sufficient focus.

The *Declaration of Independence*, the brainchild predominantly of Thomas Jefferson (along with some prudent editing by Ben Franklin), is a prime example of neoclassical writing—balanced, well crafted, and focused.

Epistles include the exquisitely-written, moving correspondence between John Adams and Abigail Adams. The poignancy of their separation—she in Boston, he in Philadelphia—is palpable and real.

The Romantic Period

Early American folktales, and the emergence of a distinctly American writing, not just a stepchild to English forms, constitute the next period.

Washington Irving's characters, Ichabod Crane and Rip Van Winkle, represent a uniquely American folklore devoid of English influences. The characters are indelibly marked by their environment and the superstitions of the New Englander. The early American writings of James Fenimore Cooper and his *Leatherstocking Tales* allow readers a window into their uniquely American world through the stirring accounts of drums along the Mohawk, the French and Indian Wars, the futile British defense of Fort William Henry and the brutalities of this period. Natty Bumppo, Chingachgook, Uncas, and Magua are unforgettable characters who reflect the American spirit in thought and action.

The poetry of the Fireside Poets—James Russell Lowell, Oliver Wendell Holmes, Henry Wadsworth Longfellow, and John Greenleaf Whittier— was recited by American families and read in the long New England winters. In "The Courtin'," Lowell used Yankee dialect to tell the story. Spellbinding epics by Longfellow (such as *Hiawatha*, *The Courtship of Miles Standish*, and *Evangeline)* told of adversity, sorrow, and ultimate happiness in a uniquely American fashion. "Snowbound" by Whittier relates the story of a captive family isolated by a blizzard and stresses family closeness.

Nathaniel Hawthorne and Herman Melville are the preeminent early American novelists, writing on subjects definitely regional, specific, and American, yet sharing insights about human foibles, fears, loves, doubts, and triumphs.

Hawthorne's writings range from children's stories, like the Cricket on the Hearth series, to adult fare of dark, brooding short stories such as "Dr. Heidegger's Experiment," "The Devil and Tom Walker," and "Rapuccini's

Daughter." His masterpiece, *The Scarlet Letter*, takes on the society of hypocritical Puritan New Englanders, who ostensibly left England to establish religious freedom but who have become entrenched in judgmental finger wagging. They ostracize Hester and condemn her child, Pearl, as a child of Satan. Great love, sacrifice, loyalty, suffering, and related epiphanies add universality to this tale. *The House of the Seven Gables* deals with kept secrets, loneliness, societal pariahs, and love ultimately triumphing over horrible wrong.

Herman Melville's great opus, *Moby Dick*, follows a crazed Captain Ahab on his Homeric odyssey to conquer the great white whale that has outwitted him and his whaling crews time and again. The whale has even taken Ahab's leg and, according to Ahab, wants all of him. Melville recreates in painstaking detail and with insider knowledge of the harsh life of a whaler out of New Bedford by way of Nantucket.

The Life and Works of Herman Melville
http://www.melville.org/

For those who don't want to learn about every guy rope or all parts of the whaler's rigging, Melville offers up the succinct tale of *Billy Budd* and his Christ-like sacrifice to the black-and-white maritime laws on the high seas. An accident results in the death of one of the ship's officers, a slug of a fellow, who had taken a dislike to the young, affable, shy Billy. Captain Vere must hang Billy for the death of Claggert but knows that this is not right. However, an example must be given to the rest of the crew so that discipline can be maintained.

Edgar Allan Poe creates a distinctly American version of romanticism with his 16-syllable line in "The Raven," the classical "To Helen," and his Gothic "Annabelle Lee." The horror short story can be said to originate from Poe's pen. "The Tell-Tale Heart," "The Cask of Amontillado," "The Fall of the House of Usher," and "The Masque of the Red Death" are exemplary short stories. In addition, the genre of detective story emerges with Poe's "Murders in the Rue Morgue."

American Romanticism has its own offshoot in the Transcendentalism of Ralph Waldo Emerson and Henry David Thoreau. One wrote about transcending the complexities of life; the other, who wanted to get to the marrow of life, immersed himself in nature at Walden Pond and wrote an inspiring autobiographical account of his sojourn, aptly titled *On Walden Pond*. Thoreau also wrote passionately regarding his objections to the interference of government imposed on the individual in "On the Duty of Civil Disobedience."

Emerson's elegantly-crafted essays and war poetry still validate several important universal truths. Probably most remembered for his address to Thoreau's Harvard graduating class, "The American Scholar," he defined the qualities of hard work and intellectual spirit required of Americans in their growing nation.

The Transition Between Romanticism and Realism

The Civil War period ushers in the poignant poetry of Walt Whitman and his homage to all who suffer from the ripple effects of war and presidential assassination. His "Come up from the Fields, Father" about a Civil

War soldier's death and his family's reaction and "When Lilacs Last in the Courtyard Bloom'd" about the effects of Abraham Lincoln's death on the poet and the nation should be required readings in any American literature course. Further, his *Leaves of Grass* gave America its first poetry truly unique in form, structure, and subject matter.

Emily Dickinson, like Walt Whitman, leaves her literary fingerprints on a vast array of poems, all but three of which were never published in her lifetime. Her themes of introspection and attention to nature's details and wonders are, by any measurement, world-class works. Her posthumous recognition reveals the timeliness of her work. American writing had most certainly arrived!

Mark Twain also left giant footprints with his unique blend of tall tale and fable. "The Celebrated Jumping Frog of Calaveras County" and "The Man who Stole Hadleyburg" are epitomes of short story writing. Move to novel creation, and Twain again rises above others by his bold, still-disputed, oft-banned *The Adventures of Huckleberry Finn*, which examines such taboo subjects as a white person's love of a slave, the issue of leaving children with abusive parents, and the outcomes of family feuds. Written partly in dialect and southern vernacular, *The Adventures of Huckleberry Finn* is touted by some as the greatest American novel.

The Realistic Period

The late nineteenth century saw a reaction against the tendency of romantic writers to look at the world through rose-colored glasses. Writers like Frank Norris (*The Pit*) and Upton Sinclair (*The Jungle*) used their novels to decry conditions for workers in slaughterhouses and wheat mills.

Upton Sinclair
http://www.online-literature.com/upton_sinclair/

In *The Red Badge of Courage*, Stephen Crane wrote of the daily sufferings of the common soldier in the Civil War. Realistic writers wrote of common, ordinary people and events using realistic detail to reveal the harsh realities of life. They broached taboos by creating protagonists whose environments often destroyed them. Romantic writers w have only protagonists whose indomitable wills helped them rise above adver Crane's *Maggie: A Girl of the Streets* deals with a young woman forced into prostitution to survive. In "The Occurrence at Owl Creek Bridge," Ambrose Bierc relates the unfortunate hanging of a Confederate soldier.

Short stories, like Bret Harte's "The Outcasts of Poker Flat" and Jack London's "To Build a Fire," deal with unfortunate people whose luck in life has run out. Many writers, sub-classified as naturalists, believed that man was subject to a fate over which he had no control.

Contemporary American Literature

Twentieth century American writing can be divided into the following three genres: drama, fiction, and poetry.

American Drama: The greatest and most prolific of American playwrights include these:

- Eugene O'Neill, *Long Day's Journey into Night, Mourning Becomes Electra,* and *Desire Under the Elms*
- Arthur Miller, T*he Crucible, All My Sons,* and *Death of a Salesman*
- Tennessee Williams. *Cat on a Hot Tin Roof, The Glass Menagerie,* and *A Street Car Named Desire*
- Edward Albee, *Who's Afraid of Virginia Woolf? Three Tall Women,* and *A Delicate Balance*

American Fiction: The renowned American novelists include these authors:

- Eudora Welty, *The Optimist's Daughter*
- John Updike, *Rabbit Run* and *Rabbit Redux*
- Sinclair Lewis, *Babbit* and *Elmer Gantry*
- F. Scott Fitzgerald, *The Great Gatsby* and *Tender Is the Night*
- Ernest Hemingway, *A Farewell to Arms* and *For Whom the Bell Tolls*
- William Faulkner, *The Sound and the Fury* and *Absalom, Absalom*
- Bernard Malamud, *The Fixer* and *The Natural*

American Poetry: The poetry of the twentieth century is multifaceted, as represented by Edna St. Vincent Millay, Marianne Moore, Richard Wilbur, Langston Hughes, Maya Angelou, and Rita Dove. Above all others are the many-layered poems of Robert Frost. His New England motifs of snowy evenings, birches, apple picking, stone wall mending, hired hands, and detailed nature studies relate universal truths in exquisite diction, polysyllabic words, and rare allusions to either mythology or the Bible.

North Americam literature is divided between the United States, Canada, and Mexico. The American writers have been amply discussed above. Canadian writers of note include feminist Margaret Atwood, *The Hand Maiden's Tale*; Alice Munro, a remarkable short story writer; and W. P. Kinsella, another short story writer whose two major subjects are North American Indians and baseball. Mexican writers include 1990 Nobel Prize winning poet, Octavio Paz, "The Labyrinth of Solitude" and feminist Rosarian Castillanos, *The Nine Guardians*.

Africa

African literary greats include South Africans Nadine Gordimer (Nobel Prize for literature) and Peter Abrahams, *Tell Freedom: Memories of Africa*, an auto-biography of life in Johannesburg. Chinua Achebe, *Things Fall Apart*, and the poet, Wole Soyinka, both from Nigeria. Mark Mathabane wrote an autobiography *Kaffir Boy* about growing up in South Africa. Egyptian writer, Naguib Mahfouz, and Doris Lessing from Rhodesia, now Zimbabwe, write about race relations in their respective countries. Because of her radical politics, Lessing was banned from her homeland and The Union of South Africa, as was Alan Paton whose seemingly simple story, *Cry, the Beloved Country*, brought the plight of blacks and the whites' fear of blacks under apartheid to the rest of the world.

Central American/Caribbean Literature

The Caribbean and Central America encompass a vast area and cultures that reflect oppression and colonialism by England, Spain, Portugal, France, and The Netherlands. The Caribbean writers include Samuel Selvon from Trinidad and Armado Valladres of Cuba. Central American authors include dramatist Carlos Solorzano, from Guatemala, whose plays include *Dona Beatriz, The Hapless, The Magician,* and *The Hands of God.*

South American Literature

Chilean Gabriela Mistral was the first Latin American writer to win the Nobel Prize for literature. She is best known for her collections of poetry, *Desolation and Feeling.* Chile was also home to Pablo Neruda, who, in 1971, also won the Nobel Prize for literature for his poetry. His 29 volumes of poetry have been translated into more than 60 languages, attesting to his universal appeal. *Twenty Love Poems* and *Song of Despair* are justly famous. Isabel Allende is carrying on the Chilean literary standards with her acclaimed novel, *House of Spirits.* Argentine Jorge Luis Borges is considered by many literary critics to be the most important writer of his century from South America. His collections of short stories, *Ficciones*, brought him universal recognition. Also from Argentina, Silvina Ocampo, a collaborator with Borges on a collection of poetry, is famed for her poetry and short story collections, which include *The Fury* and *The Days of the Night.*

Noncontinental European Literature

Horacio Quiroga represents Uruguay, and Brazil has Joao Guimaraes Rosa, whose novel, *The Devil to Pay*, is considered first-rank world literature.

Russian Literature

Boris Pasternak won the Nobel Prize (*Dr. Zhivago*). Aleksandr Solzhenitsyn (*The Gulag Archipelago*) is only recently back in Russia after years of expatriation in Vermont. Ilya Varshavsky, who creates fictional societies that are dystopias, or the opposite of utopias, represents the genre of science fiction.

French Literature

French literature is defined by the existentialism of Jean-Paul Sartre (*No Exit, The Flies, Nausea*), Andre Malraux, (*The Fall*), and Albert Camus (*The Stranger, The Plague*), the recipient of the 1957 Nobel Prize for literature. Feminist writings include those of Sidonie-Gabrielle Colette, known for her short stories and novels, as well as Simone de Beauvoir.

Slavic nations

Austrian writer Franz Kafka (*The Metamorphosis, The Trial,* and *The Castle*) is considered by many to be the literary voice of the first half of the twentieth century. Representing the Czech Republic is the poet Vaclav Havel. Slovakia has dramatist Karel Capek (*R.U.R.*) Romania is represented by Elie Weisel (*Night*), a Nobel Prize winner.

Far East Literature

Asia has many modern writers who are being translated for the western reading public. India's Krishan Chandar has authored more than 300 stories. Rabindranath Tagore won the Nobel Prize for literature in 1913 (*Song Offerings*). Narayan, India's most famous writer (*The Guide*) is highly interested in mythology and legends of India. Santha Rama Rau's work, *Gifts of Passage*, is her true story of life in a British school where she tries to preserve her Indian culture and traditional home.

Revered as Japan's most famous female author, Fumiko Hayashi (*Drifting Clouds*) by the time of her death had written more than 270 literary works.

In 1968 the Nobel Prize for literature was awarded to Yasunari Kawabata. *The Sound of the Mountain* and *The Snow Country* are considered to be his masterpieces. His Palm-of-the-Hand Stories take the essentials of Haiku poetry and transform them into the short story genre.

Modern feminist and political concerns are written eloquently by Ting Ling, who used the pseudonym Chiang Ping-Chih. Her stories reflect her concerns about social injustice and her commitment to the women's movement.

Skill 9.2   Demonstrate knowledge of the significance of major literary works.

The Upanishads are Hindu treatises that deal with broad philosophic problems. The term means "to sit down near" and implies sitting at the feet of a teacher. There are approximately 108 that record views of many teachers over a number of years. Read chronologically, they exhibit a development toward the concept of a single supreme being and suggest ultimate reunion with it. Of special philosophical concern is the nature of reality. Their appearance in Europe in the early 19th century captured the interest of philosophers, particularly in Germany. The work of Arthur Schopenhauer is reflective of the Upanishads.

Virgil (Publius Vergilius Maro, later called Virgilius and known in English as Virgil or Vergil, October 15, 70BC/September 21, 19BC) was a Latin poet, author of the *Eclogues,* the *Georgics,* and the *Aeneid.* The Aeneid is a poem of twelve books that became the Roman Empire's national epic.

Virgil has had a strong influence on English literature. Edmund Spenser's *The Faerie Queene* reflects that influence. It was also the model for John Milton's *Paradise Lost*, not only in structure but also in style and diction. The Augustan poets considered Virgil's poetry the ultimate perfection of form and ethical content. He was not so popular during the Romantic period, but Victorians such as Matthew Arnold and Alfred, Lord Tennyson rediscovered Virgil and were influenced by the sensitivity and pathos that had not been so appealing to the Romantics.

From Greece come Homer's epics, *The Iliad* and *The Odyssey*. No one, except Shakespeare, is more often cited. Add to these the works of Plato and Aristotle for philosophy; the dramatists Aeschylus, Euripides, and Sophocles for tragedy, and Aristophanes for comedy.

The *Canterbury Tales*, written by Geoffrey Chaucer in the medieval period, are written in the vernacular, or street language of England, not in Latin. Thus, the tales are said to be the first work of British literature.

Don Quixote, written by Spanish author, Miguel de Cervantes is best remembered for the protagonist, a middle-aged gentleman from the region of La Mancha, who sets out with his sword to defend helpless victims and to eliminate the wicked persecutors. His not-too-bright assistant, Sancho Panza, has become a symbol of misguided faithfulness. *Don Quixote* ultimately abandons his determination to make the world better and dies of a fever. The purpose of the novel, according to Cervantes is to illustrate the demise of chivalry.

Madame Bovary, considered the masterpiece of French writer, Gustave Flaubert, has become a classic in the study of literature. The protagonist, Emma Bovary, has adulterous affairs and spend extravagantly to escape a life that offers little by way of fulfillment, let along excitement. A seminal example of the Realism movement in literature, it remains influential with writers all over the world.

Leaves of Grass, a collection of poems by American poet, Walter Whitman, represent a departure from previous poetry, which used such devices as symbolism and allegory and focused on the religious and the spiritual. Whitman instead praises nature and individuality instead. He does not claim that the human form and the human mind are more important than spiritual matters; rather, he elevates them, deeming them worthy of being important poetic themes.

Ulysses, a novel by James Joyce, an Irish writer, published in 1922 in Paris ranks as one of the most important and representative works of the Modernist movement in literature. Based largely on the hero of Homer's *Odyssey*, it is a chronicle of the life of Leopold Bloom, its protagonist, for a day as he passes through Dublin.

Skill 9.3   Demonstrate knowledge of the significance of major literary movements and periods.

In literature, there are four major periods: neoclassicism, romanticism, realism, and naturalism. Certain authors, among these Chaucer, Shakespeare, and Donne, though writing during a particular literary period, are considered to have a style all their own.

Neoclassicism: Patterned after the greatest writings of classical Greece and Rome, this type of writing is characterized by balanced, graceful, well-crafted, refined, elevated style. Major proponents of this style are poet laureates John Dryden and Alexander Pope. The eras in which they wrote are called the Ages of Dryden and Pope. The self is not exalted in neoclassic writing and focus is on the group, not the individual.

Romanticism: Writings emphasize the individual. Emotions and feelings are validated. Nature acts as an inspiration for creativity; it is a balm of the spirit. Romantics hearken back to medieval, chivalric themes and ambience. They also emphasize supernatural, Gothic themes and settings, which are characterized by gloom and darkness. Imagination is stressed. New types of writings include detective and horror stories and autobiographical introspection (Wordsworth). There are two generations in British Literature: First Generation includes William Wordsworth and Samuel Taylor

Coleridge whose collaboration, *Lyrical Ballads*, defines romanticism and its exponents. Wordsworth maintained that the scenes and events of everyday life and the speech of ordinary people were the raw material of which poetry could and should be made. Romanticism spread to the United States, where Ralph Waldo Emerson and Henry David Thoreau adopted it in their transcendental romanticism, emphasizing reasoning. Further extensions of this style are found in Edgar Allan Poe's Gothic writings. Second Generation romantics include the ill-fated Englishmen Lord Byron, John Keats, and Percy Bysshe Shelley. Byron and Shelley, who for some most epitomize the romantic poet (in their personal lives as well as in their work), wrote resoundingly in protest against social and political wrongs and in defense of the struggles for liberty in Italy and Greece. The Second Generation romantics stressed personal introspection and the love of beauty and nature as requisites of inspiration.

Realism: Unlike classical and neoclassical writing, which often deal with aristocracies and nobility or the gods, realistic writers deal with the common man and his socio/economic problems in a non-sentimental way. Muckraking, social injustice, domestic abuse, and inner city conflicts are examples of this movement. Realistic writers include Thomas Hardy, George Bernard Shaw, and Henrik Ibsen.

Naturalism: This is realism pushed to the limit, writing that exposes the underbelly of society, usually lower class struggles. This is the world of penury, injustice, abuse, ghetto survival, hungry children, single parenting, and substance abuse. Émile Zola was inspired by history and medicine and attempted to apply methods of scientific observation to the depiction of pathological human character, notably in his series of novels devoted to several generations of one French family.

Skill 9.4 Demonstrate knowledge of significant literary forms, genres, and styles.

An archetype is an idealized model of a person, object, or concept from which similar instances are derived, copied, patterned, or emulated. In psychology, an archetype is a model of a person, personality or behavior. Archetypes often appear in literature. William Shakespeare, for example, is known for popularizing many archetypal characters. Although he based many of his characters on existing archetypes from fables and myths, Shakespeare's characters stand out as original by their contrast against a complex, social literary landscape. An image, character, or pattern of circumstances that reoccurs frequently in literature can be considered an archetype.

For example, *Oedipus Rex* has a structure that appears to be repeated in the lives of all men in the sense that all sons are replacements for their fathers. Faulkner, in "Barn Burning" provides an original example that calls forth this archetype.

There are many archetypes, and skillful and creative writers often rely on them to create successful fiction. Some examples of **action archetypes**:

- The search for the killer
- The search for salvation (or the holy grail)
- The search for the hero
- The descent into hell

Some examples of **character archetypes**:
- The double
- The scapegoat
- The prodigal son
- The Madonna and the Magdalene

The family has often been used as a recurring archetypal theme in literature including the Greek play *Oedipus Rex* and other Greek literature such as the *Medea*. Many of Shakespeare's plays also used this archetype: *Hamlet, Romeo and Juliet,* and *King Lear*, for example. Modern writers also use this archetype, such as *Desire Under the Elms* by Eugene O'Neill and *A Streetcar Named Desire* by Tennessee Williams. Toni Morrison in her popular novel *Beloved* uses the archetype of family by chronicling the difficulties the protagonist Sethe and her family face before, during, and after the Civil War. The result is a compelling picture of a family's response to the devastation brought on by slavery.

The major literary genres include allegory, ballad, drama, epic, epistle, essay, fable, novel, poem, romance, and the short story.

Allegory: A story in verse or prose with characters representing virtues and vices. There are two meanings, symbolic and literal. John Bunyan's *The Pilgrim's Progress* is the most renowned of this genre.

Ballad: An *in medias res* story told or sung, usually in verse and accompanied by music. Literary devices found in ballads include the refrain, or repeated section, and incremental repetition, or anaphora, for effect. Earliest forms were anonymous folk ballads. Later forms include Coleridge's Romantic masterpiece, "The Rime of the Ancient Mariner."

Drama: Plays—comedy, modern, or tragedy—typically in five acts. Traditionalists and neoclassicists adhere to Aristotle's unities of time, place, and action. Plot development is advanced via dialogue. Literary devices include asides, soliloquies and the chorus representing public opinion. William Shakespeare is considered the greatest of all dramatists/playwrights. Other dramaturges include Ibsen, Williams, Miller, Shaw, Stoppard, Racine, Moliére, Sophocles, Aeschylus, Euripides, and Aristophanes.

Epic: Long poem usually of book length reflecting values inherent in the generative society. Epic devices include an invocation to a Muse for inspiration, purpose for writing, universal setting, protagonist and antagonist who possess supernatural strength and acumen, and interventions of a God or the gods. Understandably, there are very few epics: Homer's *Iliad* and *Odyssey*; Virgil's *Aeneid*; Milton's *Paradise Lost*; Spenser's *The Fairie Queene*; Barrett Browning's *Aurora Leigh*; and Pope's mock-epic, *The Rape of the Lock*.

Epistle: A letter that is not always originally intended for public distribution, but due to the fame of the sender and/or recipient, becomes public domain. Paul wrote epistles that were later placed in the *Bible*.

Essay: Typically a limited-length prose work focusing on a topic and propounding a definite point of view and authoritative tone. Great essayists include Carlyle, Lamb, DeQuincy, Emerson, and Montaigne, who is credited with defining this genre.

Fable: Terse tale offering up a moral or exemplum. Chaucer's "The Nun's Priest's Tale" is a fine example of a *bête fabliau* or beast fable in which animals speak and act characteristically human, illustrating human foibles.

Legend: A traditional narrative or collection of related narratives, popularly regarded as historically factual but actually a mixture of fact and fiction.

Myth: Stories that are more or less universally shared within a culture to explain its history and traditions.

Novel: The longest form of fictional prose containing a variety of characterizations, settings, local color, and regionalism. Most have complex plots, expanded description, and attention to detail. Some of the great novelists include Austin, the Brontes, Twain, Tolstoy, Hugo, Hardy, Dickens, Hawthorne, Forster, and Flaubert.

Poem: The only requirement is rhythm. Sub-genres include fixed types of literature such as the sonnet, elegy, ode, pastoral, and villanelle. Unfixed types of literature include blank verse and dramatic monologue.

Romance: A highly imaginative tale set in a fantastical realm dealing with the conflicts between heroes, villains and/or monsters. "The Knight's Tale" from Chaucer's *Canterbury Tales*, *Sir Gawain and the Green Knight* and Keats' "The Eve of St. Agnes" are prime representatives.

Short Story: Typically a terse narrative, with less developmental background about characters than in a novel. May include description, author's point of view, and tone. Poe emphasized that a successful short story should create one focused impact. Considered to be great short story writers are Hemingway, Faulkner, Twain, Joyce, Shirley Jackson, Flannery O'Connor, de Maupassant, Saki, Edgar Allen Poe, and Pushkin.

Skill 9.5   Analyze within the context of a passage the thematic concerns and stylistic and formal characteristics associated with major prose writers who have contributed to literatures from around the world.

Skill 9.6   Recognize within the context of a passage references to historical events and to political, social, and cultural movements and institutions that have influenced the development of literatures from around the world.

These two essays will have the same format and will be approached in the same way. The only distinction is the aspect of the work being discussed. See this book's preface for scoring rubric.

Each is one of four essays that you will write in a two-hour period, so you will want to budget thirty minutes per essay. Plan to spend five or ten minutes reading the prompt and selection carefully. Spend another five minutes prewriting. Use whatever method works well for you: outline, free write, make brief notes. Spend ten to fifteen minutes writing your essay and use the remaining time to edit.

Read the prompt very closely. It will typically ask you to focus on a particular theme. Make sure to focus on what the prompt is suggesting instead of discussing irrelevant aspects of the text.

Poetry: Read the poem carefully. If you cannot understand it, read it again as if you were saying it aloud. Look at the punctuation within the poem. This often helps you understand the grouping of ideas. In this discussion, we'll focus on "Do not go gentle into that good night," by Dylan Thomas.

Prose: While prose is not usually as dense as poetry and possibly more easily understood, you should still do a careful reading of the selection. In this discussion, we'll focus on "The Story of an Hour," a very short but extremely powerful short story.

OVERVIEW FOR WRITING THE ESSAY

In their training to be scorers for these essays, readers are told to think of these essays as somewhat polished first drafts. However, that does not mean you can be hasty or careless. Your essay should reflect the same standards you would expect of your students. Use the standard five paragraph essay if you are comfortable with it but you are free to use whatever development strategy in which you feel confident and capable.

Provide an introduction. In your opening paragraph, establish the purpose of your essay. Avoid direct statements, such as "In this essay, I will analyze the literary elements in Dylan Thomas' poem 'Do not go gentle into that good night.'" Avoid the obvious, such as "Kate Chopin uses diction and style in her short story 'The Story of an Hour.'" All writers have a style and use diction.

Instead, write an interesting paragraph that will hook the reader's attention and still explain your main thesis and purpose.

Develop your thesis clearly. Your essay should have unity, coherence, and balance. This is not the time to throw in everything you know about poetry or prose. You must have control of your ideas and your writing style.

Analyze; Avoid Paraphrase or Summary

In these essays, you should analyze how the various literary elements or devices develop the theme and/or enhance the effect of the poem or prose selection. Yes, Dylan Thomas writes about his father's death in "Do not go gentle into that good night"—that is obvious. What's needed, however, is an analysis of how Thomas uses metaphor, repetition, and rhyme to develop the beseeching tone. Why does he use the villanelle, a light verse form, for such a serious subject?

Summarizing the plot of "The Story of an Hour" is a low-level skill, and your goal here is to convince your reader that you have the critical thinking skills of an English teacher. Relate the events only as a way of illustrating the thesis, which leads to the next point.

Show, Don't Tell

Provide specific examples from the work to support the points you make. Do not write "Dylan Thomas uses many metaphors for death in his poem." Instead, incorporate lines from the poem to prove your point.

> Comparing death to darkness, Thomas pleads with his father to fight against "the good night" and to "rage against the dying of the light."

Do not make claims you are unsure about. An inaccurate claim is worse than a brief response. For example, in "The Story of an Hour," Chopin is deliberately ambiguous in her closing lines. But to write that "Chopin's closing line indicates that the main character dies from the joy of seeing her husband" is not supported by the details the story.

While you may be hurrying to meet the time requirements, be sure to close your essay effectively. Restate your thesis but don't merely repeat it. You have made your case and your closing should be a sound recapitulation of the main ideas.

Irritations for English Teachers

Most scorers for teacher certification essays are experienced English instructors who have developed personal biases against common problems in essays. They will overlook some of them but would hope that prospective English teachers would not make these mistakes. However, when the writer has little or no control over spelling, grammar, and punctuation, the score on the essay is naturally affected. Here's an incomplete list of thorny irritations. You should also review information in **Skills 14.1 through 14.5**.

Using *its* and *it's* incorrectly. *Its* is the possessive pronoun; *it's* is the contraction for it is.

Using the apostrophe incorrectly. Review the use of apostrophes in making nouns possessive. Review plural possessives.

Using the existential *it*. Begin sentences with strong subjects. Be sure the pronoun *it* has a clear antecedent. For example, "It is important to note" is a weak sentence beginning. Instead, you could write "Repetition is an important element in Dylan Thomas' poem." "It was a dark and stormy night" is unnecessarily repetitive. Instead, write "The night was dark and stormy."

Misspelling literary terms and incorrect word choice. For example, don't write *smile* for *simile* or confuse *affect* and *effect*.

Writing illegibly. Although scorers are trained to look past poor handwriting, this is sometimes hard and the psychological impact on your score cannot be measured. Scorers should be able to read your essay once. If your handwriting is weak, then print your response. If your handwriting is flowery and decorative, simplify it. Don't dot your *i's* with hearts or end words with fancy curlicues.

General Strategies for Writing an Essay

The strategies below, which apply to your own experience in writing essays for the certification exam, can also be adapted for your students.

The essay that you are to write must demonstrate the ability to write on a literary topic. As you practice the steps provided to prepare for this test, please keep in mind that this review will not teach you how to analyze literature. It is expected that analyzing literature has been a focus of your course of study. The following steps in writing an essay in a timed situation will aid you in preparing to write the essay in the most time efficient manner possible. Keep in mind that a good essay has focus, organization, support, and correct usage.

Understanding the Question

When you receive your question, the first task is to decide what the question is asking you to do. Look for key words that will establish the purpose of your essay. Examine the following chart and review the key words and purpose each word establishes. Please note that for each key word the purpose and an example are illustrated.

KEY WORD	PURPOSE	EXAMPLE
Analyze	To examine the parts of a literary selection	Read a passage and analyze how the author achieves tone using diction and imagery
Compare	To identify the similarities	Read "I Hear America Singing" by Walt Whitman and "Chicago" by Carl Sandburg and compare each poet's attitude about America.
Contrast	To identify the differences	Read "Thanatopsis" by Bryant and "Do not go gentle into that good night" by Dylan Thomas and contrast how each poet uses imagery to express his distinct views of death.
Discuss	Examine in detail	Read a poem and discuss how the poet establishes the mood using imagery and word choice.
Explain	Provide reasons and examples or clarify the meaning	Read the opening passage of *The Great Gatsby* and explain how the author establishes the tone of the novel.

When writing an essay on literature, consider the following before you begin to prewrite.

Identify the elements for analysis. If you are asked to examine the tone of poem, you might need to look at imagery and word choice. If you are asked to examine prose and explain how a writer creates mood, you should examine the diction, style, imagery, syntax, structure, and selection of detail.

Decide on your main idea. Use the question as a guideline. However, do not merely restate the question. Make sure that in restating the topic you have taken a position on how you will answer the prompt. For example, you might be asked to read Whitman's poem "I Hear America Singing" and discuss not only the tone of the poem but also how Whitman creates the tone. If you wish to receive a high score on the essay, state your main idea clearly.

A well-crafted thesis statement can help both writers and readers. Writers can stay on topic and develop their thesis statement with appropriate and relevant details. Readers can better understand the main idea and the supporting ideas. By following these steps, writers can develop the skill to formulate clear and strong thesis statements.

Write the Thesis Statement

First, you should identify the topic.
> I am going to write about the tone and how it is created in the poem "I Hear America Singing" by Walt Whitman.

Second, state your point of view about the topic.

> The upbeat and optimistic tone of Whitman's poem is created by his word choice, structure, and imagery.

Third, summarize the main points you will make in your essay.

> Whitman creates an optimistic tone through his choice of words, parallel structure, and images.

State the Main Point of Each Body Paragraph and Organize Support

Using a five-paragraph essay format is one of many ways to respond to literature. It is a basic structure that encourages development and coherence. As writers become more sophisticated, they will progress beyond this formula.

PARAGRAPH	PURPOSE	SUPPORT
1st Intro	Main idea statement	
2nd 1st body paragraph	Main point 1	Quotes or specifics from the text with analysis or explanation of how each detail supports your main point.
3rd 2nd body Paragraph	Main point 2	Quotes or specifics from the text with analysis or explanation of how each detail supports your main point.
4th 3rd Body Paragraph	Main point 3	Quotes or specifics from the text with analysis or explanation of how each detail supports Your main point.

5th Closing	Summarize ideas	

Consider Audience, Purpose, and Tone

Keep in mind as you write this essay that your purpose is to demonstrate literary skill by reading an unfamiliar passage or poem and examining its elements. It is crucial to avoid giving a summary of the piece or writing your personal reaction to the work. Your audience is familiar with the piece and thus does not need to have the work summarized. In fact, the readers of your essay have been trained to look for focus, organization, support, and correct usage. Finally, the tone is formal.

Techniques to Maintain Focus

- **Focus on a main point.** The point should be clear to readers, and all sentences in the paragraph should relate to it.

- **Start the paragraph with a topic sentence.** This should be a general, one-sentence summary of the paragraph's main point, relating back to the thesis and forward to the content of the paragraph. (A topic sentence is sometimes unnecessary if the paragraph continues a developing idea clearly introduced in a preceding paragraph, or if the paragraph appears in a narrative of events where generalizations might interrupt the flow of the story.)

- **Stick to the point.** Eliminate sentences that do not support the topic sentence.

- **Be flexible.** If you do not have enough evidence to support the claim of your topic sentence, do not fall into the trap of wandering or introducing new ideas within the paragraph. Either find more evidence, or adjust the topic sentence to corroborate the evidence that is available.

CRITICAL APPROACHES

To analyze a work of literature, no matter the genre, you can use the critical approaches discussed below. Some are more appropriate than others for particular texts. Not all works can be viewed through the lens of feminism or Marxism, for example.

The New Criticism

New Criticism treats literary texts as independent entities requiring little or no consideration of external factors such as the identity of the author or the society in which he or she lives. Proponents of the New Criticism believe that the literary text itself is the paramount concern.

Works are analyzed, evaluated, and interpreted through what is called "close reading." Close reading emphasizes genre and literary form; a work's theme and a writer's rendition of it; plot and character development; poetic meter, rhythm, and, if applicable, rhyme; metaphor, simile, and other figurative or literal imagery; evaluation of literary quality; analysis and interpretation of a work's meaning.

The goal of close reading is to arrive, without biographical or sociological distractions, at an objective understanding and appreciation of a literary work

> **Resources for Literary Theory**
> http://vos.ucsb.edu/browse.asp?id=2718

The New Criticism's approach is summed up in two key literary anthologies: *Understanding Poetry* (4th ed.) and *Understanding Fiction*, both edited by Cleanth Brooks and Robert Penn Warren.

Structuralism and Deconstructionism

The structural approach is to examine the structure of a literary work without regard for external influences. This is an attempt to quantify objectively certain criteria that a work must follow. Emphasis is placed on the work as a whole and its place within its genre.

In deconstruction theory, only the text itself is examined. This is done through a very close reading. Formulated by Jacques Derrida in the 1960s, it has been unjustly called "destruction criticism" because of its detailed analytical approach.

Both of these theories are much more complex than explained here and require further study.

Marxist Criticism

Based on the ideas of Karl Marx, some of the key components of this critical theory follow:

- Class conflict drives the history of human civilization.

- The capitalists or bourgeoisie (those who possess and control economic capital) exploit and oppress the proletariat (the working classes) for their own economic and political benefit.

- The workers must therefore unite to overthrow the capitalists and their socio-economic system. This will result in a "dictatorship of the proletariat" that will create a classless society in which most, if not all, private property is abolished in favor of collective ownership. The result will be a "workers' paradise"; eventually the nation-states themselves will dissolve and be replaced by a unitary, worldwide communist society free of class conflict.

- Marxist orthodoxy holds that the triumph of communism is inevitable, and that Marxist doctrine is validated by its scientific and materialist approach to history.

- Therefore the Marxist critic uses these ideas to scrutinize literary works, which are analyzed and interpreted to determine their "revolutionary" or "proletarian," "bourgeois" or "reactionary," character.

- Works focused primarily on social injustice and abuses of power have drawn sustained attention from Marxist critics. These include: *The Jungle* by Upton Sinclair; Stephen Crane's *Maggie, a Girl of the Streets*; Theodore Dreiser's *Sister Carrie* and *An American Tragedy*; John Steinbeck's *Grapes of Wrath*; Virginia Woolf's *A Room of One's Own*; and Dostoevsky's *Crime and Punishment* and *The Brothers Karamazov*.

Feminist Criticism

Feminist critics emphasize the ways that literary works are informed and inspired by an author's gender, by an author's ideas about gender and gender roles, and by social norms regarding gender. Of prime concern to the feminist critical enterprise is the advocacy of women as intellectual, social, and artistic equals to men. Feminist criticism is not limited to works by women, nor is it hostile or opposed to male writers or males in general.

"Feminism" could just as easily be referred to as "feminisms." There are a variety of schools of thought that make the plural form more accurate than the singular. Some feminists emphasize class, others race, still others sexual orientation, when critiquing texts or social norms and conditions affecting women's lives.

When introducing feminist writing and criticism to high school students, teachers should consider giving a comprehensive summary of what feminism is, and when, where, and why it arose. Some students will likely have the impression that feminism originated in the 1960s despite the fact that it has existed for over 200 years. To counter any such misconceptions, teachers can assign excerpts or entire works by these 18th or 19th century authors:

- Mary Wollstonecraft
- Margaret Fuller
- Sojourner Truth
- Susan B. Anthony
- Elizabeth Cady Stanton
- Frederick Douglass

Some popular 20th century works relevant to feminist thought and suitable for high school students are listed below.

- *A Room of One's Own* by Virginia Woolf (nonfiction)
- *The Yellow Wallpaper* by Charlotte Perkins Gilman (novella)
- *The Color Purple* by Alice Walker (novel)
- *Beloved* by Toni Morrison (novel)
- *Good Woman* by Lucille Clifton (poems)
- *She Had Some Horses* by Joy Harjo (poems)
- *The Joy Luck Club* by Amy Tan (novel)
- *The Secret Life of Bees* by Sue Monk Kidd (novel)

There are numerous up-to-date anthologies of women's literature and feminist criticism available through major publishers. The groundbreaking anthology, *The New Feminist Criticism*, edited by Elaine Showalter, offers an excellent variety of feminist essays on Western literature. Some of these essays are rather dated but the collection does give a solid overview of key concerns that animated "second wave" feminism in the 1960s and 70s.

Psychoanalytic, or Freudian, Criticism

Based initially on the works of Sigmund Freud, this theory has been expanded to include the ideas of other psychoanalysts.

Freudian psychoanalysis holds that the human mind is a tripartite structure composed of the id, which generates and seeks to satisfy all of a person's urges and desires; the superego, which "polices" and counters the id; and the ego, which is the psychic result of the id/superego conflict. The ego is characterized by a person's thoughts and behaviors.

The formation of human character—including sexual behavior—begins at birth. The infant is said to pass through various stages—the oral stage, the anal stage, and so on—as its needs and urges arise and are either satisfied or frustrated; and as it learns (or doesn't learn) to master human relationships and bodily functions.

All humans are said to have inexorable conflicts between drives such as Eros and Thanatos (the sex drive and the death wish), which are also played out in the contests between id and superego.

Neurotic behavior results from fixations on one of the above physical factors or from an imbalance in the powers of the id and superego or from deeply embedded (unconscious) memories of pleasant or unpleasant experiences, or from a combination of these. Neurosis is usually rooted in infancy or early childhood.

To discover the nature of a person's mind, the psychoanalyst looks for recurrent thoughts, images, speech patterns, and behaviors evident in the person being analyzed. By carefully observing (especially listening to) a patient, the psychoanalyst uncovers previously unknown truths about the hows and whys of the patient's predicament.

The psychoanalytic literary critic applies Freudian theories to writings and authors in order to better understand the psychological underpinnings of literary works, writers, and, sometimes society itself.

Writers that have garnered much attention from Freudian critics include Edgar Allen Poe, the Marquis de Sade, Moses, Madame de Stahl, and William S. Burroughs. Not surprisingly, sex and violence feature prominently in these writers' works. Representative examples of psychoanalytic criticism include "Moses and Monotheism" by Sigmund Freud, and *Edgar Allen Poe* by Marie Bonaparte.

Reader-Response

In this critical theory, the readers create meaning through their individual understandings and responses. Some critics focus solely on the readers' experiences; other critics experiment on defined groups to determine reader response.

Resources for Literary Theory:
http://vos.ucsb.edu/browse.asp?id=2718

COMPETENCY 10 HISTORICAL, SOCIAL, AND CULTURAL ASPECTS OF LITERATURES FROM AROUND THE WORLD

Skill 10.1   Demonstrate knowledge of the common structural and stylistic elements of and shared themes in literary works from the oral tradition.

Encyclopedia Britannica points out that even in the oral literature of preliterate people, the important literary genres all existed: heroic epic; songs in praise of priests and kings; stories of mystery and the supernatural; love lyrics; personal songs; love stories; tales of adventure and heroism; satire; satirical combats; ballads; folktales of tragedy and murder; folk stories; animal fables; riddles, proverbs, and philosophical observations; hymns, incantations, and mysterious songs of priests; and mythology.

The epic, a natural manifestation of oral poetic tradition in preliterate societies where the poetry was transmitted to the audience and from performer to performer by purely oral means, is one of the major forms of narrative literature, which retells chronologically the life of a mythological person or group of persons. This genre has become uncommon since the early 20th century although the term has been used to define certain extraordinarily long prose works and films. Usually a large number of characters, multiple settings, and a long span of time are features that lead to its designation as an epic. This change in the use of this term might indicate that some prose works of the past might be called epics although they were not composed or originally understood as such. It was composed of short episodes, each of equal status, interest, and importance, which facilitated memorization. The poet recalls each episode and uses it to recreate the entire epic.

Some Ancient Epics:
The *Iliad* and the *Odyssey*, both ascribed to Homer
Lost Greek epics ascribed to the Cyclic poets:
      Trojan War cycle
      Theban Cycle
      Argonautica by Apollonius of Rhodes
      Mahabharata and *Ramayana*, Hindu mythologies
Aeneid by Virgil
Metamorphoses by Ovid
Argonautica by Gaius Valerius Flaccus

Some Medieval Epics (500-1500)
Beowulf (Anglo-Saxon mythology)
Bhagavata Purana (Sanskrit "Stories of the Lord")
Divina Commedia (*The Divine Comedy*) by Dante Alighieri
The Canterbury Tales by Geoffrey Chaucer
Alliterative Morte Arthure

An Ode is generally a long lyric poem and as a form or poetry or song has an extensive history. Though odes vary in topic and occasionally structure, three forms have risen to the foreground in literature. These three forms are identifiable by their different features, and all odes carry characteristics that line up somewhere among the three. They may contain parts from one form and pieces from another, but this is generally true. The two best-known and best-established ode forms are the Pindaric and the Horatian odes of the Greek and Roman traditions respectively.

Named after a 5th century B.C. Greek poet, the Pindaric ode consists of a triadic structure, which emulates the musical movement of the early Greek chorus. Though infrequently attempted in English, some examples do exist. The Horatian ode is also named after a poet. The Roman poet Horace is given credit for this form, which typically has equal-length stanzas with the same rhyme scheme and meter. The Horatian ode, unlike the Pindaric ode, also has a tendency to be personal rather than formal.

Pastoral odes differ from others mostly in subject matter. "Pastoral" designates a literary work that has to do with the lives of shepherds or rural life and usually draws a contrast between the innocence and serenity of the simple life and the discomforts and corruptions of the city and especially court life. The poet's moral, social, and literary views are usually expressed.

The Upanishads are Hindu treatises that deal with broad philosophic problems. The term means "to sit down near" and implies sitting at the feet of a teacher. There are approximately 108 that record views of many teachers over a number of years. Read chronologically, they exhibit a development toward the concept of a single supreme being and suggest ultimate reunion with it. Of special philosophical concern is the nature of reality.

Virgil (Publius Vergilius Maro, later called Virgilius and known in English as Virgil or Vergil (October 15, 70BC/September 21, 19BC) was a Latin poet, author of the *Eclogues,* the *Georgics,* and the *Aeneid.* The Aeneid is a poem of twelve books that became the Roman Empire's national epic.

Virgil has had a strong influence on English literature. Edmund Spenser's *The Faerie Queene* reflects that influence. It was also the model for John Milton's *Paradise Lost*, not only in structure but also in style and diction. The Augustan poets considered Virgil's poetry the ultimate perfection of form and ethical content. He was not so popular during the Romantic period, but Victorians such as Matthew Arnold and Alfred, Lord Tennyson rediscovered Virgil and were influenced by the sensitivity and pathos that had not been so appealing to the Romantics.

Skill 10.2   Analyze how social and cultural issues and issues relating to gender, sexual orientation, and ethnicity are explored in traditional and contemporary literature for adolescents and young adults.

Adolescent literature, because of the age range of readers, is extremely diverse. Fiction for the middle group, usually ages ten/eleven to fourteen/fifteen, deals with issues of coping with internal and external changes in their lives. Because children's writers in the twentieth century have produced increasingly realistic fiction, adolescents can now find problems dealt with honestly in novels.

Teachers of middle/junior high school students see the greatest change in interests and reading abilities. Fifth and sixth graders, included in elementary grades in many schools, are viewed as older children while seventh and eighth graders are preadolescent.

Ninth graders, included sometimes as upper tier in junior high school and sometimes as underlings in high school, definitely view themselves as teenagers. Their literature choices will often be governed more by interest than by ability—thus, the wealth of high-interest, low readability books that have flooded the market in recent years. Tenth through twelfth graders will still select high-interest books for pleasure reading but are also easily encouraged to stretch their literature muscles by reading more classics.

At the same time, because of the complex changes affecting adolescents, the teacher must be well versed in learning theory and child development in addition to being competent to teach the subject matter of language and literature.

Child/adolescent literature has always been to some degree didactic, whether non-fiction or fiction. Until the twentieth century, "kiddie" lit was also morally prescriptive. Written by adults who determined either what they believed children needed or liked or what they should need or like, most books, stories, poems, and essays dealt with experiences or issues that would make children into better adults. The fables, fairy tales, and epics of old set the moral/social standards of their times while entertaining the child in every reader/listener. These tales are still popular because they have a universal appeal. Except for the rare exceptions discussed earlier in this section, most books were written for literate adults. Educated children found their pleasure in the literature that was available.

Because of the rapid social changes, topics that once did not interest young people until they reached their teens—suicide, gangs, homosexuality—are now subjects of books for even younger readers. The plethora of high-interest books reveals how desperately schools have failed to produce on-level readers and how the market has adapted to that need. However, these high-interest books are now readable for younger children whose reading levels are at or above normal. No matter how tastefully written, some contents are inappropriate for younger readers. The problem becomes not so much steering them toward books that they have the reading ability to handle but encouraging them toward books whose content is appropriate to their levels of cognitive and social development. A fifth-grader may be able to read V.C. Andrews' book *Flowers in the Attic* but not possess the social/moral development to handle the deviant behavior of the characters.

Skill 10.3   Analyze how writers from diverse cultural backgrounds and various historical periods have commented on major historical events.

Local Color is defined as the presenting of the peculiarities of a particular locality and its inhabitants. This genre began to be seen primarily after the Civil War although there were certainly precursors such as Washington Irving and his depiction of life in the Catskill Mountains of New York. However, the local colorist movement is generally considered to have begun in 1865, when humor began to permeate the writing of those who were focusing on a particular region of the country. Samuel L. Clemens (Mark Twain) is best-known for his humorous works about the southwest such as *The Notorious Jumping Frog of Calaveras County*. The country had just emerged from its "long night of the soul," a time when death, despair, and disaster had preoccupied the nation for almost five years. It's no wonder that the artists sought to relieve the grief and pain and lift spirits nor is it surprising that their efforts brought such a strong response. Mark Twain is generally considered to be not only one of America's funniest writers but one who also wrote great and enduring fiction.

Other examples of local colorists who used many of the same devices are Harriet Beecher Stowe, Bret Harte, George Washington Cable, Joel Chandler Harris, and Sarah Orne Jewett.

Slavery

The best-known of the early writers who used fiction as a political statement about slavery is Harriet Beecher Stowe, author of *Uncle Tom's Cabin*. This was her first novel, and it was published first as a serial in 1851 then as a book in 1852. This antislavery book infuriated Southerners. However, Stowe, herself, had been angered by the 1850 Fugitive Slave Law that made it legal to indict those who assisted runaway slaves. It also took away rights not only of the runaways but also of the free slaves. She intended to generate a protest of the law and slavery. It was the first effort to present the lives of slaves from their standpoint.

The novel is about three slaves, Tom, Eliza, and George who are together in Kentucky. Eliza and George are married to each other but have different masters. They successfully escape with their little boy, but Tom does not. Although he has a wife and children, he is sold, ending up finally with the monstrous Simon Legree, where he dies at last. Stowe cleverly uses depictions of motherhood and Christianity to stir her readers. When President Lincoln finally met her, he told her it was her book that started the war.

Many writers used the printed word to protest slavery. Some of them:
Frederick Douglas
William Lloyd Garrison
Benjamin Lay, a Quaker
Connecticut theologian Jonathan Edward
Susan B. Anthony

Civil Rights

Many of the abolitionists were also early crusaders for civil rights. However, the 1960s movement focused attention on the plight of the people who had been "freed" by the Civil War in ways that brought about long overdue changes in the opportunities and rights of African Americans. David Halberstam, who had been a reporter in Nashville at the time of the sit-ins by eight young black college students that initiated the revolution, wrote *The Children*, published in 1998 by Random House, for the purpose of reminding Americans of their courage, suffering, and achievements. Congressman John Lewis, Fifth District, Georgia, was one of those eight young men who has gone on to a life of public service. Halberstam records that when older black ministers tried to persuade these young people not to pursue their protest, John Lewis responded: "If not us, then who? If not now, then when?"

Some examples of protest literature:
James Baldwin, *Blues for Mister Charlie*
Martin Luther King, *Where Do We Go from Here?*
Langston Hughes, *Fight for Freedom: The Story of the NAACP*
Eldridge Cleaver, *Soul on Ice*
Malcolm X, *The Autobiography of Malcolm X*
Stokely Carmichael and Charles V. Hamilton, *Black Power*
Leroi Jones, *Home*

Vietnam:

An America that was already divided over the civil-rights movement faced even greater divisions over the war in Vietnam. Those who were in favor of the war and who opposed withdrawal saw it as the major front in the war against communism. Those who opposed the war and who favored withdrawal of the troops believed that it would not serve to defeat communism and was a quagmire.

Catch-22 by Joseph Heller was a popular antiwar novel that became a successful movie of the time. *Authors Take Sides on Vietnam*, edited by Cecil Woolf and John Bagguley is a collection of essays by 168 well-known authors throughout the world. *Where is Vietnam?* edited by Walter Lowenfels consists of 92 poems about the war.

Many writers were publishing works for and against the war, but the genre that had the most impact was rock music. Bob Dylan was an example of the musicians of the time. His music represented the hippie aesthetic using brilliant, swirling colors and hallucinogenic imagery, creating a style that came to be called psychedelic. Some other bands that originated during this time and became well-known for their psychedelic music, primarily about the Vietnam War in the early years, are the Grateful Dead, Jefferson Airplane, Big Brother, and Sly and the Family Stone. In England, the movement attracted the Beatles and the Rolling Stones.

Immigration

This has been a popular topic for literature from the time of the Louisiana Purchase in 1804. The recent *Undaunted Courage* by Stephen E. Ambrose is ostensibly the autobiography of Meriwether Lewis but is actually a recounting of the Lewis and Clark expedition. Presented as a scientific expedition by President Jefferson, the expedition was actually intended to provide maps and information for the opening up of the west. A well-known novel of the settling of the west by immigrants from other countries is *Giants in the Earth* by Ole Edvart Rolvaag, himself a descendant of immigrants.

John Steinbeck's *Cannery Row* and *Tortilla Flats* glorifies the lives of Mexican migrants in California. Amy Tan's *The Joy Luck Club* deals with the problems faced by Chinese immigrants.

Leon Uris' *Exodus* deals with the social history that led to the founding of the modern state of Israel. It was published in 1958, only a short time after the Holocaust. It also deals with attempts of concentration camp survivors to get to the land that has become the new Israel. In many ways, it is the quintessential work on immigration—causes and effects.

Skill 10.4 Analyze how writers from diverse cultural backgrounds and various historical periods have influenced public opinion about and understanding of social and cultural issues through their literary works.

Literature is powerful in influencing the thinking of individual readers and all of society. Waves of philosophical ideas have swept over the reading world almost from the time of the invention of the printing press. It's possible to trace the emergence of a particular set of values over centuries. Feminism is a case in point. While the matter of women's rights didn't reach a boiling point until the 1960s, it can be traced through history for many years.

For example, Empress Theodora of Byzantium was a proponent of legislation that would afford greater protections and freedoms to her female subjects; and Christine de Pizan, the first professional female writer, advanced many feminist ideas as early as the 1300s in the face of attempts to restrict female inheritance and guild membership. In 1869, John Stuart Mill published *The Subjection of Women* to demonstrate that "the legal subordination of one sex to the other is wrong…and…one of the chief hindrances to human improvement." Norwegian playwright Henrik Ibsen wrote the highly controversial play, *A Doll's House*, in 1879, a scathing criticism of the traditional roles of men and women in Victorian marriages. These and many other works with feminist themes led to changes in the way society viewed women throughout the civilized world. The impact of the literature and the changes in thinking on this issue led to many countries' granting of the vote to women in the late 1800s and the early years of the 20th century.

The feminist movement has virtually been fueled by literature going back several hundred years. Although the organized movement began with the first women's rights convention at Seneca Falls, New York, in 1948, in 1869, John Stuart Mill had already published *The Subjection of Women* to demonstrate that the legal subordination of one sex to the other is wrong. Virginia Woolf's essay, *A Room of One's Own*, first published in 1929, had a strong influence on how women were beginning to see their roles.

However, in the crusade that was ignited by the civil-rights movement of the 1960s, Betty Friedan's book, *The Feminine Mystique*, published in 1963, was very popular and influenced many women to become involved, both in changes in their own outlooks and behaviors, but also in the movement at large as activists. Feminism has been so much a part of thinking throughout the world that it should always be included in the potential themes one looks for when writing a critique of a literary work.

Regional literature has played an important role in the themes of popular literature, particularly in America. The best-known of the regional American writers is Samuel Langhorne Clemens, better known as Mark Twain with his stories about the Mississippi River and the state of Missouri. Although his home state was a slave state and considered by many to be part of the South, it declined to join the Confederacy and remained loyal to the union. He wrote sympathetic slave characters in many of his stories.

Some regional American writers:
Harriet Beecher Stowe
Sarah Orne Jewett
George Washington Cable
Joel Chandler Harris
Edward Eggleston
James Whitcomb Riley
Bret Harte

Ethnic themes are also very popular in American literature. Toni Morrison, who writes African-American stories, is considered to be the most important American writer of the last 25 years and won the Nobel Prize for Literature in 1993 for her collected works. Saul Bellow wrote of his own Jewish backgrounds and also won the Nobel Prize in 1976.

James Michener wrote history as fiction in his many novels: *Tales of the South Pacific* (for which he won the Pulitzer Prize for Fiction in 1948), *Hawaii*, *The Drifters*, *Centennial*, *The Source*, *The Fires of Spring*, *Chesapeake*, *Caribbean*, *Caravans*, *Alaska*, *Texas*, and *Poland*.

Literature about a particular period has also been very popular with American writers. The Civil War era has been a very successful subject for novelists, most notable of which is *Gone with the Wind* by Margaret Mitchell.

Some novels about the American Civil War:
- *The Red Badge of Courage* by Stephen Crane
- *Cold Mountain* by Charles Frazier
- *Love and War* by John Jakes
- *Gods and Generals*; *The Last Full Measure* by Jeffrey Shaara
- *By Valour and Arms* by James Street
- *Fort Pillow* by Harry Turtledove
- *Lincoln* by Gore Vidal

Skill 10.4   Analyze the expression of specific cultural values, ideas, and attitudes in literary works.

World folk-epics are poems (or prose sometimes) that are an integral part of the world view of a people. In many cases, they were original oral texts that were eventually written by a single author or several.

Some examples of world folk-epics:

Soundiata, an African epic
Tunkashila, an American Indian epic
Epic of Gilgamesh, the oldest epic from Mesopotamia and the Mediterranean world
Aeneid, a Roman epic
Moby Dick is considered by some to be an American folk epic.

A **national myth** is an inspiring narrative or anecdote about a nation's past. These often over-dramatize true events, omit important historical details, or add details for which there is no evidence. It can be a fictional story that no one takes to be true, such as *Paul Bunyan,* which was created by French Canadians during the Papineau Rebellion of 1837, when they revolted against the young English Queen. In older nations, national myths may be spiritual and refer to the nation's founding by God or gods or other supernatural beings.

Some national myths:
The legend of King Arthur in Great Britain
Sir Francis Drake in England
The Pilgrims and the Mayflower in the United States
Pocahontas, who is said to have saved the life of John Smith from her savage father, Powhatan
The legendary ride of Paul Revere
The last words of Nathan Hale

The person of George Washington and apocryphal tales about him such as his cutting down a cherry tree with a hatchet and then facing up to the truth: "I cannot tell a lie."

COMPETENCY 11 THE SHAPING OF THE ENGLISH LANGUAGE BY HISTORICAL, SOCIAL, CULTURAL, AND TECHNOLOGICAL INFLUENCES

Skill 11.1   Recognize the significance of historical events that have influenced the development of the English language.

English is an Indo-European language that evolved through several periods. The origin of English dates to the settlement of the British Isles in the fifth and sixth centuries by Germanic tribes called the Angles, Saxons, and Jutes. The original Britons spoke a Celtic tongue while the Angles spoke a Germanic dialect.

Modern English derives from the speech of the Anglo-Saxons who imposed not only their language but also their social customs and laws on their new land. From the fifth to the

> Learn more about the
> **History of the English Language**
> http://ebbs.english.vt.edu/hel/hel.html

tenth century, Britain's language was the tongue we now refer to as Old English. ⟵ 5 – 10th cent During the next four centuries, the many French attempts at English conquest introduced many French words to English. However, the grammar and syntax of the language remained Germanic.

Middle English, most evident in the writings of Geoffrey Chaucer, dates loosely from 1066 to 1509. William Caxton brought the printing press to England in 1474 and increased literacy. Old English words required numerous inflections to indicate noun cases and plurals as well as verb conjugations. Middle English continued the use of many inflections and pronunciations that treated these inflections as separately pronounced syllables. English in 1300 would have been written "Olde Anglishe" with the e's at the ends of the words pronounced as our short a vowel. Even adjectives had plural inflections: "long dai" became "longe daies" pronounced "long-a day-as." Spelling was phonetic; thus every vowel had multiple pronunciations, a fact that continues to affect the language.

Modern English dates from the introduction of The Great Vowels Shift because it created guidelines for spelling and pronunciation. Before the printing press, books were copied laboriously by hand; the language was subject to the individual interpretation of the scribes. Printers and subsequently lexicographers like Samuel Johnson and America's Noah Webster influenced the guidelines. As reading matter was mass produced, the reading public was forced to adopt the speech and writing habits developed by those who wrote and printed books.

Despite many students' insistence to the contrary, Shakespeare's writings are in Modern English. Teachers should stress to students that language, like customs, morals, and other social factors, is constantly subject to change. Immigration, inventions, and cataclysmic events change language as much as any other facet of life is affected by these changes.

The domination of one race or nation over another can change a language significantly. Beginning with the colonization of the New World by England and Spain, English and Spanish became dominant languages in the Western hemisphere.

American English today is somewhat different in pronunciation and sometimes vocabulary from British English. The British call a truck a "lorry," baby carriages a "pram" (short for "perambulator"), and an elevator a "lift." The two languages have very few syntactical differences, and even the tonal qualities that were once so clearly different are converging.

Though Modern English is less complex than Middle English, having lost many unnecessary inflections, it is still considered difficult to learn because of its many exceptions to the rules. It has, however, become the world's dominant language by reason of the great political, military, and social power of England from the fifteenth to the nineteenth century and of America in the twentieth century.

Modern inventions—the telephone, phonograph, radio, television, and motion pictures—have especially affected English pronunciation. Regional dialects, once a hindrance to clear understanding, have fewer distinct characteristics. The speakers from different parts of the United States of America can be identified by their accents, but more and more as educators and media personalities stress uniform pronunciations and proper grammar, the differences are diminishing.

The English language has a more extensive vocabulary than any other language. Ours is a language of synonyms, words borrowed from other languages, and coined words—many of them introduced by the rapid expansion of technology.

Students should understand that language is in constant flux. They can demonstrate this when they use language for specific purposes and audiences. Negative criticism of a student's errors in word choice or sentence structures will inhibit creativity. Positive criticism that suggests ways to enhance communication skills will encourage exploration.

Language changes in all its manifestations: At the phonetic level, the sounds of a language will change as will its orthography (spelling). The vocabulary level will probably manifest the greatest changes. Changes in syntax are slower and less likely to occur. For example, English has changed in response to the influences of many other languages and cultures as well as internal cultural changes such as the development of the railroad and the computer; however, its syntax still relies on word order—it has not shifted to an inflected system even though many of the cultures that have impacted it do, in fact, have an inflected language, such as Spanish.

The most significance influence on a language is the blending of cultures. The Norman Conquest (1066 AD) that brought the English speakers in the British Isles under the rule of French speakers changed the language, but the fact that English speakers did not adopt the language of the ruling class is significant— they did not become speakers of French. Even so, many vocabulary items entered the language during that period. The Great Vowel Shift that occurred between the 14th and 16th centuries is somewhat of a mystery although it's generally attributed to the migration to Southeast England following the plague of the Black Death. The Great Vowel Shift largely accounts for the discrepancy between orthography and speech—the difficult spelling system in modern English.

Colonization of other countries has also brought new vocabulary items into the language. Indian English has its own easily recognizable attributes as does Australian and North American English, and these cultural interactions have added to items in the usages of each other and in the language at large. The fact that English is the most widely spoken and understood language all over the world in the 21st century implies that it is constantly being changed by the globalized world.

Other influences, of course, impact language. The introduction of television and its domination by the United States has had great influence on the English that is spoken and understood all over the world. The same is true of the computerizing of the world (Tom Friedman called it "flattening" in his *The World is Flat: A Brief History of the Twenty-first Century*). New terms have been added ("blog"), old terms have changed meaning ("mouse"), and nouns have been verbalized ("prioritize").

Skill 11.2   Recognize the effects of technological innovations on the English language.

Just as countries and families have histories, so do words. Knowing and understanding the origin of a word, where and how it has been used through the years, and the history of its meaning as it has changed are important components of the writing and language teacher's tool kit.

Never in the history of the English language, or any other language for that matter, have the forms and meanings of words changed so rapidly. When America was settled originally, immigration from many countries made it a "melting pot." Immigration accelerated rapidly within the first hundred years, resulting in pockets of language throughout the country.

When trains began to make transportation available and affordable, individuals from those various pockets came in contact with each other, shared vocabularies, and attempted to converse. From that time forward, every generation brought the introduction of a technology that made language interchange not only more possible but more important.

Radio began the trend to standardize dialects. A Bostonian might not be understood by a Houstonian, who might not be interested in turning the dial to hear the news or a drama or the advertisements of the vendors that had a vested interest in being heard and understood. Soap and soup producers knew a goldmine when they saw it and created a market for radio announcers and actors who spoke without a pronounced dialect. In return, listeners began to hear the English language in a dialect very different from the one they spoke, and as it settled into their thinking processes, it eventually made its way to their tongues; consequently, spoken English began to lose some of its local peculiarities.

This change has been a slow process, but most Americans can easily understand other Americans, no matter where they come from. They can even converse with a native of Great Britain with little difficulty. The introduction of television carried the evolution further as did the explosion of electronic communicating devices over the past fifty years.

An excellent example of the changes that have occurred in English is a comparison of Shakespeare's original works with modern translations. Without help, twenty-first-century Americans are unable to read the *Folio*.

On the other hand, teachers must constantly be mindful of the vocabularies and etymologies of their students, who are on the receiving end of the escalation brought about by technology and increased global influence and contact.

> Check out the
> **Learning Resources of the OED**
> http://www.oed.com/learning/

In the past, the Oxford English Dictionary has been the most reliable source for etymologies. Some of the collegiate dictionaries are also useful. *Merriam-Webster's 3rd Unabridged Dictionary* is useful in tracing the sources of words in American English. *Merriam-Webster's Unabridged Dictionary* may be out of date, so a teacher should also have a *Merriam-Webster's Collegiate Dictionary*, which is updated regularly.

In addition to etymologies, knowing how and when to label a usage "jargon" or "colloquial" is important. The teacher must be aware of the possibility that it's a word that is now accepted as standard. To be on top of this, the teacher must continually keep up with the etymological aids that are available, particularly online.

If you google "etymology," for instance, or even the word you're unsure of, you can find a multitude of sources. Don't trust a single one. The information should be validated by at least three sources. Wikipedia is very useful, but it can be changed by anyone who chooses, so any information on it should be backed up by other sources. If you go to http://www.etymonline.com/sources.php, you will find a long list of resources on etymology.

Skill 11.3   Relate English derivatives and borrowings, including slang terms, to their origins in other languages.

Words come into the language from many sources. Following are the most common:
1. Created from scratch. Examples: Kodak, Kleenex
2. Coinage. Often roots from existing words are used in coinage. For example: political, apolitical; Gnostic, agnostic
3. Borrowing. This is the largest one. Some say 80% are from this source. Some examples: bouquet from the French; sputnik from the Russian; veranda from the Hindi; porch from Old English, from the Latin.
4. Compounding: black + bird became blackbird, a particular species; wall + paper became wallpaper; black + board became blackboard; under + world became underworld; brow + beat became browbeat.
5. Acronyms: CARE; UNICEF; RADAR; SCUBA; ROTC.
6. Onomatopoeia: hiss, fizz, meow, bow-wow, baa, moo.
7. Portmanteau, blend words: chuckle + snort = chortle; breakfast + lunch = brunch; electric + execute = electrocute; smoke + fog = smog.
8. Shortening: gasoline becomes gas; pianoforte becomes piano; fanatic becomes fan.
9. Change in meaning, often resulting in slang: Gay once meant happy; it has virtually been taken over to mean homosexual. Spam, which was a brand of canned meat, is now used to mean unwanted internet messages. *Cold one* has come to mean a glass or can of beer. To drink has come to mean alcohol, not water. Moonshine means illegally-made hard liquor.

Skill 11.4   Recognize regional and social variations in language in the United States.

Geographical Influences

Dialect differences are basically in pronunciation. Bostoners say "pahty" for "party" and Southerners blend words like "you all" into "y'all." Besides the dialect differences already mentioned, the biggest geographical factors in American English stem from minor word choice variances. Depending on the region where you live, when you order a carbonated, syrupy beverage most generically called a soft drink, you might ask for a "soda" in the South, or a "pop" in the Midwest. If you order a soda in New York, then you will get a scoop of ice cream in your soft drink, while in other areas you would have to ask for a "float."

Social Influences

Social influences are mostly those imposed by family, peer groups, and mass media. The economic and educational levels of families determine language use. Exposure to adults who encourage and assist children to speak well enhances readiness for other areas of learning and contributes to their ability to communicate their needs. Historically, children learned language, speech patterns, and grammar from members of the extended family just as they learned the rules of conduct within their family unit and community. In modern times, the mother in a nuclear family became the dominant force in influencing children's development. With increasing social changes, many children are not receiving the proper guidance in all areas of development, especially language.

Those who are fortunate to be in educational day-care programs like Head Start or in certified preschools develop better language skills than those whose care is entrusted to untrained care providers. Once children enter elementary school, they are also greatly influenced by peer language. This peer influence becomes significant in adolescence as the use of teen jargon gives teenagers a sense of identity within their chosen group(s) and independence from the influence of adults. In some lower socio-economic groups, children use Standard English in school and street language outside the school. Some children of immigrant families become bilingual by necessity if no English is spoken in the home.

Research has shown a strong correlation between socio-economic characteristics and all areas of intellectual development. Traditional measurement instruments rely on verbal ability to establish intelligence. Research findings and test scores reflect that children reared in nuclear families providing cultural experiences and individual attention become more language proficient than those who are denied that security and stimulation.

Personal Influences

In adolescence, children's choice of role models and decisions about their future determine the growth of identity. Rapid physical and emotional changes and the stress of coping with the pressure of sexual awareness make concentration on any educational pursuits difficult. The easier the transition from childhood to adulthood, the better the competence will be in all learning areas.

Middle school and junior high school teachers are confronted by a student body ranging from fifth graders who are still childish to eighth or ninth graders who, if not in fact, at least in their minds, are young adults. Teachers must approach language instruction as a social development tool with more emphasis on vocabulary acquisition, reading improvement, and speaking/writing skills. High school teachers can deal with the more formalized instruction of grammar, usage, and literature meant for older adolescents whose social development allows them to pay more attention to studies that will improve their chances for a better adult life.

As a tool, language must have relevance to students' real environment. Many high schools have developed practical English classes for business/ vocational students whose specific needs are determined by their desire to enter the workforce upon graduation. More emphasis is placed upon accuracy of mechanics and understanding verbal and written directions because these are skills desired by employers. Writing résumés, completing forms, reading policy and operations manuals, and generating reports are some of the desired skills. Emphasis is placed on higher-level thinking skills, including inferential thinking and literary interpretation, in literature classes for college-bound students.

The explosion of hand-held communication devices and their long-term effect on language development and vocabulary in children, especially teenagers, is unknown at this time. However, any teacher of these young people is very well aware that they have developed and are developing a vocabulary and a short-hand that has an impact language development.

COMPETENCY 12 THE WRITING PROCESS.

Skill 12.1   Demonstrate knowledge of ways to generate content for writing.

Prewriting Strategies

Students gather ideas before writing. Prewriting may include clustering, listing, brainstorming, mapping, free writing, and charting. If you provide many ways for students to develop ideas on a topic, you will increase their chances for success.

Listed below are the most common prewriting strategies students can use to explore, plan, and write on a topic. When teaching these strategies, remember that not all prewriting must eventually produce a finished piece of writing. In fact, in the initial lesson of teaching prewriting strategies, you might have students practice prewriting strategies without the pressure of having to write a finished product.

- Keep an idea book so that they can jot down ideas that come to mind.
- Write in a daily journal.

- Write down whatever comes to mind; this is called **free writing**. Students do not stop to make corrections or interrupt the flow of ideas. A variation of this technique is focused free writing—writing on a specific topic—to prepare for an essay.
- Make a list of all ideas connected with their topic; this is called **brainstorming**. Make sure students know that this technique works best when they let their mind work freely. After completing the list, students should analyze the list to see if a pattern or way to group the ideas can be seen.
- Ask the questions who, what, when, where, why, and how. Help the writer approach a topic from several perspectives.
- Create a visual map on paper to gather ideas. Cluster circles and lines to show connections between ideas. Students should try to identify the relationship that exists between their ideas. If they cannot see the relationships, have them pair up, exchange papers and have their partners look for some related ideas.
- Observe details of sight, hearing, taste, touch, and taste.
- Visualize by making mental images of something and write down the details in a list.

Skill 12.2   Demonstrate knowledge of ways to organize ideas before writing.

Once prewriting is complete, several decisions need to be made. The first is what the *purpose* of the speech is. Does the speaker want to persuade the audience to believe something or to act on something, or does the speaker simply want to present information that the audience might not have? Once that decision is made, a thesis should be developed. What point does the speaker want to make? And what are the points that will support that point? And in what order will those points be arranged? Introductions and conclusions should be written last. The purpose of the introduction is to draw the audience into the topic. The purpose of the conclusion is to polish off the speech, making sure the thesis is clear, reinforcing the thesis, or summarizing the points that have been made.

Visual organizers are often used by writers and writing teachers.

Visual Organizer 1.

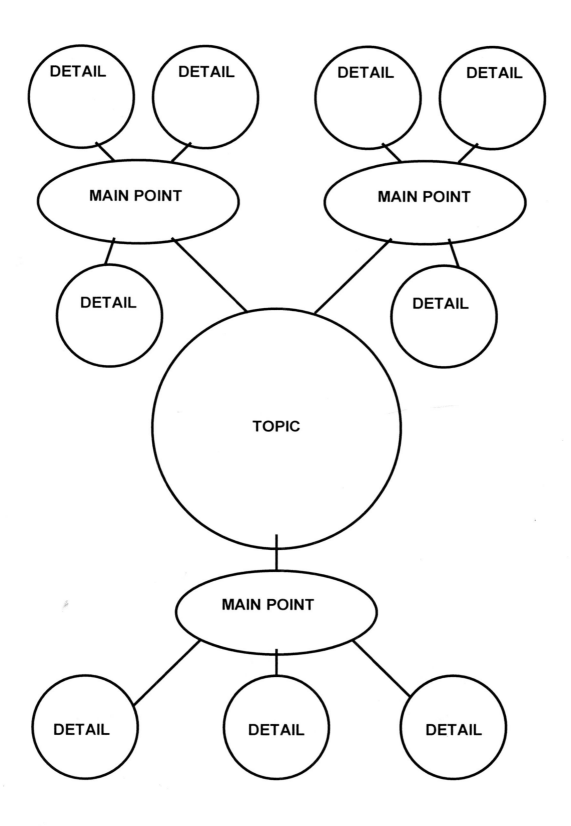

Visual Organizer 2.

The Venn diagram, invented around 1880 by John Venn and used in several fields to show logical relationships between groups of things, is often used by teachers of writing to help students grasp the organization of concepts. Venn diagrams are overlapping circles. Because one challenge to organizing ideas is that concepts overlap, this provides a visual way to see where the overlapping occurs.

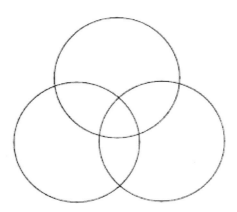

Skill 12.3 Determine the audience and purpose of writing.

In determining the purpose for a piece of writing or a speech, the author will need to decide what he wants to accomplish. Does he want to persuade his readers/listeners to a particular point of view? Does he want to persuade them to take some action? Does he simply want to convey certain information or is his purpose to entertain them? This is a decision that should be made early in the planning for a speech or a written piece. Once that decision is made, everything flows from it.

The more information a writer or speaker has about an audience, the more likely he/she is to communicate effectively with them. Several factors figure into the speaker/audience equation: age, ethnic background, educational level, knowledge of the subject, and interest in the subject.

Speaking about computers to senior citizens who have, at best, rudimentary knowledge about the way computers work must take that into account. Perhaps handing out a glossary would be useful for this audience. Speaking to first-graders about computers presents its own challenges. On the other hand, the average high-school student has more experience with computers than most adults and that should be taken into account. Speaking to a room full of computer systems engineers requires a rather thorough understanding of the jargon related to the field.

In considering the age of the audience, it's best not to make assumptions. The gathering of senior citizens might include retired systems engineers or people who have made their livings using computers, so research about the audience is important. It might not be wise to assume that high-school students have a certain level of understanding, either.

With an audience that is primarily Hispanic with varying levels of competence in English, the speaker is obligated to adjust the presentation to fit that audience. The same would be true when the audience is composed of people who may have been in the country for a long time but whose families speak their first language at home. Black English presents its own peculiarities, and if the audience is composed primarily of African-Americans whose contacts in the larger community are not great, some efforts need to be made to acquaint oneself with the specific peculiarities of the community those listeners come from.

It's unwise to "speak down" to an audience; they will almost certainly be insulted. On the other hand, speaking to an audience of college graduates will require different skills than speaking to an audience of people who have never attended college.

Finally, has the audience come because of an interest in the topic or because they have been influenced or forced to come to the presentation? If the audience comes with an interest in the subject already, efforts to motivate or draw them into the discussion might not be needed. On the other hand, if the speaker knows the audience does not have a high level of interest in the topic, it would be wise to use devices to draw them into it, to motivate them to listen.

Skill 12.4   Recognize methods of drafting text so that it shows consistent development of a central idea.

Once pencil is put to paper or hands are put to computer keys, decisions must be made about how to proceed to accomplish the purpose. The first step is to draft a thesis statement—the *point* of the discourse. If the purpose is to persuade, then the thesis will be a statement of the author's position on a topic, either pro or con. If the purpose is merely to present information, then the thesis statement will be the organizing device that will lead readers/audience to an understanding of that information.

The next decisions will have to do with the points that will support that thesis statement. They should provide strong supporting details and organizing key points. In a persuasive discourse, three points are usually sufficient although there is no hard and fast rule. The organization of supporting information in an exposition will vary according to the information being conveyed. For example, if the purpose is to tell how to put together a cabinet, then the supporting paragraphs will be the steps in the process. On the other hand, if it's to explain the melt-down on Wall Street of 2008, the paragraphs will probably reflect the history of the failures that led to it. An effective writer or speaker reasons in a straight line and does not veer away into irrelevancies. It's always a good idea to keep going back to the thesis in developing an idea to make certain you're staying on track.

Skill 12.5   Recognize methods of revising text to eliminate wordiness, ambiguity, redundancy, and clichés

and

Skill 12.6   Recognize methods of revising text to clarify meaning.

- Ask students to read their writing and check for specific errors such as using a subordinate clause as a sentence.
- Provide students with a proofreading checklist to guide them as they edit their work.

You may think this exercise is simply catching errors in spelling or word use, but you should reframe your thinking about revising and editing. This is an extremely important step that often is ignored. Here are some questions you could ask:

Is the reasoning coherent?
Is the point established?
Does the introduction make the reader want to read this discourse?
What is the thesis? Is it proven?
What is the purpose? Is it clear? Is it useful, valuable, and interesting?
Is the style of writing so wordy that it exhausts the reader and interferes with engagement?
Is the writing so spare that it is boring?
Is the language appropriate? Is it too formal? Too informal? If jargon is used, is it appropriate?
Are the sentences too uniform in structure?
Are there too many simple sentences?
Are too many of the complex sentences the same structure?
Are the compounds truly compounds, or are they unbalanced?
Are parallel structures truly parallel?
If there are characters, are they believable?
If there is dialogue, is it natural or stilted?
Is the title appropriate?
Does the writing show creativity, or is it boring?

 Studies have clearly demonstrated that the most fertile area in teaching writing is this one. If students can learn to revise their own work effectively, they are well on their way to becoming effective, mature writers.

Word processing is an important tool for teaching this stage in the writing process. Requiring extensive revision in writing classrooms nowadays is not unreasonable and can be an important stage in the production of papers.

Microsoft Word has had a "tracking" capability in its last several upgrades, which carries revision a step further. Now the teacher and student can carry on a dialogue on the paper itself. The teacher's deletions and additions can be tracked, the student can respond, and the tracking will be facilitated by automatically putting the changes in a different color. The "comment" function makes it possible for both teacher and student to write notes at the exactly relevant point in the manuscript.

While a spelling checker is an appropriate first step, students should be reminded that they should not rely solely on spell checkers for proofreading. Noted for their failure to understand context, spell checkers will not help with incorrect homonyms or typos.

Skill 12.7   Recognize methods of editing text so that it conforms to the conventions of Standard American English.

Sentence completeness

Avoid fragments and run-on sentences. Recognition of sentence elements necessary to make a complete thought, proper use of independent and dependent clauses (see *Use correct coordination and subordination*), and proper punctuation will correct such errors.

Sentence structure

Recognize simple, compound, complex, and compound-complex sentences. Use dependent (subordinate) and independent clauses correctly to create these sentence structures.

Simple	Joyce wrote a letter.
Compound	Joyce wrote a letter, and Dot drew a picture.
Complex	While Joyce wrote a letter, Dot drew a picture.
Compound/Complex	When Mother asked the girls to demonstrate their new-found skills, Joyce wrote a letter, and Dot drew a picture.

Note: Do **not** confuse compound sentence elements with compound sentences.

   Simple sentence with compound subject
      Joyce and Dot wrote letters.

The <u>girl</u> in row three and the <u>boy</u> next to her were passing notes across the aisle.

Simple sentence with compound predicate
Joyce <u>wrote letters</u> and <u>drew pictures</u>.
The captain of the high school debate team <u>graduated with honors</u> and <u>studied broadcast journalism in college</u>.

Simple sentence with compound object of preposition
Coleen graded the students' essays for <u>style</u> and <u>mechanical accuracy</u>.

Parallelism

Recognize parallel structures using phrases (prepositional, gerund, participial, and infinitive) and omissions from sentences that create the lack of parallelism.

Prepositional phrase/single modifier

Incorrect: Coleen ate the ice cream with enthusiasm and hurriedly.
Correct: Coleen ate the ice cream with enthusiasm and in a hurry.
Correct: Coleen ate the ice cream enthusiastically and hurriedly.

Participial phrase/infinitive phrase

Incorrect: After hiking for hours and to sweat profusely, Joe sat down to rest and drinking water.
Correct: After hiking for hours and sweating profusely, Joe sat down to rest and drink water.

Recognition of dangling modifiers

Dangling phrases are attached to sentence parts in such a way that they create ambiguity and incorrectness of meaning.

Participial phrase

Incorrect: Hanging from her skirt, Dot tugged at a loose thread.
Correct: Dot tugged at a loose thread hanging from her skirt.

Incorrect: Relaxing in the bathtub, the telephone rang.
Correct: While I was relaxing in the bathtub, the telephone rang.

Infinitive phrase

Incorrect: To improve his behavior, the dean warned Fred.

Correct: The dean warned Fred to improve his behavior.

Prepositional phrase

Incorrect: On the floor, Father saw the dog eating table scraps.
Correct: Father saw the dog eating table scraps on the floor.

Recognition of syntactical redundancy or omission

These errors occur when superfluous words have been added to a sentence or key words have been omitted from a sentence.

Redundancy

Incorrect: Joyce made sure that when her plane arrived that she retrieved all of her luggage.
Correct: Joyce made sure that when her plane arrived she retrieved all of her luggage.

Incorrect: He was a mere skeleton of his former self.
Correct: He was a skeleton of his former self.

Omission

Incorrect: Dot opened her book, recited her textbook, and answered the teacher's subsequent question.
Correct: Dot opened her book, recited from the textbook, and answered the teacher's subsequent question.

Avoidance of double negatives

This error occurs from positioning two negatives that, in fact, cancel each other in meaning.

Incorrect: Harold couldn't care less whether he passes this class.
Correct: Harold could care less whether he passes this class.

Incorrect: Dot didn't have no double negatives in her paper.
Correct: Dot didn't have any double negatives in her paper.

In learning to write and in improving one's writing, the most useful exercise is editing/revising. Extensive revision is the hallmark of most successful writers. In the past, writers, student writers in particular, have been reluctant to revise because it meant beginning over to prepare the document for final presentation. However, that time is long gone. The writing of graduate dissertations took on a whole new dimension after the creation of the word processor and before long, classroom writing teachers were able to use this function to help students improve their writing.

Skill 12.8 Demonstrate familiarity with proofreading techniques and other tools used to finalize a text for publishing.

Things to look for in proofreading and getting a text ready for the publisher:
1. Only one space following a sentence, not two.
2. Repeated words or parts of words.
3. Substitutions and omissions, especially those that change meaning.
4. Errors in copying data.
5. Transposition of letters.
6. Spelling.
7. Incomplete sentences.
8. Punctuation.
9. Paragraphing.
10. Style—for example, spacing.
11. Follow up on alerts of word-processor.

COMPETENCY 13 ELEMENTS OF EFFECTIVE COMPOSITION

Skill 13.1 Recognize effective ways to present original ideas or perspectives in a text clearly, concisely, and coherently.

In studies of professional writers and how they produce their successful works, it has been revealed that writing is a process that can be clearly defined although in practice it must have enough flexibility to allow for creativity. The teacher must be able to define the various stages that successful writers go through in order to make a statement that has value. There must be a discovery stage when ideas, materials, supporting details, etc., are deliberately collected. These may come from many possible sources: the writer's own experience and observations, deliberate research of written sources, interviews of live persons, television presentations, or the internet.

The next stage is organization where the purpose, thesis, and supporting points are determined. Most writers will put forth more than one possible thesis and in the next stage, the writing of the paper, settle on one as the result of trial and error. Once the paper is written, the editing stage is necessary and is probably the most important stage. This is not just the polishing stage. At this point, decisions must be made regarding whether the reasoning is cohesive—does it hold together? Is the arrangement the best possible one or should the points be rearranged? Are there holes that need to be filled? What form will the introduction take? Does the conclusion lead the reader out of the discourse or is it inadequate or too abrupt, etc.

It's important to remember that the best writers engage in all of these stages recursively. They may go back to discovery at any point in the process. They may go back and rethink the organization, etc. To help students become effective writers, the teacher needs to give them adequate practice in the various stages and encourage them to engage deliberately in the creative thinking that makes writers successful.

Skill 13.2   Recognize the appropriate organizational structure/format, tone/voice, and word choice for various writing purposes and audiences.

The Internet has transformed all kinds of communications all over the world. Very few people write letters in the 21st century that will be delivered physically to an individual's mailbox. However, there are still important reasons for writing letters. For one thing, they are more personal and convey a quite different message from an e-mail, especially if they are handwritten. For another, not everybody has and uses e-mail regularly.

An electronic mailbox will retain what has been sent and received, sometimes to the writer's regret; even so, those messages and exchanges will not endure in the way that paper letters sometimes do over long periods. A husband and wife who married in 1954 always corresponded with his parents by mail approximately once a week in the first thirty years of their marriage. The three children often included a note of their own. It was before the long-distance call became routine and affordable. After the grandmother and grandfather died, the family discovered that they had kept all of those letters. It's a priceless record of a period in the family's life. If that correspondence had occurred via e-mail, it would be lost to history.

Sometimes there's a business reason for a paper letter. It may contain a receipt or legal information that needs to be retained. For those people who do not yet have a computer or access to e-mail, paper letters are necessary. Sometimes a company or organization wishes to advertise a product or even issue invitations to an event when not all e-mail addresses are known. Mass-mailings can be sent quite easily to make sure that everyone on the list can be reached. Advertisers, of course, use mass-mail more than anyone else because they do not even need to know the addresses to get their literature into all the mailboxes in a zip code.

Sometimes courtesy requires a personally written letter either typed or handwritten. If a person in high office has taken the time to do something for an individual, certainly a handwritten letter of thanks would be in order. In the U.S., the form of the letter can be full block (all lines blocked at the left margin); modified block (all lines blocked at the left margin except the date and closing lines, which begin at the center point); and semi-block (same as modified block except that the first lines of paragraphs are indented by five points). Microsoft

Word's letter wizard will automatically format a business letter according to these three styles.

Social notes should be handwritten on note paper, which varies in size but is smaller than letter-sized paper. They should be courteous and brief and should be specific about what is intended. For example, if the note is to say thank you, then the gift or favor should be specifically acknowledged in the note. If the note is an invitation, the same rule applies: the language should be courteous, the place and time specified, and any useful information such as "casual dress" or parking recommendations should be included.

A high percentage of communications between individuals, groups, and businesses is conducted nowadays over the Internet. It has even replaced many telephone calls. Internet language should be courteous, free of words that might be offensive, and clear. In the early days of e-mail, a writer was censured for using bold or capital letters. That has relaxed somewhat. Nowadays, almost anything goes although it's generally accepted that restrained language is assumed for business people and personal communications. The blog, where a person has his/her own website and uses it to send messages, is a new wrinkle. Chat is available on most blogs as well as other Internet sites. The language and the messages tend to be unrestrained there.

Some people use the same styles for letters via e-mail that are recommended for paper letters; however, the formatting has tended to become less and less formal. It is not uncommon for thank-you letters and invitations to be sent via e-mail. One important feature of the Internet that makes it so valuable is that it reaches everywhere—to small communities, all the way across the country, and overseas. It's possible to dash off an e-mail note to a person or business or several persons or businesses in Europe as quickly as to a person in the next office, and it costs no extra money beyond the cost of equipment and Internet services.

The fax machine is yet another dimension of electronic communications. At first, it was used primarily by businesses, but it has become so affordable that many people have them in their homes. The fax makes possible an actual picture of a document. This may be preferable to retyping it or sending it by paper mail because it can go immediately. Sometimes people who are exchanging contracts will use the fax to cut down on the time it takes to get them signed and sent back and forth. The scanner will do the same thing but will produce a document that can be e-mailed.

Skill 13.3   Recognize methods of developing an introduction to a text that draws a reader's attention, specifies the topic or issue, or provides a thesis.

It's important to remember that in the writing process, the introduction should be written last. Until the body of the paper has been determined—thesis, development—it's difficult to make strategic decisions regarding the introduction. The Greek rhetoricians called this part of a discourse _exordium_, a "leading into." The basic purpose of the introduction, then, is to lead the audience into the discourse. It can let the reader know what the purpose of the discourse is and it can condition the audience to be receptive to what the writer wants to say. It can be very brief or it can take up a large percentage of the total word count. Aristotle said that the introduction could be compared to the flourishes that flute players make before their performance—an overture in which the musicians display what they can play best in order to gain the favor and attention of the audience for the main performance.

In order to do this, we must first of all know what we are going to say; who the readership is likely to be; what the social, political, economic, etc., climate is; what preconceived notions the audience is likely to have regarding the subject; and how long the discourse is going to be.

There are many ways to do this:
- Show that the subject is important.
- Show that although the points we are presenting may seem improbable, they are true.
- Show that the subject has been neglected, misunderstood, or misrepresented.
- Explain an unusual mode of development.
- Forestall any misconception of the purpose.
- Apologize for a deficiency.
- Arouse interest in the subject with an anecdotal lead-in.
- Ingratiate oneself with the readership.
- Establish one's own credibility.

The introduction often ends with the thesis, the point or purpose of the paper. However, this is not set in stone. The thesis may open the body of the discussion, or it may conclude the discourse. The most important thing to remember is that the purpose and structure of the introduction should be deliberate if it is to serve the purpose of "leading the reader into the discussion."

Skill 13.4   Recognize effective ways to organize ideas in a text.

Is it better to put your strongest supporting material first and arrange the rest in a declining order of strength or importance? Is it better to simply use chronology to arrange your supporting ideas? Is it better to generalize and then develop your supports starting with the most general and moving to the most specific?

Students often ask these questions of their writing teachers. The answer is "yes." However, the decision depends on the topic, the thesis, and the supporting ideas themselves. If the writer feels that the interest of the reader might be lost if not-very-interesting ideas come early in the speech or essay, then he will want to invert the order. If, on the other hand, the reader or listener might be difficult to persuade, it might be better to start with the least convincing support and move toward a climax of the strongest support.

If the reader needs to see the situation chronologically in order to understand, then that will determine the order of the development. Also, many theses are generalizations and the proof is in the specifics. In this case, probably least specific to most specific or weakest to strongest might work best.

Skill 13.5   Recognize effective ways to emphasize, link, and contrast important ideas in a text.

Repetition, if used judiciously, can be very effective in achieving emphasis. However, locating the most important ideas strategically is another way to achieve emphasis.

A mark of maturity in writing is the effective use of transitional devices at all levels. For example, a topic sentence can be used to establish continuity, especially if it is positioned at the beginning of a paragraph. The most common use would be to refer to what has preceded, repeat it, or summarize it and then go on to introduce a new topic. An essay by W. H. Hudson uses this device: "Although the potato was very much to me in those early years, it grew to be more when I heard its history." It summarizes what has preceded, makes a comment on the author's interest, and introduces a new topic: the history of the potato.

Another example of a transitional sentence could be, "Not all matters end so happily." This refers to the previous information and prepares for the next paragraph, which will be about matters that do not end happily. This transitional sentence is a little more forthright: "The increase in drug use in our community leads us to another general question."

Another fairly simple and straightforward transitional device is the use of numbers or their approximation: "First, I want to talk about the dangers of immigration; second, I will discuss the enormity of the problem; third, I will propose a reasonable solution."

An entire paragraph may be transitional in purpose and form. In "Darwiniana," Thomas Huxley used a transitional paragraph:

> So much, then, by way of proof that the method of establishing laws in science is exactly the same as that pursued in common life. Let us now turn to another matter (though really it is but another phase of the same question), and that is, the method by which, from the relations of certain phenomena, we prove that some stand in the position of causes toward the others.

The most common transitional device is a single word. Some examples: *and, furthermore, next, moreover, in addition, again, also, likewise, similarly, finally, second,* etc. There are many.

In marking student papers, a teacher can encourage a student to think in terms of moving coherently from one idea to the next by making transitions between the two. If the shift from one thought to another is too abrupt, the student can be asked to provide a transitional paragraph. Lists of possible transitions can be put on a handout and students can be encouraged to have the list at hand when they are composing essays. These are good tools for nudging students to more mature writing styles.

Skill 13.6   Recognize effective ways to incorporate graphic features in a text.

The old adage that a picture is worth a thousand words is never more evident than in the use of charts, graphs, and tables in expository writing. It's one thing to say that the GDP of the United States rose fifteen percentage points in the last five years; it's an entirely different thing to show a graph that depicts that rapid rise. If the point being made is that the increase in the GDP is better than it has ever been in the past fifty years, then a graph showing that growth cinches the point. If the point being made is that the growth in the GDP corresponds to the growth of the stock market for the same period, then that also can be graphed.

It's important that data in charts and graphs be simple and comprehensive. Also, it should only be used if it does, in fact, display the information more effectively than words alone can. However, it should also be able to stand alone. It should make the point by itself. If two or more charts or tables are used within a work, they should be consistent in style. Whatever graphic is used, elements of the same kind must always be represented in the same way. This is not a time to be artistic graphically; visual effects should be used only for the purpose of making the point, not for variety.

In graphs, both the horizontal and vertical axes should be labeled. In a column, both column heads and stubs should be labeled. In a graph, the vertical axis is always read from the bottom up and curves or bars should be graphically distinct (color or dotted lines, for example) and all elements should be clearly identified in a key. The title appears in a caption rather than as a title and is lowercased except for names that would normally be capitalized in the text. If abbreviations are used, care should be taken to make them easily recognizable unless they are explained in the key or in the caption.

A table can often give information that would take several paragraphs to present and can do so more clearly. Tables should be as simple as the material allows and should be understandable without explanation even to a reader who might be unfamiliar with the subject matter. Only necessary explanations should be presented in the text; the table should be able to stand alone.

The advent of word processing makes the creation and insertion of charts, graphs, and tables much more practical than ever before. It takes very little knowledge or skill to create these illustrative devices, and helping students develop those skills is a valuable enhancement to a writing course.

Skill 13.7   Recognize methods of developing a conclusion to a text that provides a restatement or summary of ideas, a resolution, or a suggested course of action.

It's easier to write a conclusion after the decisions regarding the introduction have been made. Aristotle taught that the conclusion should strive to do four things:

- Inspire the reader with a favorable opinion of the writer.
- Amplify the force of the points made in the body of the paper.
- Reinforce the points made in the body.
- Rouse appropriate emotions in the reader.
- Restate in a summary way what has been said.

The conclusion may be short or it may be long depending on its purpose in the paper. Recapitulation, a brief restatement of the main points or certainly of the thesis is the most common form of effective conclusions. A good example is the closing argument in a court trial.

COMPETENCY 14 CONVENTIONS OF STANDARD AMERICAN ENGLISH

Skill 14.1   Demonstrate knowledge of the conventions of capitalization.

Capitalize all proper names of persons (including specific organizations or agencies of government); places (countries, states, cities, parks, and specific geographical areas); and things (political parties, structures, historical and cultural terms, and calendar and time designations); and religious terms (any deity, revered person or group, sacred writings).

> Percy Bysshe Shelley, Argentina, Mount Rainier National Park, Grand Canyon, League of Nations, the Sears Tower, Birmingham, Lyric Theater, Americans, Midwesterners, Democrats, Renaissance, Boy Scouts of America, Easter, God, Bible, Dead Sea Scrolls, Koran

Capitalize proper adjectives and titles used with proper names.

> California gold rush, President John Adams, French fries, Homeric epic, Romanesque architecture, Senator John Glenn

Note: Some words that represent titles and offices are not capitalized unless used with a proper name.

Capitalized	Not Capitalized
Congressman McKay	the congressman from Florida
Commander Alger	commander of the Pacific Fleet
Queen Elizabeth	the queen of England

Capitalize all main words in titles of works of literature, art, and music.

Skill 14.2   Demonstrate knowledge of the conventions of punctuation.

A basic way to show relationship of ideas in sentences is to use punctuation correctly and effectively. Competency exams will generally test the ability to apply the more advanced skills; thus, a limited number of more frustrating rules are presented here. Rules should be applied according to the American style of English, i.e. spelling *theater* instead of *theatre* and placing terminal marks of punctuation almost exclusively within other marks of punctuation.

Quotation Marks

The more troublesome punctuation marks involve the use of quotations.

Using Terminal Punctuation in Relation to Quotation Marks: In a quoted statement that is either declarative or imperative, place the period inside the closing quotation marks.

"The airplane crashed on the runway during takeoff."

If the quotation is followed by other words in the sentence, place a comma inside the closing quotations marks and a period at the end of the sentence.

"The airplane crashed on the runway during takeoff," said the announcer.

In most instances in which a quoted title or expression occurs at the end of a sentence, the period is placed before either the single or double quotation marks.

The educator worried, "The middle school readers were unprepared to understand Bryant's poem 'Thanatopsis.'"

Early book-length adventure stories like *Don Quixote* and *The Three Musketeers* are known as "picaresque novels."

There is an instance in which the final quotation mark would precede the period: when the content of the sentence is about a speech or quote so that the understanding of the meaning would be confused by the placement of the period.

The first thing out of his mouth was "Hi, I'm home." *but*
The first line of his speech began "I arrived home to an empty house".

In sentences that are interrogatory or exclamatory, the question mark or exclamation point should be positioned outside the closing quotation marks if the quote itself is a question or command or cited title.

Who decided to lead us in the recitation of the "Pledge of Allegiance"?

Why was Tillie shaking as she began her recitation, "Once upon a midnight dreary..."?

I was embarrassed when Mrs. White said, "Your slip is showing"!

In sentences that are declarative but the quotation is a question or an exclamation, place the question mark or exclamation point inside the quotation marks.

The hall monitor yelled, "Fire! Fire!"

"Fire! Fire!" yelled the hall monitor.

TEACHER CERTIFICATION STUDY GUIDE

Cory shrieked, "Is there a mouse in the room?" (In this instance, the question supersedes the exclamation.)

Using Double Quotation Marks with Other Punctuation: Quotations—whether words, phrases, or clauses—should be punctuated according to the rules of the grammatical function they serve in the sentence.

The works of Shakespeare, "the bard of Avon," have been contested as originating with other authors.

"You'll get my money," the old man warned, "when 'Hell freezes over'."

Sheila cited the passage that began "Four score and seven years ago...." (Note the ellipsis followed by an enclosed period.)

"Old Ironsides" inspired the preservation of the U.S.S. Constitution.

Use quotation marks to enclose the titles of shorter works: songs, short poems, short stories, essays, and chapters of books. (See "Using Italics" for punctuating longer titles.)

"The Tell-Tale Heart"—short story
"Casey at the Bat"—poem
"America the Beautiful"—song

Using Commas

Separate two or more coordinate adjectives modifying the same word and three or more nouns, phrases, or clauses in a list.

Maggie's hair was dull, dirty, and lice-ridden.

Dickens portrayed the Artful Dodger as skillful pickpocket, loyal follower of Fagin, and defendant of Oliver Twist.

Ellen daydreamed about getting out of the rain, taking a shower, and eating a hot dinner.

In Elizabethan England, Ben Jonson wrote comedy, Christopher Marlowe wrote tragedies, and William Shakespeare composed both.

Use commas to separate antithetical or complementary expressions from the rest of the sentence.

The veterinarian, not his assistant, would perform the delicate surgery.

The more he knew about her, the less he wished he had known.

Randy hopes to, and probably will, get an appointment to the Naval Academy.

Using Semicolons

Use semicolons to separate independent clauses when the second clause is introduced by a transitional adverb. (These clauses may also be written as separate sentences, preferably by placing the adverb within the second sentence.)

> The Elizabethans modified the rhyme scheme of the sonnet; thus, it was called the English sonnet.
> *or*
> The Elizabethans modified the rhyme scheme of the sonnet. It thus was called the English sonnet.

Use semicolons to separate items in a series that are long and complex or have internal punctuation.

> The Italian Renaissance produced masters in the fine arts: Dante Alighieri, author of the *Divine Comedy;* Leonardo da Vinci, painter of *The Last Supper;* and Donatello, sculptor of the *Quattro Coronati*, the four saints.

> The leading scorers in the WNBA were Haizhaw Zheng, averaging 23.9 points per game; Lisa Leslie, 22; and Cynthia Cooper, 19.5.

Using Colons

Place a colon at the beginning of a list of items. (Note its use in the sentence about Renaissance Italians above.)

> The teacher directed us to compare Faulkner's three symbolic novels: *Absalom, Absalom; As I Lay Dying;* and *Light in August.*

Do **not** use a comma if the list is preceded by a verb.

> Three of Faulkner's symbolic novels are *Absalom, Absalom; As I Lay Dying*; and *Light in August.*

Using Dashes

Place dashes (called an "em" dash) to denote sudden breaks in thought.

Some periods in literature—the Romantic Age, for example—spanned different time periods in different countries.

Use dashes instead of commas if commas are already used elsewhere in the sentence for amplification or explanation.

The Fireside Poets included three Brahmans—James Russell Lowell, Henry David Wadsworth, Oliver Wendell Holmes—and John Greenleaf Whittier.

Using Italics

Use italics to punctuate the titles of long works of literature, names of periodical publications, musical scores, works of art, motion pictures, television shows, and radio programs. (When unable to write in italics, you can instruct students to underline in their own writing where italics would be appropriate.)

| *The Idylls of the King* | *Hiawatha* | *The Sound and the Fury* |
| *Mary Poppins* | *Newsweek* | *The Nutcracker Suite* |

Skill 14.3 Demonstrate knowledge of the conventions of spelling.

Spelling in English is complicated because it is not phonetic—that is, it is not based on the one-sound/one letter formula used by many other languages. It is based on the Latin alphabet, which originally had twenty letters, consisting of the present English alphabet minus J, K, V, W, Y, and Z. The Romans added K to be used in abbreviations and Y and Z in words that came from the Greek. This 23-letter alphabet was adopted by the English, who developed W as a ligatured doubling of U and later J and V as consonantal variants of I and U. The result was our alphabet of 26 letters with upper case (capital) and lower case forms.

Spelling is based primarily on 15th century English. The problem is that pronunciation has changed drastically since then, especially long vowels and diphthongs. This Great Vowel Shift affected the seven long vowels.

For a long time, spelling was erratic—there were no standards. As long as the meaning was clear, spelling was not considered very important. Samuel Johnson tackled this problem, and his *Dictionary of the English Language* (1755) brought standards to spelling, so important once printing presses were invented. There have been some changes, of course, through the years, but spelling is still not strictly phonetic.

Despite many attempts to nudge the spelling into a more phonetic representation of the sounds, all have failed for the most part. A good example is Noah Webster's *Spelling Book* (1783), which was a precursor to the first edition (1828) of his *American Dictionary of the English Language*. While there are rules for spelling, and it's important that students learn the rules, there are also many exceptions; and memorizing exceptions and giving plenty of opportunities for practicing them seems the only solution for the teacher of English.

Skill 14.4 Demonstrate knowledge of the correct use of the parts of speech in sentences.

The eight parts of speech form the syntactical framework on our language. While the study of grammar can be detailed, let's review some of the basics.

- Noun—names a person, place, or thing
- Pronoun—takes the place of one or more noun
- Verb—expresses action or state of being
- Adjective—describes, or modifies, a noun or a pronoun
- Adverb—modifies a verb, an adjective, or another adverb
- Conjunction—is a connecting word
- Preposition—relates a noun or a pronoun to another word in a sentence
- Interjection—expresses emotions

Nouns

A **noun** names a person, place, or thing/idea. A common noun names any person, place, or thing/idea; a proper noun names a particular person, place, thing/idea and will be capitalized.

	Person	Place	Thing/Idea	Idea
Common Noun	Actor	museum	ship	bravery
Proper Noun	Meryl Streep	The Smithsonian	*Titanic*	

Plural Nouns

The multiplicity and complexity of spelling rules based on phonics, letter doubling, and exceptions to rules—not mastered by adulthood—should be replaced by a good dictionary. As spelling mastery is also difficult for adolescents, our recommendation is the same. Learning the use of a dictionary and thesaurus will be a more rewarding use of time.

Most plurals of nouns that end in hard consonants or hard consonant sounds followed by a silent *e* are made by adding *s*. Some words ending in vowels only add *s*.

    fingers, numerals, banks, bugs, riots, homes, gates, radios, bananas

Nouns that end in soft consonant sounds *s, j, x, z, ch,* and *sh,* add *es*. Some nouns ending in *o* add *es*.

    dresses, waxes, churches, brushes, tomatoes

Nouns ending in *y* preceded by a vowel just add *s*.

    boys, alleys

Nouns ending in *y* preceded by a consonant change the *y* to *i* and add *es*.

    babies, corollaries, frugalities, poppies

Some nouns' plurals are formed irregularly or remain the same.

    sheep, deer, children, leaves, oxen

Some nouns derived from foreign words, especially Latin, may make their plurals in two different ways—one of them Anglicized. Sometimes, the meanings are the same; other times, the two plurals are used in slightly different contexts. It is always wise to consult the dictionary.

    appendices, appendixes   criterions, criteria
    indexes, indices

Make the plurals of closed (solid) compound words in the usual way except for words ending in *ful* which make their plurals on the root word.

    timelines, hairpins, spoonsful

Make the plurals of open or hyphenated compounds by adding the change in inflection to the word that changes in number.

    fathers-in-law, courts-martial, masters of art, doctors of medicine

Make the plurals of letters, numbers, and abbreviations by adding *s*.

    fives and tens, IBMs, 1990s, *p*s and *q*s (Note that letters are italicized.)

Possessive Nouns

Make the possessives of singular nouns by adding an apostrophe followed by the letter s ('s).

> baby's bottle, father's job, elephant's eye, teacher's desk, sympathizer's protests, week's postponement

Make the possessive of singular nouns ending in s by adding either an apostrophe or an ('s) depending upon common usage or sound. When making the possessive causes difficulty, use a prepositional phrase instead. Even with the sibilant ending, with a few exceptions, it is advisable to use the ('s) construction.

> dress's color, species' characteristics or characteristics of the species, James' hat or James's hat, Delores's shirt. Make the possessive of plural nouns ending in s by adding the apostrophe after the s; horses' coats, jockeys' times, four days' time

Make possessives of plural nouns that do not end in s the same as singular nouns by adding 's.

> children's shoes, deer's antlers, cattle's horns

Make possessives of compound nouns by adding the inflection at the end of the word or phrase.

> the mayor of Los Angeles' campaign, the mailman's new truck, the mailmen's new trucks, my father-in-law's first wife, the keepsakes' values, several daughters-in-laws husbands

Note: Because a gerund functions as a noun, any noun preceding it and operating as a possessive adjective must reflect the necessary inflection. However, if the gerundive following the noun is a participle, no inflection is added.

> The general was perturbed by the private's sleeping on duty. (The word *sleeping* is a gerund, the object of the preposition *by.)*
> *but*
> The general was perturbed to see the private sleeping on duty. (The word *sleeping* is a participle modifying private.)

Pronoun

A pronoun takes the place of one or more noun and must agree with that noun in case and number. The noun to which the pronoun refers is called the "antecedent."

Proper Case Forms

Pronouns, unlike nouns, change case forms. Pronouns must be in the subjective, objective, or possessive form according to their function in the sentence.

Subjective (Nominative)		Possessive		Objective	
Singular	Plural	Singular	Plural	Singular	Plural
1st person: I	we	my	our	me	us
2nd person: You	you	your	your	you	you
3rd person: He she it	they	his her its	their	him her it	them

Relative Pronouns

Who   Subjective/Nominative
Whom   Objective
Whose   Possessive

Rules for Clearly Identifying Pronoun Reference

Misuse of pronouns creates agreement errors and clouds the meaning of the sentence. Here are a few tips to correct this common grammatical error.

Make sure that the antecedent reference is clear and cannot refer to something else. A "distant relative" is a relative pronoun or a relative clause that has been placed too far away from the antecedent to which it refers. It is a common error to place a verb between the relative pronoun and its antecedent.

Error: Return the books to the library that are overdue.

Problem: The relative clause "that are overdue" refers to the "books" and should be placed immediately after the antecedent.

Correction: *Return the books that are overdue to the library.*
                or
                Return the overdue books to the library.

A pronoun should not refer to adjectives or possessive nouns. Adjectives, nouns, or possessive pronouns should not be used as antecedents. This will create ambiguity in sentences.

Error: In Todd's letter he told his mom he'd broken the priceless vase.

Problem:	In this sentence the pronoun "he" seems to refer to the noun phrase "Todd's letter" though it was probably meant to refer to the possessive noun "Todd's."
Correction:	*In his letter, Todd told his mom that he had broken the priceless vase.*

A pronoun should not refer to an implied idea. A pronoun must refer to a specific antecedent rather than an implied antecedent. When an antecedent is not stated specifically, the reader has to guess or assume the meaning of a sentence. Pronouns that do not have antecedents are called expletives. "It" and "there" are the most common expletives, though other pronouns can also become expletives as well. In informal conversation, expletives allow for casual presentation of ideas without supporting evidence. However, in more formal writing, it is best to be more precise.

Error:	She said that it is important to floss every day.
Problem:	The pronoun "it" refers to an implied idea.
Correction:	*She said that flossing every day is important.*

Error:	They returned the book because there were missing pages.
Problem:	The pronouns "they" and "there" do not refer to the antecedent.
Correction:	*The customer returned the book with missing pages.*

Using Who, That, and Which

Who, whom and **whose** refer to human beings and can either introduce essential or nonessential clauses. **That** refers to things other than humans and is used to introduce essential clauses. **Which** refers to things other than humans and is used to introduce nonessential clauses.

Error:	The doctor that performed the surgery said the man would be fully recovered.
Problem:	Since the relative pronoun is referring to a human, who should be used.
Correction:	*The doctor who performed the surgery said the man would be fully recovered.*

Error:	That ice cream cone that you just ate looked really delicious.

Problem: That has already been used so you must use *which* to introduce the next clause, whether it is essential or nonessential.

Correction: *That ice cream cone, which you just ate, looked really delicious.*

Error: Tom and me have reserved seats for next week's baseball game.

Problem: The pronoun me is the subject of the verb have reserved and should be in the subjective form.

Correction: *Tom and I have reserved seats for next week's baseball game.*

Error: Who's coat is this?

Problem: The interrogative possessive pronoun is whose; who's is the contraction for who is.

Correction: *Whose coat is this?*

Error: The voters will choose the candidate whom has the best qualifications for the job.

Problem: The case of the relative pronoun *who* or *whom* is determined by the pronoun's function in the clause in which it appears. The word *who* is in the subjective case, and whom is in the objective. Analyze how the pronoun is being used within the sentence.

Correction: *The voters will choose the candidate who has the best qualifications for the job.*

Verbs

A verb expresses action or state of being. Most verbs show time (tense) by an inflectional ending to the word. Other irregular verbs take completely different forms.

Both regular and irregular verbs must appear in their standard forms for each tense. Note: the *ed* or *d* ending is added to regular verbs in the past tense and for past participles.

Infinitive	Past Tense	Past Participle
Bake	baked	baked

Irregular Verb Forms

Infinitive	Past Tense	Past Participle
Be	was, were	been
become	became	become
break	broke	broken
bring	brought	brought
choose	chose	chosen
come	came	come
do	did	done
draw	drew	drawn
eat	ate	eaten
fall	fell	fallen
forget	forgot	forgotten
freeze	froze	frozen
give	gave	given
go	went	gone
grow	grew	grown
have/has	had	had
hide	hid	hidden
know	knew	known
lay	laid	laid
lie	lay	lain
ride	rode	ridden
rise	rose	risen
run	ran	run
see	saw	seen
steal	stole	stolen
take	took	taken
tell	told	told
throw	threw	thrown
wear	wore	worn
write	wrote	written

Error: She should have went to her doctor's appointment at the scheduled time.

Problem: The past participle of the verb *to go* is *gone*. *Went* expresses the simple past tense.

Correction: *She should have gone to her doctor's appointment at the scheduled time.*

Error: My train is suppose to arrive before two o'clock.

Problem: The verb following *train* is a present tense passive construction which requires the present tense verb *to be* and the past participle.

Correction: *My train is supposed to arrive before two o'clock.*

Error: Linda should of known that the car wouldn't start after leaving it out in the cold all night.

Problem: *Should of* is a nonstandard expression. Of is not a verb.

Correction: *Linda should have known that the car wouldn't start after leaving it out in the cold all night.*

Subject-Verb Agreement

A verb agrees in number with its subject. Making them agree relies on the ability to identify the correct subject.

One of the boys *was playing* too rough.

No one in the class, not the teacher nor the students, was listening to the message from the intercom.

The candidates, including a grandmother and a teenager, are debating some controversial issues.

If two singular subjects are connected by *and* the verb must be plural.

A *man* and his *dog* were jogging on the beach.

If two singular subjects are connected by *or,* or *nor*, a singular verb is required.

Neither Dot nor Joyce has missed a day of school this year.
Either Fran or Paul is missing.

If one singular subject and one plural subject are connected by *or,* or *nor*, the verb agrees with the subject nearest to the verb.

Neither the coach nor the players were able to sleep on the bus.

If the subject is a collective noun, its sense of number in the sentence determines the verb: singular if the noun represents a group or unit and plural if the noun represents individuals.

The House of Representatives has adjourned for the holidays.

The House of Representatives have failed to reach agreement on the subject of adjournment.

Use of Verbs (Tense)

Present tense is used to express that which is currently happening or is always true.

Randy is playing the piano.

Randy plays the piano like a pro.

Past tense is used to express action that occurred in a past time.

Randy learned to play the piano when he was six years old.

Future tense is used to express action or a condition of future time.

Randy will probably earn a music scholarship.

Present perfect tense is used to express action or a condition that started in the past and is continued to or completed in the present.

Randy has practiced piano every day for the last ten years.

Randy has never been bored with practice.

Past perfect tense expresses action or a condition that occurred as a precedent to some other past action or condition.

Randy had considered playing clarinet before he discovered the piano.

Future perfect tense expresses action that started in the past or the present and will conclude at some time in the future.

By the time he goes to college, Randy will have been an accomplished pianist for more than half of his life.

Use of Verbs: Mood

Indicative mood is used to make unconditional statements; subjunctive mood is used for conditional clauses or wish statements that pose conditions that are untrue. Verbs in subjunctive mood are plural with both singular and plural subjects.

If I were a bird, I would fly.

I wish I <u>were</u> as rich as Donald Trump.

Use of Verbs: Voice

A verb is in the **active voice** when its subject is the doer of the action. A verb is in the **passive voice** when its subject is the receiver of the action.

Active Voice	Passive Voice
The director adjourned the meeting. The subject, *director*, performs the action, *adjourned*.	**The meeting was adjourned by the director.** The subject, *meeting*, is not performing the action; instead, it is receiving the action, *was adjourned*.
The mechanic at the Shell station inspected Mrs. Johnson's automobile. The subject, *mechanic*, performed the action, *inspected*.	**Mrs. Johnson's automobile was inspected by the mechanic at the Shell station.** The subject, *automobile*, is not acting; it is receiving the action, *was inspected*.

How do you recognize passive voice? Look at the verb. A passive voice verb has at least two parts:
1. a form of the verb *to be (am, is, are, was, were, be, been)*
   The computer *was* installed by Datacorp.
2. a past participle form of the main verb (thrown, driven, planted, talked)
   The computer was *installed* by Datacorp.

* Sometimes the subject is in an object position in the sentence.
   The computer was installed by *Datacorp*. (object of preposition)

* Watch for a "by" statement between the verb phrase and the object.
   The computer was installed *by* Datacorp. (preposition)

* Sometimes the doer is not even present.
   The computer was installed. (By whom?)

Verb Conjugation

The conjugation of verbs follows the patterns used in the discussion of tense above. However, the most frequent problems in verb use stem from the improper formation of past and past participial forms.

Regular verb: believe, believed, (have) believed

Irregular verbs: run, ran, run; sit, sat, sat; teach, taught, taught

Other problems stem from the use of verbs that are the same in some tenses but have different forms and different meanings in other tenses.

I lie on the ground. I lay on the ground yesterday. I have lain down. I lay the blanket on the bed. I laid the blanket there yesterday. I have laid the blanket down every night.

The sun rises. The sun rose. The sun has risen.

He raises the flag. He raised the flag. He had raised the flag.

I sit on the porch. I sat on the porch. I have sat in the porch swing.

I set the plate on the table. I set the plate there yesterday. I had set the table before dinner.

Adjectives and Adverbs

Adjectives are words that modify or describe nouns or pronouns. Adjectives usually precede the words they modify, but not always; for example, an adjective occurs after a linking verb. Adjectives answer what kind, how many, or which one.

Adverbs are words that modify verbs, adjectives, or other adverbs. They cannot modify nouns. Adverbs answer such questions as how, why, when, where, how much, or how often something is done. Many adverbs are formed by adding *ly*.

Error: The birthday cake tasted sweetly.

Problem: *Tasted* is a linking verb; the modifier that follows should be an adjective, not an adverb.

Correction: *The birthday cake tasted sweet.*

Error: You have done good with this project.

Problem: *Good* is an adjective and cannot be used to modify a verb phrase such as have done.

Correction: *You have done well with this project.*

Error: The coach was positive happy about the team's chance of winning.

Problem: The adjective *positive* cannot be used to modify another adjective, *happy*. An adverb is needed instead.

Correction: *The coach was positively happy about the team's chance of winning.*

Error: The fireman acted quick and brave to save the child from the burning building.

Problem: *Quick and brave* are adjectives and cannot be used to describe a verb. Adverbs are needed instead.

Correction: *The fireman acted quickly and bravely to save the child from the burning building.*

Conjunctions

A conjunction connects words, phrases, or clauses. It acts as a signal, indicating when a thought is added, contrasted, or altered.

Meet the FANBOYS! This mnemonic device will help students remember the seven coordinating conjunctions.

For, And, Nor, But, Or, Yet, So

These are **coordinating conjunctions** that join similar elements.
Strong and tall (adjectives)
Easily and quickly (adverbs)
Of the people, by the people, for the people (prepositional phrases)
We disagreed, but we reached a compromise. (sentences)

Subordinating conjunctions connect clauses (subject-verb combinations) in a sentence. They signal that the clause is subordinate and cannot stand alone.

Subordinating Conjunctions			
after	because	though	whenever
although	before	till	where
as	if	unless	whereas
as if	since	until	wherever
as though	than	when	while

I will be grateful *if you will work on this project with me.*
Because I am running late, you will need to cover for me.

Prepositions

A preposition relates a noun or a pronoun to another word in a sentence. Think of prepositions as words that show relationships. Below is a partial list.

> Check out this
> **Guide to Grammar and Writing**
> http://grammar.ccc.commnet.edu/grammar/

about	above	according to	across	after	against
along	along with	among	apart from	around	as/as for
at	because of	before	behind	below	beneath
beside	between	beyond	by	by means of	concerning
despite	down	during	except	except for	excepting
for	from	in	in addition to	in back of	in case of
in front of	in place of	inside	in spite of	instead of	into
like	near	next	of	off/off of	on
onto	on top of	out/out of	outside	over	past
regarding	round	since	through	throughout	till
to	toward	under	underneath	unlike	until
up/upon	up to	with	within	without	

Guidelines
- Include necessary prepositions.
    I graduated from high school. (not *I graduated high school.*)

- Omit unnecessary prepositions
    Both printers work well. (Not *Both of the printers* work well.)
    Where are the printers? (Not *Where are the printers at?*)

- Avoid the overuse of prepositions.
    We have received your application for credit at our branch in the Fresno area.
    We have received your Fresno credit application.

Interjections

An **interjection** is a word or group of words that express emotion, surprise, or disbelief. It has no grammatical connection to other words in a sentence.

Some Common Interjections			
aha	great	my	ouch
alas	ha	no	well

gee	hey	oh	wow
good grief	hooray	oops	yes

Guidelines

*   When an interjection expresses strong emotion, it usually stands alone; it begins with a capital letter and ends with an exclamation point.
    Ouch! That paper cut really hurts.
    Good grief! My favorite store has closed.

*   When an interjection expresses mild feeling, it is written as part of the sentence and is set off with commas.
    Yes, we will comply with your request.

Skill 14.5   Recognize ways to form simple, compound, complex, and compound-complex sentences in which there is subject–verb and pronoun–antecedent agreement.

Recognize the sentence elements necessary to make a complete thought and use independent and dependent clauses properly. Proper punctuation will correct such errors.

Sentence Structure

You should recognize simple, compound, complex, and compound-complex sentences. Use dependent (subordinate) and independent clauses correctly to create these sentence structures.

Simple	Joyce wrote a letter.
Compound	Joyce wrote a letter, and Dot drew a picture.
Complex	While Joyce wrote a letter, Dot drew a picture.
Compound/Complex	When Mother asked the girls to demonstrate their new-found skills, Joyce wrote a letter, and Dot drew a picture.

Note: Do **not** confuse compound sentence elements with compound sentences.

Simple sentence with compound subject
    <u>Joyce</u> and <u>Dot</u> wrote letters.
    The <u>girl</u> in row three and the <u>boy</u> next to her were passing notes across the aisle.

Simple sentence with compound predicate
    Joyce <u>wrote letters</u> and <u>drew pictures</u>.

The captain of the high school debate team <u>graduated with honors</u> and <u>studied broadcast journalism in college</u>.

Simple sentence with compound object of preposition
Coleen graded the students' essays for <u>style</u> and <u>mechanical accuracy</u>.

Clauses and Phrases

Clauses are connected word groups that are composed of *at least* one subject and one verb. (A subject is the doer of an action or the element that is being joined. A verb conveys either the action or the link.)

<u>Students</u> <u>are waiting</u> for the start of the assembly.
Subject   Verb

At the end of the play, <u>students</u> <u>wait</u> for the curtain to come down.
Subject   Verb

Clauses can be **independent** or **dependent**. Independent clauses can stand alone or can be joined to other clauses. Connect independent clauses with the coordinating conjunctions—*and, but, or, for,* or *nor*—when their content is of equal importance. Use subordinating conjunctions—*although, because, before, if, since, though, until, when, whenever, where*—and relative pronouns—*that, who, whom, which*—introduce clauses that express ideas that are subordinate to main ideas expressed in independent clauses.

Comma and coordinating conjunction
Independent clause	, for	Independent clause
	, and	Independent clause
	, nor	Independent clause
	, but	Independent clause
	, or	Independent clause
	, yet	Independent clause
	, so	Independent clause

Semicolon
Independent clause	;	Independent clause

Subordinating conjunction, dependent clause, and comma
Dependent clause	,	Independent clause

Independent clause followed by a subordinating conjunction that introduces a dependent clause
Independent clause	Dependent clause

Dependent clauses, by definition, contain at least one subject and one verb. However, they cannot stand alone as a complete sentence. They are structurally dependent on the main clause.

There are two types of dependent clauses: (1) those with a subordinating conjunction, and (2) those with a relative pronoun.

Sample subordinating conjunctions: *although, when, if, unless, because*

<u>Unless a cure is discovered</u>, <u>many more people will die of the disease</u>.
     Dependent clause   +   Independent clause

Sample relative pronouns: *who, whom, which, that*

<u>The White House has an official website</u>, <u>which</u> <u>contains press releases, news updates, and biographies of the President and Vice-President</u>. (<u>Independent clause</u> + <u>relative pronoun</u> + <u>relative dependent clause</u>)

Be sure to place the conjunctions so that they express the proper relationship between ideas (cause/effect, condition, time, space).

Incorrect: Because mother scolded me, I was late.
Correct: *Mother scolded me because I was late.*

Incorrect: The sun rose after the fog lifted.
Correct: *The fog lifted after the sun rose.*

Notice that placement of the conjunction can completely change the meaning of the sentence. Main emphasis is shifted by the change.

Although Jenny was pleased, the teacher was disappointed.
Although the teacher was disappointed, Jenny was pleased.

The boys who had written the essay won the contest.
The boys who won the contest had written the essay.

While not syntactically incorrect, the second sentence makes it appear that the boys won the contest for something else before they wrote the essay.

Misplaced and Dangling Modifiers

Particular phrases that are not placed near the one word they modify often result in misplaced modifiers. Particular phrases that do not relate to the subject being modified result in dangling modifiers.

Error: Weighing the options carefully, a decision was made regarding the punishment of the convicted murderer.

Problem: Who is weighing the options? No one capable of weighing is named in the sentence; thus, the participle phrase weighing the options carefully dangles. This problem can be corrected by adding a subject of the sentence capable of doing the action.

Correction: *Weighing the options carefully, the judge made a decision regarding the punishment of the convicted murderer.*

Error: Returning to my favorite watering hole brought back many fond memories.

Problem: The person who returned is never indicated, and the participle phrase dangles. This problem can be corrected by creating a dependent clause from the modifying phrase.

Correction: *When I returned to my favorite watering hole, many fond memories came back to me.*

Error: One damaged house stood only to remind townspeople of the hurricane.

Problem: The placement of the misplaced modifier only suggests that the sole reason the house remained was to serve as a reminder. The faulty modifier creates ambiguity.

Correction: *Only one damaged house stood, reminding townspeople of the hurricane.*

Parallelism

You should recognize parallel structures using phrases (prepositional, gerund, participial, and infinitive) and omissions from sentences that create the lack of parallelism. Parallelism provides balance to the grammar and the ideas.

> Learn more about
> **Parallel Structure vs.**
> **Faulty Parallelism**
> http://jerz.setonhill.edu/writing/
> grammar/parallel.html

Prepositional phrase/single modifier
Incorrect: Coleen ate the ice cream with enthusiasm and hurriedly.
Correct: *Coleen ate the ice cream with enthusiasm and in a hurry.*
Correct: *Coleen ate the ice cream enthusiastically and hurriedly.*

Participial phrase/infinitive phrase

Incorrect: After hiking for hours and to sweat profusely, Joe sat down to rest and drinking water.

Correct: *After hiking for hours and sweating profusely, Joe sat down to rest and drink water.*

COMPETENCY 15 EXPOSITORY WRITING

Skill 15.1   Demonstrate knowledge of forms of writing that are appropriate for describing events, providing information, or answering questions.

Basic expository writing simply gives information not previously known about a topic or is used to explain or define one. Facts, examples, statistics, cause and effect, direct tone, objective rather than subjective delivery, and non-emotional information are presented in a formal manner.

Descriptive writing centers on person, place, or object, using concrete and sensory words to create a mood or impression and arranging details in a chronological or spatial sequence.

Narrative writing is developed using an incident or anecdote or related series of events. Chronology, the 5 W's, topic sentence, and conclusion are essential ingredients.

Answering questions: The best way to form an answer is by forming a thesis statement, which will be what you think to be true about the question that is being asked. Then develop the answer—the thesis—by using standard methods of support. For example, reason logically either inductively or deductively. Use examples to clarify your point.

Skill 15.2   Demonstrate the ability to select an appropriate subject or topic for writing and to formulate a fundamental question for addressing through writing.

In studies of professional writers and how they produce their successful works, it has been revealed that writing is a process that can be clearly defined although in practice it must have enough flexibility to allow for creativity. The teacher must be able to define the various stages that a successful writer goes through in order to make a statement that has value. There must be a discovery stage when ideas, materials, supporting details, etc., are deliberately collected. These may come from many possible sources: the writer's own experience and observations, deliberate research of written sources, interviews of live persons, television presentations, or the internet.

In selecting a thesis for developing an essay, the following questions should be asked:

1. Is it broad enough to allow for a significant statement?
2. Is there enough information to develop this thesis?

3. Is it worthwhile? In other words, is it anything that the average person would care about?
4. Is it narrow enough to develop in a paper of this size?

A thesis will have two sides; it is an arguable statement. Before making a final selection of a thesis, both sides should be considered. Only then can you develop a question that will make a paper worthwhile.

Skill 15.3   Determine appropriate primary sources and secondary sources for locating and gathering information about a subject or topic.

(Refer to Skill 3.6 for a discussion of primary and secondary sources.)

The best place to start research is usually at your local library. Not only does it have numerous books, videos, and periodicals to use for references, the librarian is always a valuable resource for information, or where to get that information.

"Those who declared librarians obsolete when the internet rage first appeared are now red-faced. We need them more than ever.The internet is full of 'stuff' but its value and readability is often questionable. 'Stuff' doesn't give you a competitive edge, high-quality related information does" (Patricia Schroeder, President of the Association of American Publishers).

The internet is a multi-faceted goldmine of information, but you must be careful to discriminate between reliable and unreliable sources. Stick to sites that are associated with an academic institution, whether it be a college or university or a scholarly organization.

Keep **content** and **context** in mind when researching. Don't be so wrapped up in how you are going to apply your resource to your project that you miss the author's entire purpose or message. Remember that there are multiple ways to get the information you need. Read an encyclopedia article about your topic to get a general overview, and then focus in from there. Note important names of people associated with your subject, time periods, and geographic areas. Make a list of key words and their synonyms to use while searching for information. And finally, don't forget about articles in magazines and newspapers, or even personal interviews with experts related to your field of interest.

Don't overlook primary sources. Search for experts on your topic whom you can interview. You may find them locally so you can sit down with them and ask questions. If you do, in fact, have a person who has experienced what you are writing about, you will have a rich resource. The best kind of interview in this case would be to encourage him or her to talk about the experience and then tell you what conclusions he or she has come to as a result of it. The possibility of an e-mail interview or a telephone interview should not be ignored. Many of the things you can accomplish one-on-one can be achieved using one of these media.

Beware of limiting the number of resources.If you have, in fact, posed a significant question, there should be a variety of views. If you are impressed with one of your interviewees, you might be overly influenced by his or her views. Always test the views of a source until you are sure that you have a thesis you can defend.

Skill 15.4   Evaluate the relevance and reliability of information sources.

When evaluating sources, first go through this checklist to make sure the source is even worth reading:
- Title (How relevant is it to your topic?)
- Date (How current is the source?)
- Reliability (What institution is this source coming from?)
- Length (How in depth does it go?)

Check for signs of bias:
- Does the author or publisher have political ties or religious views that could affect his objectivity?
- Is the author or publisher associated with any special-interest groups that might only see one side of an issue, such as Greenpeace or the National Rifle Association?
- How fairly does the author treat opposing views?
- Does the language of the piece show signs of bias?

Keep an open mind while reading, and don't let opposing viewpoints prevent you from absorbing the text. Remember that you are not judging the author's work; you are examining its assumptions, assessing its evidence and weighing its conclusions.

Skill 15.5   Recognize methods of developing a thesis statement that expresses the central idea of a piece of writing.

Seeing writing as a process is very helpful in saving preparation time, particularly in the taking of notes and the development of drafts. Once a decision is made about the topic to be developed, some preliminary review of literature is helpful in thinking about the next step, which is to determine what the purpose of the written document will be. For example, if the topic is immigration, a cursory review of the various points of view in the debate going on in the country will help the writer decide what this particular written piece will try to accomplish. The purpose could just be a review of the various points of view, which would be an informative purpose. On the other hand, the writer might want to take a point of view and provide proof and support with the purpose of changing the reader's mind. The writer might even want the reader to take some action as the result of reading. Another possible purpose might be simply to write a description of a family of immigrants.

Once that cursory review has been completed, it's time to begin research in earnest and to prepare to take notes. If the thesis has been clearly defined, and some thought has been given to what will be used to prove or support it, a tentative outline can be developed. A thesis plus three points is typical. Decisions about introduction and conclusion should be deferred until the body of the paper is written. Note-taking is much more effective if the notes are being taken to provide information for an outline. There is much less danger that the writer will go off on time-consuming tangents.

Formal outlines inhibit effective writing. However, a loosely constructed outline can be an effective device for note-taking that will yield the information for a worthwhile statement about a topic. Sentence outlines are better than topic outlines because they require the writer to do some thinking about the direction a subtopic will take.

Once this preliminary note-taking phase is over, the first draft can be developed. The writing at this stage is likely to be highly individualistic. However, successful writers tend to just write, keeping in mind the purpose of the paper, the point that is going to be made in it, and the information that has been turned up in the research. Student writers need to understand that this first draft is just that—the first one. It takes more than one draft to write a worthwhile statement about a topic. This is what successful writers do. It's sometimes helpful to have students read the various drafts of a story by a well-known writer.

The writing process is *recursive*. Until the very last draft, the door should be left open to go back and redo one stage or another. For example, if it appears that the research has not been complete enough, then more discovery should take place. If the preliminary outline cannot be developed, then changes should be made at this time. It may be that the writer must go back to the drawing board, so to speak. Students tend to be impatient with this, so they should be taught that this is the way effective writing occurs.

Skill 15.6   Demonstrate the ability to select an appropriate organizational structure or pattern for developing ideas in writing.

Organizational Structures

Authors use a particular organization to best present the concepts they are writing about. Teaching students to recognize organizational structures helps them to understand authors' literary intentions, and helps them decide which structure to use in their own writing.

Cause and Effect: When writing about *why* things happen, as well as *what* happens, authors commonly use the cause and effect structure. For example, when writing about how he became so successful, a CEO might talk about how he excelled in math in high school, moved to New York after college, and stuck to his goals even after multiple failures. These are all *causes* that led to the *effect*, or result, of his becoming a wealthy and powerful businessman.

Compare and Contrast: When examining the merits of multiple concepts or products, compare and contrast lends itself easily to organization of ideas. For example, a person writing about foreign policy in different countries will put them against each other to point out differences and similarities, easily highlighting the concepts the author wishes to emphasize.

Problem and Solution: This structure is used in a lot of handbooks and manuals. Anything organized around procedure-oriented tasks, such as a computer repair manual, gravitates toward a problem and solution format, because it offers such clear, sequential text organization.

An easy and effective way of organizing information to be used in a work of nonfiction is by asking specific questions that are geared towards a particular mode of presentation. An example of these questions follows:

Useful research questions:

What is it?

It is the process of thinking up and writing down a set of questions that you want to answer about the research topic you have selected.

Why should I do it?

It will keep you from getting lost or off-track when looking for information. You will try to find the answers to these questions when you do your research.

When do I do it?

After you have written your statement of purpose, and have a focused topic to ask questions about, begin research.

How do I do it?

Make two lists of questions. Label one "factual" questions and one "interpretive" questions. The answers to factual questions will give your reader the basic background information they need to understand your topic. The answers to interpretive questions show your creative thinking in your project and can become the basis for your thesis statement.

Asking factual questions:

Assume your readers know nothing about your subject. Make an effort to tell them everything they need to know to understand what you will say in your project.

Make a list of specific questions that ask: Who? What? When? Where?

Example: For a report about President Abraham Lincoln's attitude and policies towards slavery, people will have to know the following: Who was Abraham Lincoln? Where and when was he born? What political party did he belong to? When was he elected president? What were the attitudes and laws about slavery during his lifetime? How did his actions affect slavery?

Asking Interpretive Questions:

These kinds of questions are the result of your own original thinking. They can be based on the preliminary research you have done on your chosen topic. Select one or two to answer in your presentation. They can be the basis of forming a thesis statement.

- **Hypothetical**: How would things be different today if something in the past had been different?

Example: How would our lives be different today if the Confederate (southern) states had won the United States Civil War? What would have happened to the course of World War Two if the Atomic Bomb hadn't been dropped on Hiroshima and Nagasaki?

- **Prediction**: How will something look or be in the future, based on the way it is now?

Example: What will happen to sea levels if global warming due to ozone-layer depletion continues and the polar caps melt significantly? If the population of China continues to grow at the current rate for the next fifty years, how will that impact its role in world politics?

- **Solution**: What solutions can be offered to a problem that exists today?

Example: How could global warming be stopped? What can be done to stop the spread of sexually transmitted diseases among teenagers?

- **Comparison or Analogy**: Find the similarities and differences between your main subject and a similar subject, or with another subject in the same time period or place.

Example: In what ways is the Civil War in the former Yugoslavia similar to (or different from) the United States Civil War? What is the difference in performance between a Porsche and a Lamborghini?

- **Judgment**: Based on the information you find, what can you say as your informed opinion about the subject?

Example: How does tobacco advertising affect teen cigarette smoking? What are the major causes of eating disorders among young women? How does teen parenthood affect the future lives of young women and men?

Introductions:

It's important to remember that in the writing process, the introduction should be written last. Until the body of the paper has been determined—thesis, development—it's difficult to make strategic decisions regarding the introduction. The Greek rhetoricians called this part of a discourse *exordium*, a "leading into." The basic purpose of the introduction, then, is to lead the audience into the discourse. It can let the reader know what the purpose of the discourse is and it can condition the audience to be receptive to what the writer wants to say. It can be very brief or it can take up a large percentage of the total word count. Aristotle said that the introduction could be compared to the flourishes that flute players make before their performance—an overture in which the musicians display what they can play best in order to gain the favor and attention of the audience for the main performance.

In order to do this, we must first of all know what we are going to say; who the readership is likely to be; what the social, political, economic, etc., climate is; what preconceived notions the audience is likely to have regarding the subject; and how long the discourse is going to be.

There are many ways to do this:
- Show that the subject is important.
- Show that although the points we are presenting may seem improbable, they are true.
- Show that the subject has been neglected, misunderstood, or misrepresented.
- Explain an unusual mode of development.
- Forestall any misconception of the purpose.
- Apologize for a deficiency.
- Arouse interest in the subject with an anecdotal lead-in.
- Ingratiate oneself with the readership.
- Establish one's own credibility.

The introduction often ends with the thesis, the point or purpose of the paper. However, this is not set in stone. The thesis may open the body of the discussion, or it may conclude the discourse. The most important thing to remember is that the purpose and structure of the introduction should be deliberate if it is to serve the purpose of "leading the reader into the discussion."

Conclusions:

It's easier to write a conclusion after the decisions regarding the introduction have been made. Aristotle taught that the conclusion should strive to do five things:

1. Inspire the reader with a favorable opinion of the writer.
2. Amplify the force of the points made in the body of the paper.
3. Reinforce the points made in the body.
4. Rouse appropriate emotions in the reader.
5. Restate in a summary way what has been said.

The conclusion may be short or it may be long depending on its purpose in the paper. Recapitulation, a brief restatement of the main points or certainly of the thesis is the most common form of effective conclusions. A good example is the closing argument in a court trial.

Skill 15.7   Demonstrate knowledge of methods of paraphrasing, summarizing, and quoting sources appropriately and of acknowledging and documenting sources to avoid plagiarism.

Paraphrasing is the art of rewording text. The goal is to maintain the original purpose of the statement while translating it into your own words. Your newly-generated sentence can be longer or shorter than the original. Concentrate on the meaning, not on the words. Do not change concept words, special terms, or proper names. There are numerous ways to effectively paraphrase:

- Change the key words' form or part of speech. Example: "American news **coverage** is frequently **biased** in favor of Western views," becomes "When American journalists **cover** events, they often display a Western **bias**."
- Use synonyms of "relationship words." Look for relationship words, such as **contrast, cause,** or **effect,** and replace them with words that convey a similar meaning, thus creating a different structure for your sentence. Example: "**Unlike** many cats, Purrdy can sit on command," becomes "Most cats are not able to be trained, **but** Purrdy can sit on command."
- Use synonyms of phrases and words. Example: "The Beatnik writers were relatively unknown at **the start of the decade**," becomes "**Around the early 1950s**, the Beatnik writers were still relatively unknown."
- Change passive voice to active voice or move phrases and modifiers. Example: "Not to be outdone by the third graders, the fourth grade class

added a musical medley to their Christmas performance," becomes "The fourth grade class added a musical medley to their Christmas performance to avoid being showed up by the third graders."

- Use reversals or negatives that do not change the meaning of the sentence. Example: "That burger chain is only found in California," becomes "That burger chain is not found on the east coast."

Summarizing engages the reader in pulling together into a cohesive whole the essential bits of information within a longer passage or excerpt of text. Readers can be taught to summarize informational or expository text by following these guidelines: first they should look at the topic sentence of the paragraph or the text and ignore the trivia. Then they should search for information which has been mentioned more than once and make sure it is included only once in their summary. Find related ideas or items and group them under a unifying heading. Search for and identify a main idea sentence. Finally, put the summary together using all these guidelines.

The ethical attributes of responsible research and reporting.

Plagiarism, whether intentional or accidental, has ethical implications, and anyone who writes needs to have a clear understanding of what it is. Basically, it means passing off the words or ideas of another person as one's own without giving proper credit to the source.

It's acceptable to paraphrase someone else's words just as long as you provide a citation—that is, announce where and whom it came from. Remember, though, that any exact words or phrases that come from the original work must be set off in quotation marks and the point in the original where it came from indicated. These rules apply to all words and ideas whether they are written, are from a speech, from a television or radio program, from e-mail messages, from interviews, or from conversations. It's even more important to be careful about lifting any such information from a website because nowadays there are very powerful search engines that identify plagiarism, and many people who provide information on the Internet use them to make sure their words and information are not being stolen. Fines for plagiarism are very steep.

Lifting another person's words or ideas and presenting them as one's own is no different from thievery. Many people who wouldn't think of committing a theft of material or property think nothing of presenting the words and ideas of others as their own.

A second kind of unethical misuse of information is falsely reporting or attributing words or ideas. This can be putting words in another's mouth or bending what was said to create a false impression. Sometimes, simply failing to report the context in which something was said becomes false reporting. So many misuses of the printed and spoken word have taken place in a world that is constantly flooded with communications from all directions that students sometimes feel that it is acceptable to commit these misuses themselves. The writing classroom is an ideal forum for teaching and discussing what is ethical and moral in the use of language from a source and what is not.

COMPETENCY 16 NARRATIVE WRITING

Skill 16.1 Demonstrate knowledge of forms of writing that are appropriate for expressing personal thoughts and feelings, exploring various points of view, or telling a story.

Teaching students and encouraging them to keep journals is a beneficial way to encourage writing. You may ask the students to turn their journals in so you may look at them from time-to-time, but if you choose this method of being sure they are keeping them, you will need to assure them that you will respect their confidences. If a journal is to be helpful, the writer must feel free to express personal thoughts and recollections. To gain the most useful effects from this, the students must feel certain that their privacy will be protected.

Personal essays are another form of writing that has its origin in the self—the writer's own opinions, experiences, or conclusions. The standard essay, "What I Did Last Summer," is often used by teachers to get students started writing about themselves. However, these essays are only valuable if students have been taught some principles about such writing, such as making a point, making careful selections of details to include, and organizing the information in a meaningful way.

The sketch is useful in helping students learn to encapsulate or distill a story or a description. Also, by showing that an idea or an event can be expanded or retracted—more can be said about it or it can have meaning even without a lot of details or development—students are able to see the possibilities for meaningful development of such an idea or event. This is particularly helpful when students are learning to write answers to essay questions.

A short story is not just a novel shortened. Effectiveness in a short story is achieved by keeping the number of characters few, and the characters are not as fully developed as in a novel. Setting plays an important role in many short stories such as in Poe's "Fall of the House of Usher." However, the setting should be limited and only include enough details to set the stage for the story itself. In other words, the setting should be highly concentrated and distilled. A study of the short story is a useful way to introduce students to the analysis of literature because they can practice their skills over and over rather than just once or twice in a course where a novel or two is read over the space of a semester.

In a study of poetry, language and its power to evoke feelings can be taught and practiced better than with any other form. It is here that the power of image can most easily be seen. Reading and analyzing poetry is a good place to start in leading students to work with language themselves to write poetry that is expressive of their innermost thoughts.

Song lyrics are must like poetry in that the language relies on image, symbol, and sound to achieve meaning. Most students are very aware of the songs that are popular at the moment and are able to talk about meanings and effects. Having them attempt to write a song may be a good introduction to poetry.

Skill 16.2 Recognize specific details that are important to include in narrative writing to achieve an effect or fulfill a purpose.

Narrative writing is developed using an incident or anecdote or related series of events. Chronology, the 5 W's, topic sentence, and conclusion are essential ingredients. Point of view plays an important role in the effect a narrative. See skill 6.4 for a thorough explanation of point of view. Believability and interest in narrative depend largely on the development of the characters. See skill 16.3 (below) for more on this important aspect of narrative construction. Action or plot is also vital if the narrative is to be effective.

Skill 16.3 Apply strategies for composing narrative writing by presenting characters and actions.

Plot is sometimes called action, or the sequence of the events. If the plot does not *move*, the story quickly dies. Therefore, the successful writer of stories uses a wide variety of active verbs in creative and unusual ways. If a reader is kept interested by the movement of the story, the experience of reading it will be pleasurable. The reader will probably want to read more of this author's work. Careful, unique, and unusual choices of active verbs will bring about that effect.

William Faulkner is a good example of a successful writer whose stories are lively and memorable because of his use of unusual active verbs. In analyzing the development of plot, analytical readers will look at the verbs. However, the development of believable conflicts is also vital. If there is no conflict, there is no story. In critical thinking, readers should ask: What devices does a writer use to develop the conflicts, and are they real and believable?

Character is portrayed in many ways: description of physical characteristics, dialogue, interior monologue, the thoughts of the character, the attitudes of other characters toward this one, and so on. Descriptive language depends on the ability to recreate a sensory experience for the reader. If the description of the character's appearance is a visual one, then the reader must be able to *see* the character. What's the shape of the nose? What color are the eyes? How tall or how short is this character? Thin or chubby? How does the character move? How does the character walk? Writers choose terms that will create a picture for the reader. It's not enough to say the eyes are blue, for example. What kind of blue? Often the color of eyes is compared to something else to enhance the readers' ability to visualize the character.

A good test of characterization is the level of emotional involvement of the reader in the character. If the reader is to become involved, the description must provide an actual experience—seeing, smelling, hearing, tasting, or feeling. In the following example, Isaac Asimov deftly describes a character both directly and indirectly.

> Undersecretary Albert Minnim was a small, compact man, ruddy of skin, and graying, with the angles of his body smoothed down and softened. He exuded an air of cleanliness and smelled faintly of tonic. It all spoke of the good things of life that came with the liberal rations obtained by those high in Administration.
>
> Isaac Asimov, *The Robot Series: The Naked Sun*

Dialogue will reflect characteristics. Is it clipped? Is it highly dialectal? Does a character rely on colloquialisms (*dis me*, *bling*)? The ability to portray the speech of a character can make or break a story.

The kind of person the character is in the mind of the reader is dependent on impressions created by description and dialogue. How do other characters feel about this one as revealed by their treatment of him/her, their discussions of him/her with each other, or their overt descriptions of the character? For example, "John, of course, can't be trusted with another person's possessions." In analyzing a story, it's useful to discuss the devices used to produce character.

Skill 16.4   Apply strategies for interpreting and evaluating the motives of characters and the causes of actions.

Motivations are the reasons that cause a character to engage in a particular behavior. It may be rooted in the need to minimize physical pain and maximize pleasure; however, it also may include such specific needs as eating and resting. It also may be because of not-so-apparent reasons such as altruism, morality, or avoiding mortality. At a very basic level, it is similar to Pavlov's discoveries concerning dogs. Humans may simply repeat behaviors that have brought rewards in the past. Motivation can also be divided into those actions that bring about enjoyment and those that are engaged in because of an obligation.

A character can be presented in such a way that the causes of his behavior are obvious. On the other hand, a mystery may sometimes be solved by the revealing of a character's background. A pathological killer may sometimes be tracked down and identified by a discovery of his background—he might have been abused as a child or a person close to him might have been mistreated or killed unfairly. In CBS's television series, *Criminal Minds,* a team of experts in motivation create profiles of serial killers in order to find them and bring them to justice. When they look at who the victims are and how they were killed, they can deduce what would motivate a person to behave in that way.

Actions by a character should have some motivating circumstance or situation. If those motivations cannot be determined by the reader, then a question remains and the story may not work for that reader. The writer is obliged to write coherent characters whose behaviors are explainable by the circumstances of the characters' lives and backgrounds. Having a college professor of English speaking in colloquial, rustic dialogue, for example, will not make this character coherent unless this disconnect is explained by some circumstance or other.

Basic frame sentence for character analysis:
"Since my character is or has been _____, then he/she would act like _____."

Skill 16.5   Apply strategies for composing narrative writing that makes effective and appropriate use of various literary elements.

Many of the literary elements we associate with fiction or poetry are also useful for other kinds of writing.

Antithesis: Balanced writing about conflicting ideas, usually expressed in sentence form. Some examples are expanding from the center, shedding old habits, and searching never finding.

Aphorism: A focused, succinct expression about life from a sagacious viewpoint. Writings by Ben Franklin, Sir Francis Bacon, and Alexander Pope contain many aphorisms. "Whatever is begun in anger ends in shame" is an aphorism.

Apostrophe: Literary device of addressing an absent or dead person, an abstract idea, or an inanimate object. Sonneteers, such as Sir Thomas Wyatt, John Keats, and William Wordsworth, address the moon, stars, and the dead Milton. For example, in William Shakespeare's *Julius Caesar*, Mark Antony addresses the corpse of Caesar in the speech that begins: "O, pardon me, thou bleeding piece of earth, That I am meek and gentle with these butchers! Thou art the ruins of the noblest man That ever lived in the tide of times. Woe to the hand that shed this costly blood!"

Conceit: A comparison, usually in verse, between seemingly disparate objects or concepts. John Donne's metaphysical poetry contains many clever conceits. For instance, Donne's "The Flea" (1633) compares a flea bite to the act of love; and in "A Valediction: Forbidding Mourning" (1633) separated lovers are likened to the legs of a compass, the leg drawing the circle eventually returning home to "the fixed foot."

Connotation: The ripple effect surrounding the implications and associations of a given word, distinct from the denotative, or literal meaning. For example, the word "love" evokes a range of meanings. What those meanings are will vary from person to person. It's the effective writer who is in control of the connotations in his writing.

Consonance: The repeated usage of similar consonant sounds although most often used in poetry, many writers of narrative prose use it effectively. "Sally sat sifting seashells by the seashore" is a familiar example.

Denotation: What a word literally means, as opposed to its connotative meaning. For example, the word love means positive feelings of one person for another. However, the connotations of the word vary by context and by audience.

Diction: The right word in the right spot for the right purpose. The hallmark of a great writer is precise, unusual, and memorable diction.

Epiphany: The moment when the proverbial light bulb goes off in one's head and comprehension sets in.

Exposition: Fill-in or background information about characters meant to clarify and add to the narrative; the initial plot element which precedes the buildup of conflict.

Figurative Language: Not meant in a literal sense, but to be interpreted through symbolism. Figurative language is made up of such literary devices as hyperbole, metonymy, synecdoche, and oxymoron. A synecdoche is a figure of speech in which the word for part of something is used to mean the whole; for example, "sail" for "boat," or vice versa.

Hyperbole: Exaggeration for a specific effect. For example, "I'm so hungry that I could eat a million of these."

Inversion: A typical sentence order to create a given effect or interest. Bacon's and Milton's works use inversion successfully. Emily Dickinson was fond of arranging words outside of their familiar order. For example in "Chartless" she writes "Yet know I how the heather looks" and "Yet certain am I of the spot."

Instead of saying "Yet I know" and "Yet I am certain" she reverses the usual order and shifts the emphasis to the more important words.

Irony: An unexpected disparity between what is written or stated and what is really meant or implied by the author. Verbal, situational, and dramatic are the three literary ironies. Verbal irony is when an author says one thing and means something else. Dramatic irony is when an audience perceives something that a character in the literature does not know. Irony of situation is a discrepancy between the expected and actual results. Shakespeare's plays contain numerous and highly effective use of irony. O. Henry's short stories have ironic endings.

Kenning: An alternate way to describe a person, place, or thing so as to avoid prosaic repetition. The earliest examples can be found in Anglo-Saxon literature such as *Beowulf* and "The Seafarer." Instead of writing King Hrothgar, the anonymous monk wrote, great Ring-Giver, or Father of his people. A lake becomes the swans' way, and the ocean or sea becomes the great whale's way. In ancient Greek literature, this device was called an "epithet."

Metonymy: Use of an object or idea closely identified with another object or idea to represent the second. "Hit the books" means "go study." Washington, D.C. means the U.S. government and the White House means the U.S. President.

Motif: A key, oft-repeated phrase, name, or idea in a literary work. Dorset/Wessex in Hardy's novels and the moors and the harsh weather in the Bronte sisters' novels are effective use of motifs. Shakespeare's *Romeo and Juliet* represents the ill-fated young lovers' motif.

Onomatopoeia: Word used to evoke the sound in its meaning. The early Batman series used *pow, zap, whop, zonk* and *eek* in an onomatopoetic way.

Oxymoron: A contradictory form of speech, such as jumbo shrimp, unkindly kind, or singer John Mellencamp's "It hurts so good."

Paradox: Seemingly untrue statement, which when examined more closely proves to be true. John Donne's sonnet "Death Be Not Proud" postulates that death shall die and humans will triumph over death, at first thought not true, but ultimately explained and proven in this sonnet.

Parallelism: A type of close repetition of clauses or phrases that emphasize key topics or ideas in writing. The psalms in the King James Version of the *Bible* contain many examples.

Personification: Giving human characteristics to inanimate objects or concepts. Great writers, with few exceptions, are masters of this literary device.

Stream of Consciousness: A style of writing that reflects the mental processes of the characters, expressing, at times, jumbled memories, feelings, and dreams. "Big time players" in this type of expression are James Joyce, Virginia Woolf, and William Faulkner.

Tone: The discernible attitude inherent in an author's work regarding the subject, readership, or characters. Swift's or Pope's tone is satirical. Boswell's tone toward Johnson is admiring.

Wit: Writing of genius, keenness, and sagacity expressed through clever use of language. Alexander Pope and the Augustans wrote about and were themselves said to possess wit.

Skill 16.6 Apply strategies for writing personal notes, letters, and stories that convey a message or point of view clearly and concisely and that engage and maintain the reader's interest.

In both formal and informal writing, there exists a **tone**, the writer's attitude toward the material and/or readers. Tone may be playful, formal, intimate, angry, serious, ironic, outraged, baffled, tender, serene, depressed, and so on. The overall tone of a piece of writing is dictated by both the subject matter and the audience. Tone is also related to the actual word choices that make up the document, as we attach affective meanings to words, called their **connotations**. Gaining this conscious control over language makes it possible to use language appropriately in various situations and to evaluate its uses in literature and other forms of communication. By evoking the proper responses from readers or listeners, we can prompt them to take action.

[handwritten: What tone to take?]

Using the following questions is an excellent way to determine audience and tone in a piece of writing.

- Who is your audience (friend, teacher, businessperson, someone else)?
- How much does this person know about you and/or your topic?
- What is your purpose (to defend a point of view, to persuade, to amuse, to register a complaint, to ask for a raise, etc)?
- What emotions do you have about the topic (nervous, happy, confident, angry, sad, no feelings at all)?
- What emotions do you want to register with your audience (anger, nervousness, happiness, boredom, interest)?
- What persona do you need to create in order to achieve your purpose?
- What choice of language is best suited to achieving your purpose with your particular subject (slang, friendly but respectful, formal)?

- What emotional quality do you want to transmit to achieve your purpose (matter of fact, informative, authoritative, inquisitive, sympathetic, angry), and to what degree do you want to express this tone?

Writing for different audiences and aims enables students to be more involved in their writing. If they write for the same audience and purpose, they will continue to see writing as just another assignment.

COMPETENCY 17 PERSUASIVE WRITING

Skill 17.1   Demonstrate knowledge of forms of writing that are appropriate for influencing beliefs, arguing a point, or expressing an opinion.

News reporters often become distinguished writers because they get a lot of practice, which is a principle most writing teachers try to employ with their students. Also, news writing is instructive in skills for writing clearly and coherently. The instant feedback that comes from a news piece helps the writer make changes to achieve better understanding on the part of his readers. Reporters generally write in two modes: straight reporting and feature writing. In both modes, the writer must be concerned with accuracy and objectivity. The reporter does not write his opinions. He/she does not write persuasive discourse. The topic is typically assigned, although some experienced reporters have the opportunity to seek out and develop their own stories.

Investigative reporting is sometimes seen as a distinct class although, technically, all reporters are "investigative." That is, they research the background of the story they're reporting, using as many means as are available. For example, the wife of a conservative, model minister murders him premeditatively and in cold blood. The reporter reports the murder and the arrest of the wife, but the story is far from complete until some questions are answered, the most obvious one being "why?" The reporter is obligated to try to answer that question and to do so will interview as many people as will talk to him about the lives of both minister and wife, their parents, members of the church, their neighbors, etc. The reporter will also look at newspaper archives in the town where the murder took place as well as in newspapers in any town the husband and/or wife has lived in previously. High-school yearbooks are sources that are often explored in these cases.

When Bob Woodward and Carl Bernstein, reporters for *The Washington Post,* began to break the Watergate story in 1972 and 1973, they set new standards for investigative reporting and had a strong influence on journalistic writing. Most reporters wanted to be Woodward and Bernstein and became more aggressive than in the past. Even so, the basic techniques and principles still apply. The reporting of these two talented journalists demonstrated that while newspapers keep communities aware of what's going on, they also have the power to influence it.

A good news story is written as an "inverted pyramid." That is, the reasoning is deductive. The "thesis" or point is stated first and is supported with details. It reasons from general to specific. The lead sentence might be, "The body of John Smith was found in the street in front of his home with a bullet wound through his skull." The headline will be a trimmed-down version of that sentence and shaped to grab attention. It might read: "Murdered man found on Spruce Street." The news article might fill several columns, the first details having to do with the finding of the body, the next the role of the police; the third will spread out and include details about the victim's life, then the scope will broaden to details about his family, friends, neighbors, etc. If he held a position of prominence in the community, those details will broaden further and include information about his relationships to fellow-workers and his day-to-day contacts in the community. The successful reporter's skills include the ability to do thorough research, to maintain an objective stance (not to become involved personally in the story), and to write an effective "inverted pyramid."

Feature writing is more like an informative essay although it may also follow the inverted pyramid model. This form of reporting focuses on a topic designed to be interesting to at least one segment of the readership—possible sports enthusiasts, travelers, vacationers, families, women, food lovers, etc. The article will focus on one aspect of the area of interest such as a particular experience for the vacationing family. The first sentence might read something like this: "Lake Lure offers a close-to-home relaxing weekend getaway for families in East Tennessee." The development can be an ever-widening pyramid of details focused particularly on what the family can experience at Lake Lure but also directions for how to get there.

While the headline is intended to contain in capsule form the point that an article makes, it is rarely written by the reporter. This can sometimes result in a disconnection between headline and article. Well-written headlines will provide a guide for the reader as to what is in the article; they will also be attention-grabbers. This requires a special kind of writing, quite different from the inverted pyramid that distinguishes these writers from the investigative or feature reporter.

Business Letters

It may seem sometimes that the **business letter** is a thing of the past. Although much business-letter writing has been relegated to e-mail communications, letters are still a potentially valuable form of communication. A carefully-written letter can be powerful. It can alienate, convince, persuade, entice, motivate, and/or create good-will.

As with any other communication, it's worthwhile to learn as much as possible about the receiver. This may be complicated if there will be more than one receiver of the message; in these cases, it's best to aim for the lowest common denominator if that can be achieved without "writing down" to any of those who will read and be affected or influenced by the letter. It may be better to send more than one form of the letter to the various receivers in some cases.

Purpose is the most powerful factor in writing a business letter. What is the letter expected to accomplish? Is it intended to get the receiver to act or to act in a specific manner? Are you hoping to see some action take place as the result of the letter? If so, you should clearly define for yourself what the purpose is before you craft the letter, and it's good to include a time deadline for the response.

Reasons for choosing the letter as the channel of communication include the following:
1. It's easy to keep a record of the transaction.
2. The message can be edited and perfected before it is transmitted.
3. It facilitates the handling of details.
4. It's ideal for communicating complex information.
5. It's a good way to disseminate mass messages at a relatively low cost.

The parts of a business letter are as follow: date line, inside address, salutation, subject line*, body, complimentary close, company name*, signature block, reference initials*, enclosure notation*, copy notation*, and postscript*.

*not required but sometimes useful.

Business letters typically use formal language. They should be straightforward and courteous. The writing should be concise, and special care should be taken to leave no important information out. Clarity is very important; otherwise, it may take more than one exchange of letters or phone calls to get the message across.

A complaint is a different kind of business letter. It can come under the classification of a "bad news" business letter, and there are some guidelines that are helpful when writing this kind of letter. A positive writing style can overcome much of the inherent negativity of a letter of complaint. No matter how much in the right you may be, maintaining self-control and courtesy and avoiding demeaning or blaming language is more likely to be effective. Abruptness, condescension, or harshness of tone will not help achieve your purpose, particularly if you are requesting a positive response such as reimbursement for a bad product or some help in righting a wrong that may have been done to you. It's important to remember that you want to solve the specific problem and to retain the good will of the receiver if possible.

Induction is better than deduction for this type of communication. Beginning with the details and building to the statement of the problem generally has the effect of softening the bad news. It's also useful to begin with an opening that will serve as a buffer. The same is true for the closing. It's good to leave the reader with a favorable impression by writing a closing paragraph that will generate good will rather than bad.

A formal essay, on the other hand, may be persuasive, informative, descriptive, or narrative in nature. The purpose should be clearly defined, and development must be coherent and easy to follow.

E-mail has revolutionized business communications. It has most of the advantages of business letters and the added ones of immediacy, lower costs, and convenience. Even very long reports can be attached to an email. On the other hand, a two-line message can be sent and a response received immediately bringing together the features of a postal system and the telephone. Instant messaging goes even one step further. It can do all of the above—send messages, attach reports, etc.—and still have many of the advantages of a telephone conversation. E-mail has an unwritten code of behavior that includes restrictions on how informal the writing can be. The level of accepted business conversation is usually also acceptable in e-mails. Capital letters and bolding are considered shouting and are usually frowned on.

Skill 17.2   Demonstrate the ability to assess the interests and knowledge of the intended audience for persuasive writing.

Tailoring language for a particular **audience** is an important skill. Writing to be read by a business associate will surely sound different from writing to be read by a younger sibling. Not only are the vocabularies different, but the formality or informality of the discourse will need to be adjusted.

Two characteristics that determine language style are **degree of formality** and **word choice**. The most formal language does not use contractions or slang while the most informal language will probably feature a more casual use of common sayings and anecdotes. Formal language will use longer sentences and will not sound like a conversation. The most informal language will use shorter sentences (not necessarily simple sentences—but shorter constructions) and may sound like a conversation.

In both formal and informal writing, there exists a **tone**, the writer's attitude toward the material and/or readers. Tone may be playful, formal, intimate, angry, serious, ironic, outraged, baffled, tender, serene, depressed, and so on. The overall tone of a piece of writing is dictated by both the subject matter and the audience. Tone is also related to the actual word choices that make up the document, as we attach affective meanings to words, called their **connotations**.

Gaining this conscious control over language makes it possible to use language appropriately in various situations and to evaluate its uses in literature and other forms of communication. By evoking the proper responses from readers or listeners, we can prompt them to take action.

Using the following questions is an excellent way to assess the audience and tone of a given piece of writing.

- Who is your audience (friend, teacher, businessperson, someone else)?
- How much does this person know about you and/or your topic?
- What is your purpose (to prove an argument, to persuade, to amuse, to register a complaint, to ask for a raise, etc)?
- What emotions do you have about the topic (nervous, happy, confident, angry, sad, no feelings at all)?
- What emotions do you want to register with your audience (anger, nervousness, happiness, boredom, interest)?
- What persona do you need to create in order to achieve your purpose?
- What choice of language is best suited to achieving your purpose with your particular subject (slang, friendly but respectful, formal)?
- What emotional quality do you want to transmit to achieve your purpose (matter of fact, informative, authoritative, inquisitive, sympathetic, angry), and to what degree do you want to express this tone?

In the past, teachers have assigned reports, paragraphs, and essays that focused on the teacher as the audience with the purpose of explaining information. However, for students to be meaningfully engaged in their writing, they must write for a variety of reasons. Writing for different audiences and aims enables students to be more involved in their writing. If they write for the same audience and purpose, they will continue to see writing as just another assignment. Listed below are suggestions that give students an opportunity to write in more creative and critical ways.

- Write letters to the editor, to a college, to a friend, to another student that would actually be sent to the intended audience.
- Write stories that would be read aloud to a group (the class, another group of students, to a group of elementary school students) or published in a literary magazine or class anthology.
- Write plays that would be performed.
- Have students discuss the parallels between the different speech styles we use and writing styles for different readers or audiences.
- Allow students to write a particular piece for various audiences.

As part of the prewriting exercises, have students identify the audience. Expose students to writing that is on the same topic but with a different audience and have them identify the variations in sentence structure and style. Remind your students that it is not necessary to identify all the specifics of the audience in the initial stage of the writing process but that at some point they must make some determinations about audience.

Guidelines for Assessing your Audience

Now that you know your purpose and have the information, you need to assess your audience. What does your audience know and what does it need to know? Here are some questions to consider.

Values: What is important to this group of people? What is their background and how will that affect their perception of your speech?

Needs: Find out in advance what the audience's needs are. Why are they listening to you? Find a way to satisfy their needs.

Constraints: What might hold the audience back from being fully engaged in what you are saying, or agreeing with your point of view, or processing what you are trying to say? These could be political reasons, which make them wary of your presentation's ideology from the start, or knowledge reasons, in which the audience lacks the appropriate background information to grasp your ideas. Avoid this last constraint by staying away from technical terminology, slang, or abbreviations that may be unclear to your audience.

Demographic Information: Take the audience's size into account as well as the location of the presentation. Demographics could include age, gender, education, religion, income level, and other such countable characteristics.

Skill 17.3	Demonstrate the ability to establish a clear position or controlling idea.

Once a topic is assigned or chosen, the next step is to begin to gather supporting materials. Those materials may come from the writer's own experience, and the best way to collect them is in prewriting—simply putting on paper whatever is there by way of past experience relevant to the topic; observations concerning it; newspaper articles or books that have been read on the topic; and television or radio presentations that have to do with the topic. The writer needs to keep in mind the need to make a statement about the topic—to declare something about it. Very often, once the writer has gone through this exercise, getting his/her own ideas and thoughts down on paper, a thesis or several theses may emerge. If not, then it is time to do active research on the topic.

It's better to write more than one thesis statement before research begins if possible. However, a successful writer will set a point when a single one must be chosen so the development of the paper may proceed. Once that decision has been made, the narrowing process begins. The writer should be asking such questions as "Is the scope too broad to cover in a 500-word paper?" For example, if the thesis statement is "Democracy is the best form of government," it will take a book or even several books to develop. However, if the thesis statement is "Democracy is the best form of government for Iraq," then it begins to become more doable. Even so, some narrowing of the predicate may still be in order. "The development of a democratic government will solve the problems of cultural and religious divisions in Iraq" may be a thesis that could be developed in one classroom assignment.

Skill 17.4   Demonstrate the ability to present an argument logically through the use of meaningful examples or details, sound reasoning, and effective transitions.

Once a thesis is put forth, there are various ways to support it. The most obvious one is reasons. Usually a reason will answer the question why. Another technique is to give examples. A third is to give details.

The presentation of a prosecutor in a court trial is a good example of an argument that uses all of these.

The **thesis** of the prosecutor may be: John O'Hara stole construction materials from a house being built at 223 Hudson Ave. by the Jones Construction Company. As a **reason**, he might cite the following: He is building his own home on Green Street and needs materials and tools. This will answer the question why. He might give **examples**: 20 bags of concrete disappeared the night before Mr. O'Hara poured the basement for his house on Green Street. The electronic nail-setter disappeared from the building site on Hudson Ave. the day before Mr. O'Hara began to erect the frame of his house on Green Street. He might fill in the **details**: Mr. O'Hara's truck was observed by a witness on Hudson Ave. in the vicinity of the Jones Construction Company site the night the concrete disappeared. Mr. O'Hara's truck was observed again on that street by a witness the night the nail-setter disappeared.

Another example of a trial might be: **Thesis,** Adam Andrews murdered Joan Rogers in cold blood on the night of December 20. **Reason #1**: She was about to reveal their affair to his wife. **Reason #2**: Andrews' wife would inherit half of his sizeable estate in case of a divorce since there is no prenuptial agreement. **Example #1**: Rogers has demonstrated that he is capable of violence in an incident with a partner in his firm. **Example #2**: Rogers has had previous affairs where he was accused of violence. **Detail #1**: Andrews' wife once called the police and signed a warrant. **Detail #2**: A previous lover sought police protection from Andrews.

An opinion is a thesis and requires support. It can also use reasons, examples, and details.

For example:

Opinion: Our borders must be protected.

Reason #1: Terrorists can get into the country undetected. **Example #1**: An Iranian national was able to cross the Mexican border and live in this country for years before being detected. **Detail**: The Iranian national came up through Central America to Mexico then followed the route that Mexican illegal immigrants regularly took. **Example #2**: a group of Middle Eastern terrorists were arrested in Oregon after they had crossed the Canadian border. **Detail**: There was no screening at that border.

Reason #2: Illegal aliens are an enormous drain on resources such as health care. **Example**: The states of California and Texas bear enormous burdens for health care and education for illegal immigrants. **Detail**: Legal citizens are often denied care in those states because resources are stretched so thin.

Using Transition

A mark of maturity in writing is the effective use of transitional devices at all levels. For example, a topic sentence can be used to establish continuity, especially if it is positioned at the beginning of a paragraph. The most common use would be to refer to what has preceded, repeat it, or summarize it and then go on to introduce a new topic. An essay by W. H. Hudson uses this device: "Although the potato was very much to me in those early years, it grew to be more when I heard its history." It summarizes what has preceded, makes a comment on the author's interest, and introduces a new topic: the history of the potato.

Another example of a transitional sentence could be, "Not all matters end so happily." This refers to the previous information and prepares for the next paragraph, which will be about matters that do not end happily. This transitional sentence is a little more forthright: "The increase in drug use in our community leads us to another general question."

Another fairly simple and straightforward transitional device is the use of numbers or their approximation: "First, I want to talk about the dangers of immigration; second, I will discuss the enormity of the problem; third, I will propose a reasonable solution."

An entire paragraph may be transitional in purpose and form. In "Darwiniana," Thomas Huxley used a transitional paragraph:

So much, then, by way of proof that the method of establishing laws in science is exactly the same as that pursued in common life. Let us now turn to another matter (though really it is but another phase of the same question), and that is, the method by which, from the relations of certain phenomena, we prove that some stand in the position of causes toward the others.

The most common transitional device is a single word. Some examples: *and, furthermore, next, moreover, in addition, again, also, likewise, similarly, finally, second*. There are many, but they should be used correctly and judiciously. In marking student papers, a teacher can encourage a student to think in terms of moving coherently from one idea to the next by making transitions between the two. If the shift from one thought to another is too abrupt, the student can be asked to provide a transitional paragraph. Provide lists of possible transitions and encourage students to have the list at hand when composing essays. These are good tools for nudging students to more mature writing styles.

Skill 17.5   Demonstrate the ability to present an argument through the use of rhetorical appeals.

Types of Appeal

- Ethos—Refers to the credibility of the writer or speaker. It utilizes the credentials of the speaker as a reliable and trustworthy authority. The education of the speaker/writer on a particular topic enhances his ethical appeal. The audience is much more likely to believe and accept a speaker or writer who is a Ph.D. in meteorology with regards to the topic of climate change than they will a speaker or writer who has no education on the topic. Experience also enhances a writer's/speaker's ethical appeal. Experience working with people in developing countries on the use of resources is more likely to be accepted with regard to foreign affairs than one who has never been out of his/her own country.
- Pathos—Refers to the emotional appeal made by the speaker to the listeners. It emphasizes the fact that the audience responds to ideas with emotion. For example, when the government is trying to persuade citizens to go to war for the sake of "the fatherland," it is using the appeal to *pathos* to target their love of their country. Rarely are minds changed or people moved to action regarding a topic unless they are touched emotionally.
- Logos—Refers to the logic of the speaker's argument. It utilizes the idea that facts, statistics, and other forms of evidence can convince an audience to accept a speaker's argument. Remember that information can be just as persuasive as appeal tactics. Even though a person may be persuaded logically, it is unlikely that he/she will experience a change of mind or be moved to act without being touched emotionally. A good argument will include all three of the appeals. The Greek Rhetoricians put it this way: "a good man with a good message." *Good men speaking well*

Skill 17.6   Demonstrate the ability to select relevant, complete, and accurate information or evidence from primary and secondary sources that can be used to support points expressed in persuasive writing.

Before accepting as gospel anything that is printed in a newspaper or advertising or presented on radio, television, or the Internet, it is wise to first of all consider the source. Even though news reporters and editors claim to be unbiased in the presentation of news, they usually take an editorial point of view. A newspaper may avow that it is Republican or conservative and may even make recommendations at election time, but it will still claim to present the *news* without bias. Sometimes this is true, and sometimes it is not. For example, Fox News declares itself to be conservative and to support the Republican Party. Its presentation of news often reveals that bias. When Vice President Cheney made a statement about his shooting of a friend in a duck-hunting accident, it was only made available to Fox News. Fox News' motto is "fair and balanced coverage."

On the other hand, CBS has tended to favor more liberal politicians although it avows that it is even-handed in its coverage. Dan Rather presented a story critical of President Bush's military service that was based on a document that could not be validated. His failure to play by the rules of certification of evidence cost him his job and his career. Even with authentication, such a story would not have gotten past the editors of a conservative-leaning news system.

Even politicians usually play by the rules of fairness in the choices they make about going public. They usually try to be even-handed. However, some channels and networks will show deference to one politician over another.

Advertising, whether in print or electronic media is another thing. Will using a certain tooth paste improve a person's love life? Is a dish better than cable? The best recourse a reader/viewer has is to ask around and find someone who has experience that is relevant or conduct research and conduct interviews of users of both.

The same rules apply when tapping into a primary source, such as a person who has experienced some aspect of the topic you're writing about. Questions need to be asked about that person's bias or lack of it when quoting him. Refer to Skill 3.6 for more information on primary and secondary sources.

Skill 17.7   Demonstrate the ability to anticipate questions, concerns, and counterarguments for points expressed in persuasive writing and to incorporate effective responses to them into the writing.

Sometimes the best argument is to explain away the opposing view. A good argument will acknowledge that there are two sides to the issue being proposed. If the thesis is: A fence should be built along the border of the US with Mexico, then dealing with the opposition is important because there are so many people who reject that thesis and because there are so many very strong arguments against it. This is not to say that answering the opposition will be adequate to persuade on its own. The thesis must be adequately supported to gain acceptance without the answer to the opposing point of view.

In dealing with the opposing view in persuasive discourse, the same techniques used in arguing the thesis should be employed. It's wise to gain reader buy-in by granting that the opposing point of view has validity. However, a good strong refutation of the opposing point of view is necessary if the reader is to be persuaded

COMPETENCY 18   LISTENING AND SPEAKING.

Skill 18.1   Identify the characteristics and purposes of various types of listening, including critical, empathic, reflective, and deliberative.

Critical Listening: Especially during a political campaign, most of us listen in this way. We want to know what each candidate has to say, and we want to weed out reliable information from the information we cannot accept as valid. Ultimately, we make our own choices about which candidate will best serve our communities using this kind of listening. Usually, if a candidate resorts to *ad hominem*, an attack on the person rather than the issues, it's because that candidate knows he is weak on the issues. It's helpful to know what the standard fallacies are in order to recognize them when the speaker tries to use means to persuade us that are not reasonable or logical.

Empathic and Reflective Listening. We often practice this in conversations, especially with friends and family. We want the speaker to know that we care about what they are saying. The very act of careful and empathic listening generates good feelings toward us and builds stronger friendships. The person who does not listen in this way often has few real friends. This kind of listening plays an important role when a tragedy happens to a family member or friend. They have a strong need to pour out their feelings at this time, and a good friend listens empathically and reflectively.

Deliberative Listening. We listen to our teachers and professors carefully for the purpose of getting the information we need to pass a test. We go to public presentations about taxes for the same reason. The speaker has information we need.

Look at Skills 4.3 and 4.6 for more information on fallacies in reasoning.

Skill 18.2   Demonstrate knowledge of the barriers to listening effectively, including selective listening.

If we listen to a speaker on a topic we already know quite a bit about and already have our minds made up about, we often tune him out. If a speaker spikes up his speech with interesting anecdotes, we may tune him out when he is talking about serious matters, even if it's information that might be useful. Even if the speaker has a different take on a topic than the listener, that listener can still benefit from hearing what the speaker has to say. Unfortunately, students often practice this kind of listening. As long as the information entertains them or is about something important to them, they listen. When the information gets into information that not only doesn't entertain but that has little to do with their own interests, their minds move on to other things.

Skill 18.3   Apply strategies for listening actively.

Letting the speaker know that you are listening and appreciate what he has to say is a good way to grasp more of what is said. It is also empathic in that it makes the going easier for the speaker. A good way to respond to a speaker is to ask questions to clarify what he has said. It's also helpful to restate or summarize what the speaker has said. This will not only help the listener but also others who might be in the audience, whether the occasion is a conversation or a formal speaking occasion. It's also useful to build on what the speaker says by asking questions, carrying the line of thinking one step further, or by reflecting or coming up with examples that demonstrate the point or points made by the speaker.

Skill 18.4   Distinguish among types of speech delivery that are appropriate for various purposes, content, audiences, and occasions.

It's a foolish person who does not prepare before he makes a formal presentation. If one has been asked to speak at an occasion, then much thought should go into how that speech may be delivered. It's entirely possible to speak from a manuscript; in other words, the speaker writes out every word of the speech and stands up and delivers it with emotion. Just reading as if one were reading a book is a mistake. Very often speeches delivered from a manuscript do move audiences, but only if they are delivered effectively. A sermon is a good example of such delivery.

On the other hand, if the speaker is very knowledgeable about the subject, he may be able to deliver a well-organized speech extemporaneously. He has the material well in hand, and it's just a matter of making a quick decision about how to organize it for delivery. In this case, the speaker may want to allow plenty of time for questions from the audience.

Some speakers memorize their speeches. If they are able to deliver a memorized speech with feeling and with pauses and inflections to keep it from seeming memorized, this can work very well.

Most speakers work from an outline. They may write out the speech ahead of time and get to know the sub-points well and then speak from the outline. This is probably the most common mode of delivery. A PowerPoint presentation that projects the outline on a screen is very helpful for a speaker if he/she feels insecure about staying on topic or remembering the points he/she wants to make.

Skill 18.5 Distinguish among styles of language that are appropriate for various purposes, content, audiences, and occasions.

Successful speakers/listeners make it a point to be aware of the context of their spoken exchanges. They think in terms of vocabulary. When are swear words appropriate? Very often, with peers and contemporaries, one is considered a fuddy-duddy if he or she does not pepper the conversation with swear words within certain parameters according to the particular group. A good conversationalist is sensitive to those nuances. In some social situations, swear words are not acceptable at all, and the one who uses them will not be well-received or, at best, will make some people uncomfortable. On the other hand, in some groups, there is gender discrimination in this matter. It's O.K. for males to swear but not females. Even if one disapproves of that discrimination, to be an accepted member of the group may require that the disapproval be kept to oneself. If one does not swear at all and is made uncomfortable by swear words, this may not be the best choice of a group to join.

The second aspect of speech successful speakers/listeners consider is syntax. Is it appropriate in conversation to speak in long, complicated sentences? Or is it better to save that sort of language for a speech or even a written communication? The person who speaks in long convoluted sentences, particularly if that person tends to hold the floor for longer periods of time than others, is often avoided and may not be invited back. However, if the speaker is making a presentation, the rules will certainly change. Speaking primarily in simple sentences is boring and annoying. Being aware of the syntactical possibilities can make the difference between an effective communicator and one who is not so well received.

Certainly, paragraph level—that level when a thought is announced and developed—needs to be scrutinized and thought about. For example, a person might say at a cocktail party, "I saw *A Prairie Home Companion* last night, and it was great!" The person might go on to speak a paragraph based on that topic sentence with subtopics about why it was so great and filling in the details, possibly even recounting one of the jokes delivered by an actor. Others will listen and ask questions, and dialogue will occur. On the other hand, if a person develops an idea that is not particularly exciting or interesting, conversation tends to die.

A job interview is a different situation. It's assumed that the applicant will be on his/her best behavior, but it's a good thing to prepare for the interview by researching the information that might be useful about the company and about the job and have control of that information. It's also good to think about what he/she will present in terms of background, interest in the particular position, desire to be successful as an employee of the company, etc. But the applicant should also give some thought to what language conventions will be appropriate in this situation. How formal should the language be? How can a mix of formal/not-so-formal be developed to polish the applicant's image but also to indicate flexibility and friendliness?

As a general rule, swear words are not well-received in the workplace. However, they are common in some environments. It's usually a good rule-of-thumb to avoid swear words there. If the workplace is an office, the level of speech will usually be a mix of formal/informal.

Formal language can be defined as that which uses no contractions, has an elevated vocabulary, and avoids slang or swear words. Informal language uses contractions, usually words of no more than three syllables, and may or may not use swear words.

Skill 18.6   Demonstrate knowledge of rhetorical strategies used to enhance clarity and generate interest in speeches.

The content in material to be presented orally plays a big role in how it is organized and delivered. For example, a literary analysis or a book report will be organized inductively, laying out the details and then presenting a conclusion, which will usually be what the author's purpose, message, and intent are. If the analysis is focusing on multiple layers in a story, that will probably follow the preliminary conclusion. On the other hand, keeping in mind that the speaker will want to keep the audience's attention, if the content has to do with difficult-to-follow facts and statistics, slides (or PowerPoint) may be used as a guide to the presentation, and the speaker will intersperse interesting anecdotes, jokes, or humor from time to time so the listeners don't fall asleep.

It's also important to take the consistency of the audience into account when organizing a presentation. If the audience can be counted on to have a high level of interest in what is being presented, little would need to be done in the way of organizing and presenting to hold interest. On the other hand, if many of those in the audience are there because they have to be, or if the level of interest can be counted on not to be very high, something like a PowerPoint presentation can be very helpful. Also the lead-in and introduction need to be structured not only to be entertaining and interest-grabbing, they should also create an interest in the topic. If the audience is senior citizens, it's important to keep the presentation lively and to be careful not to "speak down" to them. Carefully-written introductions aimed specifically at this audience will go a long way to attract their interest in the topic.

No speaker should stand up to make a presentation if the purpose has not been carefully determined ahead of time. If the speaker is not focused on the purpose, the audience will quickly lose interest. As to organizing for a particular purpose, some of the decisions to be made are where it will occur in the presentation— beginning, middle, or end—and whether displaying the purpose on a chart, PowerPoint, or banner will enhance the presentation. The purpose might be the lead-in for a presentation if it can be counted on to grab the interest of the listeners, in which case, the organization will be deductive. If it seems better to save the purpose until the end, the organization, of course, will be inductive.

The occasion, of course, plays an important role in the development and delivery of a presentation. A celebration speech when the company has achieved an important accomplishment will be organized around congratulating those who were most responsible for the accomplishment and giving some details about how it was achieved and probably something about the competition for the achievement. The presentation will be upbeat and not too long. On the other hand, if bad news is being presented, it will probably be the CEO who is making the presentation and the bad-news announcement will come first followed with details about the news itself and how it came about, and probably end with a pep talk and encouragement to do better the next time.

Skill 18.7   Recognize the different roles that voice and body language play in speech delivery.

Voice: Many people fall into one of two traps when speaking: using a monotone or talking too fast. These are both caused by anxiety. A monotone restricts your natural inflection but can be remedied by releasing tension in upper

> Learn more about
> **Using Your Voice**
> http://www.longview.k12.wa.us/mmhs
> /wyatt/pathway/voice.html

and lower body muscles. Subtle movement will keep you loose and natural.

Talking too fast, on the other hand, is not necessarily bad if you are exceptionally articulate. If you are not a strong speaker or if you are talking about very technical items, the audience will easily become lost.

When you talk too fast and begin tripping over your words, consciously pause after every sentence you say. Don't be afraid of brief silences. The audience needs time to absorb what you are saying.

Volume: Problems with volume, whether too soft or too loud, can usually be overcome with practice. If you tend to speak too softly, have someone stand in the back of the room and signal you when your volume is strong enough. If possible, have someone in the front of the room as well to make sure you're not overcompensating with excessive volume. If you plan to use a microphone, be sure to test it beforehand.

Conversely, if you have a problem with speaking too loud, have the person in the front of the room signal you when your voice is soft enough and check with the person in the back to make sure it is still loud enough to be heard. In both cases, note your volume level for future reference. Don't be shy about asking your audience, "Can you hear me in the back?" Suitable volume is beneficial for both you and the audience.

Pitch: Pitch refers to the length, tension, and thickness of your vocal bands. As your voice gets higher, the pitch gets higher. In oral performance, pitch reflects the emotional arousal level. More variation in pitch typically corresponds to more emotional arousal but can also be used to convey sarcasm or highlight specific words.

While these skills are essential for you to be an effective teacher, you want your students to develop these techniques as well. By encouraging the development of proper techniques for oral presentations, you are enabling your students to develop self-confidence for higher levels of communication.

Physicality on the part of a speaker calls for embodiment of the emotion of the words into the speaking. This can drastically alter the perception of the audience.

Take a look at the phrase, "No, I don't mind waiting." Said while leaning back in a chair with a casual wave of the hand, the speaker comes off as easygoing and calm. On the other hand, if the speaker is tapping her foot and constantly checking her watch, the message is very different. Simple gestures, from the raise of an eyebrow to a jump in the air, indicate the speaker's state of mind, supplementing vocal tone and inflection.

The best advice for a speaker regarding body language is to relax. It's best to have both feet on the floor and flat because it will contribute to conveying confidence. Using the hands for gestures works well for some people; for some, it seems stilted and distracting. Walking around also works well for some, but more often than not, it's distracting. Leaning on the podium can reinforce a relaxed attitude but it should be used with care.

It's good for a speaker to have himself or herself videotaped while giving a speech. This can be used to make adjustments to body language that will improve the effectiveness of his or her speech-making.

COMPETENCY 19 PRESENTATIONS.

Skill 19.1   Recognize methods of establishing clear objectives for a presentation.

Objective has been defined as what you want to happen as a result of an action, in this case, a presentation. Do you want your listeners' minds to be changed? Do you want them to accept a new point of view? Or do you want them to go out and take action? If so, you will need to establish a thesis along those lines. You will want to use persuasive discourse and the methods of appealing to an audience to achieve your objectives. For example, it would be a good idea to establish your own credibility. Do you have credentials that would lead your listeners to accept what you have to say on this topic? Make certain the person who introduces tells them what those credentials are. Make certain that your delivery is logical. People don't want to admit that they've been persuaded by something that doesn't make sense. On the other hand, you'll want to include some emotional appeal—an example that will move them to sympathy, for instance—because even though listeners may accept your reasoning, they probably won't make a change unless they've been moved emotionally.

On the other hand, if you only want them to have new information on a topic, that's another thing entirely. If you decide on this objective, you will want to organize your information very clearly and use liberal examples. You might even want to send something home with them, such as a handout. Using devices such as comparison/contrast, definition, or analysis of a process generally work well with this kind of presentation.

Skill 19.2   Recognize methods of organizing a presentation to achieve objectives and meet an audience's needs and expectations.

If you've done the things recommended above to organize your presentation so it will achieve your objectives, then it's time to take your audience into account. What are they expecting from you? It's important that you try to meet those expectations. Barack Obama recognizes that expectations are high for him when he stands up to speak. While his agenda has a more serious purpose than satisfying an audience, he still will take into account what they are expecting and will meet them as well as he can within the boundaries of the decisions he's making for the country. This is a good example for speakers. Trying to surmise what your audience's expectations are is valuable. If you can meet them without compromising your objectives, then your speech will be more successful.

Skill 19.3   Recognize methods of modifying a presentation to better correspond to the specific characteristics of various audiences.

The more information a speaker has about an audience, the more likely he/she is to communicate effectively with them. Several factors figure into the speaker/audience equation: age, ethnic background, educational level, knowledge of the subject, and interest in the subject.

Speaking about computers to senior citizens who have, at best, rudimentary knowledge about the way computers work must take that into account. Perhaps handing out a glossary would be useful for this audience. Speaking to first-graders about computers presents its own challenges. On the other hand, the average high-school student has more experience with computers than most adults and that should be taken into account. Speaking to a room full of computer systems engineers requires a rather thorough understanding of the jargon related to the field.

In considering the age of the audience, it's best not to make assumptions. The gathering of senior citizens might include retired systems engineers or people who have made their livings using computers, so research about the audience is important. It might not be wise to assume that high-school students have a certain level of understanding, either.

With an audience that is primarily Hispanic with varying levels of competence in English, the speaker is obligated to adjust the presentation to fit that audience. The same would be true when the audience is composed of people who may have been in the country for a long time but whose families speak their first language at home. Black English presents its own peculiarities, and if the audience is composed primarily of African-Americans whose contacts in the larger community are not great, some efforts need to be made to acquaint oneself with the specific peculiarities of the community those listeners come from.

It's unwise to "speak down" to an audience; they will almost certainly be insulted. On the other hand, speaking to an audience of college graduates will require different skills than speaking to an audience of people who have never attended college.

Finally, has the audience come because of an interest in the topic or because they have been influenced or forced to come to the presentation? If the audience comes with an interest in the subject already, efforts to motivate or draw them into the discussion might not be needed. On the other hand, if the speaker knows the audience does not have a high level of interest in the topic, it would be wise to use devices to draw them into it, to motivate them to listen.

Skill 19.4   Recognize methods of incorporating appropriate and effective visual aids into a presentation to reinforce a message, clarify a point, or create excitement and interest.

PowerPoint, a Microsoft program that comes with the various forms of Office, seems to have taken over the presentation field. In the past, slide projectors or overhead projectors were the audiovisual aids of choice in the classroom.

With PowerPoint, you can project your outline on a screen and fill in the development orally. You can also project pictures, diagrams, and graphs to help clarify your points. There are built in action devices so you can have your text or pictures zoom onto the screen or fade away with many variations in between. You can even play a video through a projector that will take PowerPoint, so you can enliven your classroom with a great deal of variety that was not possible a few years ago. What makes PowerPoint especially useful is that, while you can buy canned presentations, you can also easily create your own and individualize your presentation to your own class.

Posters and write-on pads on easels with parts of the presentation already there are another audiovisual aid that can greatly enhance a presentation. Interactive presentations where listeners will be responding and participating in the discussions are enhanced with these tools. Classes often enjoy brainstorming activities and can come to respect their own ability to make valuable and valued contributions.

Skill 19.5   Demonstrate knowledge of appropriate technologies and media to produce various types of communications and to convey specific messages.

The video camera has reached the level of common use nowadays. An assignment where students produce a video as a team is a good learning experience for all ages. They will need some guidance, of course, in planning their project and will probably need some supervision. Even so, it's a useful experience for learning the power of communication. If the project turns out to your satisfaction, the video might be taken to groups in the community for presentation, such as the Rotary Club.

See the information on PowerPoint above in Skill 19.4. Students may also prepare and present their own PowerPoint presentations with a little training and very little supervision. They might tell one of the stories in their books with pictures and words in a PowerPoint presentation. They can either take pictures with their digital cameras (the quality of images from cell phones has limitations) or scan pictures either from the book where the story appears or from other sources.

COMPETENCY 20 USING VISUAL IMAGES IN VARIOUS MEDIA

Skill 20.1   Recognize messages, meanings, and themes conveyed through various visual images in various media.

Refer to Skill 3.9 for a thorough coverage of interpreting graphics used in text.

Choice of Medium

The choices have multiplied in the past thirty or forty years. How much more impact can your message have if it pops up on a cell phone than if it appears in a newspaper? This is the crux of the choice.

Unfortunately, the medium of print is in decline. Many major newspapers have gone out of business, and it's predicted that many more are teetering. However, there are still examples of print media where the market is lively and a good buy for the advertiser. For example, in smaller towns, it's the only news in town. If you want to sell something, invite someone to an event, or make a splash in the news, you must use the newspaper. If that paper only comes out once a week, you probably get more saturation and more return simply because the readership is more likely to read every word and to rely on the paper for whatever information they want and get.

The biggest problem with advertising on television is the cost. Also, it's a little like a gun that shoots buckshot. You will be hitting a lot of people who are not good prospects. A middle-of-the-road way to go is to buy cable time. It costs less, and if your ad is an effective one although it may cost quite a bit of money to produce, and you choose your time and location wisely, this is a good buy for many advertisers.

E-mail advertising has become big business. This is a situation where you obtain e-mail addresses of people who might have an interest in what you are selling and send them a marketing e-mail. There are many companies who are making a lot of money offering e-mail addresses of people who are interested in a particular kind of product. These companies are able to do this by using spy software to determine what a person buys on the internet. Many Internet users resent this, so these unwelcome contacts often do more harm than good. Besides, people receive so many of them that they automatically delete them or set up their systems so that they are screened out and never reach them.. In addition, especially recently, word has gotten out that scams are being run this way, so e-mail users have become cautious about opening e-mails from anyone they don't know.

Another way being used for marketing by some companies is to buy the right to pop-up their information on another site. This is how some people are able to finance their site. There are several versions of this method, for example, the pop-under—you close out the site you are looking at and the advertiser's message is there waiting for you to read. Gaining marketing advantage via the Internet is a growing area and the means to use it expand all the time.

Skill 20.2   Recognize how certain media combinations are used to emphasize and reinforce messages, meanings, and themes.

If a newspaper item does not have an accompanying photo, it is more likely to be overlooked. We are conditioned to accept that any news item that is at all valuable to the readers is going to have a photo with it. Often, the photo with its caption tells its story, and the story itself may go unread. It's certainly true in the newspaper world that a picture is worth a thousand words. It's the job of the newspaper to report on serious car crashes, but the story has limited effect unless there's a photo of the vehicles and possibly an ambulance loading victims.

Many popular magazines such as *Time* continue to succeed and have subscribers because they usually include visuals that no one else has been able to get. Seeing the visual adds meaning to the coverage and is important to readers. *Life* magazine made its long-running success by the photos and pictures it ran. That magazine had on its staff some of the most noted and renowned photographers in the world. Today, old issues of *Life* sell for a lot of money because of the photos.

Music is so much a part of the television shows we view that we tend to forget it exists. However, the very shows that entertain us the most would become boring pretty quickly without the music scores that build on excitement and underscore joy when the characters are experiencing the happiness that comes from happy outcomes or relationships. In fact, the music of movies and television shows has taken on a life of its own. The musicians who write and play the music on the most popular movies and TV series have very successful careers as a result of those shows.

Skill 20.3   Analyze how the elements of visual images are manipulated to convey particular messages, meanings, and themes.

Surely anyone who lives in the United States can tell you what Coca Cola's color is. That company spends millions on getting its red images into American homes every year, especially at the Super Bowl. Branding with color may be the first element that a marketing agency will recommend for an advertising/marketing campaign. What is John Deere's color? Green, of course.

Branding with a logo is probably next on the list. A distinctive logo that also suggests the company's strength or may echo its name is very useful for capturing viewers. A good example is John Deere's deer. Type is another element that is used effectively to communicate certain messages. The next time you see a Coca Cola ad, look at the type font. Why does Coke choose that particular semi-script type?

Holiday Inn hotels have been around for a long time, and the type announcing their offerings has remained the same. Not long ago, the company changed the type. Just look at a Holiday Inn's name on the side of the hotel. For people who have been aware of Holiday Inn hotels for a long time—most adults, in fact, the new logo is a little jarring and disorienting.

How to place the elements on a page or on a billboard are also important decisions to be made by the marketer. More often than not, a graphics designer, an artist, composes logos, ads, and commercials. There are certain guidelines this graphics designer will follow when creating a logo or an ad. Graphic designers work with colors, lines, shapes, space, fonts, and textures. The guidelines include such things as don't make all the elements the same size and don't put an important message at the bottom, etc.

Coca Cola's message is and has always been, "We're the best," and for the most part, they've dominated the market. They invite comparison with Pepsi particularly, which has at times been Coke's most successful competitor. They also want their ads to appeal to the viewer's thirst, so they are designed to look wet, cold, and inviting. "Just go out and buy one now," is what they're saying.

Another successful advertiser is Target. Their bull's eye is quickly recognized and their color (again, red) catches attention. Target's television commercials don't announce who the advertiser is until the very end. However, if you look closely, you'll see various arrangements of circles that suggest that bull's eye. There is a sort of resolution that comes at the end of the commercial when the circle is now the trademark bull's eye. The message Target wants to get out is that they provide quality goods for less, thus the bull's eye. "We are on target," they announce.

Skill 20.4 Analyze how visual images are used to change behavior and influence public opinion by appealing to reason, emotion, authority, and convention.

The three appeals, according to the early Rhetoricians, are the appeal to reason, the appeal to the emotions, the so-called "ethical appeal"—the appeal of a speaker who is well-qualified to speak on a particular topic—the appeal to authority, in other words. Modern theorists have also added the appeal to convention—"everybody does it this way"—sometimes also called the "bandwagon" appeal.

The Cadillac symbol is not flashy or large, just expensive and exclusive; however, its simplicity suggests that it's sophisticated to drive a Cadillac—the appeal to reason. When you receive a letter from a university on its letterhead, that letterhead with the university's logo is usually very formal-looking and gives the impression of reasoned excellence—again, an appeal to reason.

On the other hand, a car dealer's commercials on television are highly hyped. They intend to appeal to the viewer's emotion. Even if you are not in the market for a new car, listening to one of those commercials inspires many to just go and look at this snazzy new model. Those "just looking" visits more often than not become purchases. On these commercials, you will see the automobiles pictured in such a way that they suggest reason—it's good fiscal management to buy one of these because they hold up over the long run or they are fuel-efficient; emotion—they jazz up the emotions of the viewers by suggesting what it would feel like to be behind the wheel; authority—they have a well-known figure testify about the vehicle such as Tiger Wood driving a Buick; convention—band wagon—everybody's buying this year's model, and you need to get on the bandwagon.

Skill 20.5 Recognize the role that an individual's personal experience and prior knowledge play in how the individual interprets certain visual images.

We don't come cold to these efforts to get us to buy something. We have been conditioned over our lives by our own experiences. If you've had a bad experience with a car you bought because it was cheap and affordable, Cadillac's advertising may have special resonance for you. If you grew up in a family that was down on its luck and when you were a teenager you were embarrassed by the old, broken-down car your parents drove, that advertising will no doubt reach you.

On the other hand, if you've driven a Cadillac at some time or other in your life and have had a good experience, you will be more responsive to the advertising.

Pictures of food on television commercials are very effective at getting viewers to come in and purchase what they see. A lingering shot of an ice-cream sundae with chocolate syrup slowly running down the side may inspire some people to get in their cars and go to the drive-in and get one. An ad for ice cream that ran on television several years ago showed close-ups of creamy ice cream being scooped, and it helped launch a new brand very successfully. This is, of course, pure and unadulterated appeal to the emotions. They probably wouldn't work so well on the viewer who has never eaten fresh-scooped ice cream.

We work extra hard to buy a house that represents some kind of longing in our past. Perhaps the home our parents brought us up in. Perhaps the home of the wealthiest family in the town where you grew up. Perhaps an aversion to the overt display of wealth of someone whose personality you didn't like—one whose greed was a turn-off for you.

We are conditioned to respond to advertising in certain ways by our own past experiences. Successful marketers are aware of that and use it to sell their products to us.

Resources

Abrams, M. H. ed. *The Norton Anthology of English Literature*. 6th ed. 2 vols. New York: Norton, 1979.

A comprehensive reference for English literature, containing selected works from *Beowulf* through the twentieth century and information about literary criticism.

Beach, Richard. "Strategic Teaching in Literature." *Strategic Teaching and Learning: Cognitive Instruction in the Content Areas*. Edited by Beau Fly Jones and others. ASCD Publications, 1987: 135-159.

A chapter dealing with a definition of and strategic teaching strategies for literature studies.

Brown, A. C. and others. *Grammar and Composition* 3rd Course. Boston: Houghton Mifflin, 1984.

A standard ninth-grade grammar text covering spelling, vocabulary, reading, listening, and writing skills.

Burmeister, L. E. *Reading Strategies for Middle and Secondary School Teachers*. Reading, MA: Addison-Wesley, 1978.

A resource for developing classroom strategies for reading and content area classes, using library references, and adapting reading materials to all levels of students.

Carrier, W. and B. Neumann, eds. *Literature from the World*. New York: Scribner, 1981.

A comprehensive world literature text for high school students, with a section on mythology and folklore.

Cline, R. K. J. and W. G. McBride. *A Guide to Literature for Young Adults: Background, Selection, and Use*. Glenview, IL: Scott Foresman, 1983.

A literature reference containing sample readings and an overview of adolescent literature and the developmental changes that affect reading.

Coater, R.B., Jr., ed. "Reading Research and Instruction." *Journal of the College Research Association*. Pittsburgh, PA: 1995.

A reference tool for reading and language arts teachers, covering the latest research and instructional techniques.

Corcoran, B. and E. Evans, eds. *Readers, Texts, Teachers*. Upper Montclair, NJ: Boynton/Cook, 1987.

A collection of essays concerning reader response theory, including activities that help students interpret literature and help the teacher integrate literature into the course study.

Cutting, Brian. *Moving on in Whole Language: The Complete Guide for Every Teacher*. Bothell, WA: Wright Group, 1992.

A resource of practical knowledge in whole language instruction.

Damrosch, L. and others. *Adventures in English Literature*. Orlando, FL: Harcourt, Brace, Jovanovich, 1985.

One of many standard high school English literature textbooks with a solid section on the development of the English language.

Davidson, A. *Literacy 2000 Teacher's Resource. Emergent Stages 1 & 2*.1990.

Devine, T. G. *Teaching Study Skills: A Guide for Teachers*. Boston: Allyn and Bacon, 1981.

Duffy, G. G. and others. *Comprehension Instruction: Perspectives and Suggestions*. New York: Longman, 1984.

Written by researchers at the Institute of Research on Teaching and the Center for the Study of Reading, this reference includes a variety of instructional techniques for different levels.

Fleming, M. ed. *Teaching the Epic*. Urbana, IL: NCTE, 1974.

Methods, materials, and projects for the teaching of epics with examples of Greek, religious, national, and American epics.

Flood, J. Ed. *Understanding Reading Comprehension: Cognition, Language, and the Structure of Prose*. Newark, DE: IRA, 1984.

Essays by preeminent scholars dealing with comprehension for learners of all levels and abilities.

Fry, E. B. and others. *The Reading Teacher's Book of Lists*. Edgewood Cliffs, NJ: Prentice-Hall, 1984.

A comprehensive list of book lists for students of various reading levels.

Garnica, Olga K. and Martha L. King. *Language, Children, and Society*. New York: Pergamon Press, 1981.

Gere, A. R. and E. Smith. *Attitude, Language and Change*. Urbana, IL: NCTE, 1979.

A discussion of the relationship between standard English and grammar and the vernacular usage, including various approaches to language instruction.

Hayakawa, S. I. *Language in Thought and Action*. 4th ed. Orlando, Fl: Harcourt, Brace, Jovanovich, 1979.

Hook, J. N. and others. *What Every English Teacher Should Know*. Champaign, IL: NCTE, 1970.

Research-based text that summarizes methodologies and specific application for use with students.

Johnson, D. D. and P. D. Pearson. *Teaching Reading Vocabulary*. 2nd ed. New York: Holt, Rinehart, and Winston, 1984.

A student text that stresses using vocabulary study in improving reading comprehension, with chapters on instructional components in the reading and content areas.

Kaywell, I. F. Ed. *Adolescent Literature as a Complement to the Classics*. Norwood, MA: Christopher-Gordon Pub., 1993.

A correlation of modern adolescent literature to classics of similar themes.

Mack, M. Ed. *World Masterpieces*. 3rd ed. 2 vols. New York: Norton, 1973.

A standard world literature survey, with useful introductory material on a critical approach to literature study.

McLuhan, M. *Understanding Media: The Extensions of Man*. New York: Signet, 1964.

The most classic work on the effect media has on the public and the power of the media to influence thinking.

McMichael, G. ed. *Concise Anthology of American Literature*. New York: Macmillan, 1974.

A standard survey of American literature text.

Moffett, J. *Teaching the Universe of Discourse*. Boston: Houghton Mifflin, 1983.

A significant reference text that proposes the outline for a total language arts program, emphasizing the reinforcement of each element of the language arts curriculum to the other elements.

Moffett, James and Betty Jane Wagner. *Student-Centered Language Arts K-12*. 4th ed. Boston: Houghton Mifflin, 1992.

Nelms, B. F., ed. *Literature in the Classroom: Readers, Texts, and Contexts*. Urbana, IL: NCTE, 1988.

Essays on adolescent and multicultural literature, social aspects of literature, and approaches to literature interpretation.

Nilsen, A. P. and K. L. Donelson. *Literature for Today's Young Adults*. 2nd ed. Glenview, IL: Scott, Foresman, and Co., 1985.

An excellent overview of young adult literature - its history, terminologies, bibliographies, and book reviews.

Perrine, L. *Literature: Structure, Sound, and Sense*. 5th ed. Orlando, FL: Harcourt, Brace, Jovanovich, 1988.

A much revised text for teaching literature elements, genres, and interpretation.

Piercey, Dorothy. *Reading Activities in Content Areas: An Ideabook for Middle and Secondary Schools*. 2nd ed. Boston: Allyn and Bacon, 1982.

Pooley, R. C. *The Teaching of English Usage*. Urbana, IL: NCTE, 1974.

A revision of the important 1946 text, which discusses the attitudes toward English usage through history and recommends specific techniques for usage instruction.

Probst, R. E. *Response and Analysis: Teaching Literature in Junior and Senior High School*. Upper Montclair, NJ: Boynton/Cook, 1988.

A resource that explores reader response theory and discusses student-centered methods for interpreting literature. Contains a section on the progress of adolescent literature.

Pyles, T. and J. Alges. *The Origin and Development of the English Language.* 3rd ed. Orlando, FL: Harcourt, Brace, Jovanovich, 1982.

A history of the English language; sections on social, personal, historical, and geographical influences on language usage.

Readence, J. E. and others. *Content Area Reading: An Integrated Approach.* 2nd ed. Dubuque, IA: Kendall/Hunt, 1985.

A practical instruction guide for teaching reading in the content areas.

Robinson, H. Alan. *Teaching Reading and Study Strategies: The Content Areas.* Boston: Allyn and Bacon, 1978.

Roe, B. D. and others. *Secondary School Reading Instruction: The Content Areas.* 3rd ed. Boston: Houghton Mifflin, 1987.

A resource of strategies for the teaching of reading for language arts teachers with little reading instruction background.

Rosenberg, D. *World Mythology: An Anthology of the Great Myths and Epics.* Lincolnwood, IL: National Textbook, 1986.

Presents selections of main myths from which literary allusions are drawn. Thorough literary analysis of each selection.

Rosenblatt, L. M. *The Reader, the Text, the Poem. The Transactional Theory of the Literary Work.* Southern Illinois University Press, 1978.

A discussion of reader-response theory and reader-centered methods for analyzing literature.

Santeusanio, Richard P. *A Practical Approach to Content Area Reading.* Reading, MA.: Addison-Wesley Publishing Co., 1983.

Strickland, D. S. and others. *Using Computers in the Teaching of Reading.* New York: Teachers College Press, 1987.

Resource for strategies for teaching and learning language and reading with computers and recommendations for software for all grades.

Sutherland, Zena and others. *Children and Books.* 6th ed. Glenview, IL: Scott, Foresman, and Co., 1981.

Thorough study of children's literature, with sections on language development theory and chapters on specific genres with synopses of specific classic works for child/adolescent readers.

Tchudi, S. and D. Mitchell. *Explorations in the Teaching of English.* 3rd ed. New York: Harper Row, 1989.

A thorough source of strategies for creating a more student-centered involvement in learning.

Tompkins, Gail E. *Teaching Writing: Balancing Process and Product.* 2nd ed. New York: Macmillan, 1994.

A tool to aid teachers in integrating recent research and theory about the writing process, writing reading connections, collaborative learning, and across the curriculum writing with practices in the fourth through eighth grade classrooms.

Warriners, J. E. *English Composition and Grammar.* Benchmark ed. Orlando, FL: Harcourt, Brace, Jovanovich, 1988.

Standard grammar and composition textbook, with a six-book series for seventh through twelfth grades; includes vocabulary study, language history, and diverse approaches to writing process.

Sample Test

Section I: Essay Test

Given are several prompts, reflecting the need to exhibit a variety of writing skills. In most testing situations, 30 minutes would be allowed to respond to each of the prompts. Some tests may allow 60 minutes for the essay to incorporate more than one question or allow for greater preparation and editing time. Read the directions carefully and organize your time wisely.

Section II: Multiple-choice Test

This section contains 125 questions. In most testing situations, you would be expected to answer from 35-40 questions within 30 minutes. If you time yourself on the entire battery, take no more than 90 minutes.

Section III: Answer Key

Section I: Essay Prompts

Prompt A

Write an expository essay discussing effective teaching strategies for developing literature appreciation with a heterogeneous class of ninth graders. Select any appropriate piece(s) of world literature to use as examples in the discussion.

Prompt B

After reading the following passage from Aldous Huxley's *Brave New World,* discuss the types of reader responses possible with a group of eight graders.

> He hated them all—all the men who came to visit Linda. One afternoon, when he had been playing with the other children - it was cold, he remembered, and there was snow on the mountains - he came back to the house and heard angry voices in the bedroom. They were women's voices, and they were words he didn't understand; but he knew they were dreadful words. Then suddenly, crash! something was upset; he heard people moving about quickly, and there was another crash and then a noise like hitting a mule, only not so bony; then Linda screamed. 'Oh, don't, don't, don't!' she said. He ran in. There were three women in dark blankets. Linda was on the bed. One of the women was holding her wrists. Another was lying across her legs, so she couldn't kick. The third was hitting her with a whip. Once, twice, three times; and each time Linda screamed.

Prompt C

Write a persuasive letter to the editor on any contemporary topic of special interest. Employ whatever forms of discourse, style devices, and audience appeal techniques that seem appropriate to the topic.

Section II: Multiple-choice Test

Explanation of Rigor

Easy: The majority of test takers would get this question correct. It is a simple understanding of the facts and/or the subject matter is part of the basics of an education for teaching English.

Average Rigor: This question represents a test item that most people would pass. It requires a level of analysis or reasoning and/or the subject matter exceeds the basics of an education for teaching English.

Rigorous: The majority of test takers would have difficulty answering this question. It involves critical thinking skills such as a very high level of abstract thought, analysis or reasoning, and it would require a very deep and broad education for teaching English.

Part A

Each underlined portion of sentences 1-10 contains one or more errors in grammar, usage, mechanics, or sentence structure. Circle the choice which best corrects the error without changing the meaning of the original sentence.

1. Joe <u>didn't hardly know his cousin Fred</u> who'd had a rhinoplasty. (Skill 2.3, Easy)

    A. hardly did know his cousin Fred

    B. didn't know his cousin Fred hardly

    C. hardly knew his cousin Fred

    D. didn't know his cousin Fred

    E. didn't hardly know his cousin Fred

2. <u>Mixing the batter for cookies</u>, the cat licked the Crisco from the cookie sheet. (Skill 2.3, Average Rigor)

    A. While mixing the batter for cookies

    B. While the batter for cookies was mixing

    C. While I mixed the batter for cookies

    D. While I mixed the cookies

    E. Mixing the batter for cookies

3. Mr. Smith <u>respectfully submitted his resignation and had</u> a new job. (Skill 2.3, Average Rigor)

   A. respectfully submitted his resignation and has

   B. respectfully submitted his resignation before accepting

   C. respectfully submitted his resignation because of

   D. respectfully submitted his resignation and had

4. Wally <u>groaned</u>, "Why do I have to do an oral interpretation <u>of "The Raven."</u> (Skill 2.3, Average Rigor)

   A. groaned "Why... of 'The Raven'?"

   B. groaned "Why... of "The Raven"?

   C. groaned ", Why... of "The Raven?"

   D. groaned, "Why... of "The Raven."

5. <u>The coach offered her assistance but</u> the athletes wanted to practice on their own. (Skill 2.3, Rigorous)

   A. The coach offered her assistance, however, the athletes wanted to practice on their own.

   B. The coach offered her assistance: furthermore, the athletes wanted to practice on their own.

   C. Having offered her assistance, the athletes wanted to practice on their own.

   D. The coach offered her assistance; however, the athletes wanted to practice on their own.

   E. The coach offered her assistance, and the athletes wanted to practice on their own.

6. **The Taj Mahal has been designated one of the Seven Wonders of the World, and people know it for its unique architecture. (Skill 2.3, Rigorous)**

   A. The Taj Mahal has been designated one of the Seven Wonders of the World, and it is known for its unique architecture.

   B. People know the Taj Mahal for its unique architecture, and it has been designated one of the Seven Wonders of the World.

   C. People have known the Taj Mahal for its unique architecture, and it has been designated of the Seven Wonders of the World.

   D. The Taj Mahal has designated itself one of the Seven Wonders of the World.

7. **Walt Whitman was famous for his composition, _Leaves of Grass, serving as a nurse during the Civil War, and a devoted son_ (Skill 2.3, Rigorous)**

   A. _Leaves of Grass_, his service as a nurse during the Civil War, and a devoted son

   B. composing _Leaves of Grass_, serving as a nurse during the Civil War, and being a devoted son

   C. his composition, _Leaves of Grass_, his nursing during the Civil War, and his devotion as a son

   D. his composition _Leaves of Grass,_ serving as a nurse during the Civil War and a devoted son

   E. his composition _Leaves of Grass_, serving as a nurse during the Civil War. and a devoted son

8. A teacher <u>must know not only her subject matter</u> but also the strategies of content teaching. (Skill 2.3, Rigorous)

    A. must not only know her subject matter but also the strategies of content teaching

    B. not only must know her subject matter but also the strategies of content teaching

    C. must not know only her subject matter but also the strategies of content teaching

    D. must know not only her subject matter but also the strategies of content teaching

9. There were <u>fewer pieces</u> of evidence presented during the second trial. (Skill 2.4, Easy)

    A. fewer peaces

    B. less peaces

    C. less pieces

    D. fewer pieces

10. The teacher <u>implied</u> from our angry words that there was conflict <u>between you and me</u>. (Skill 2.4, Average Rigor)

    A. Implied… between you and I

    B. Inferred… between you and I

    C. Inferred… between you and me

    D. Implied… between you and me

Part B
Directions: Select the best answer in each group of multiple choices.

11. **Sometimes readers can be asked to demonstrate their understanding of a text. This might include all of the following except** (Skill 1.1, Average Rigor)

    A. role playing.

    B. paraphrasing.

    C. storyboarding a part of the story with dialogue bubbles.

    D. reading the story aloud

12. **Which of the following reading strategies calls for higher order cognitive skills?** (Skill 1.1, Average Rigor)

    A. Making predictions

    B. Summarizing

    C. Monitoring

    D. Making inferences

13. **Which definition is the best for defining diction?** (Skill 1.2, Easy)

    A. The specific word choices of an author to create a particular mood or feeling in the reader.

    B. Writing which explains something thoroughly.

    C. The background, or exposition, for a short story or drama.

    D. Word choices that help teach a truth or moral.

14. **In the following quotation, addressing the dead body of Caesar as though he were still a living being is to employ an** (Skill 1.2, Average Rigor)

    > O, pardon me, though
    > Bleeding piece of earth
    > That I am meek and gentle with
    > These butchers.
    >   -Marc Antony from
    > *Julius Caesar*

    A. apostrophe

    B. allusion

    C. antithesis

    D. anachronism

15. The literary device of personification is used in which example below? (Skill 1.2, Average Rigor)

    A. "Beg me no beggary by soul or parents, whining dog!"

    B. "Happiness sped through the halls cajoling as it went."

    C. "O wind thy horn, thou proud fellow."

    D. "And that one talent which is death to hide."

16. An extended metaphor comparing two very dissimilar things (one lofty one lowly) is a definition of a/an (Skill 1.2, Average Rigor)

    A. antithesis.

    B. aphorism.

    C. apostrophe.

    D. conceit.

17. Which of the following is a characteristic of blank verse? (Skill 1.2, Average Rigor)

    A. Meter in iambic pentameter

    B. Clearly specified rhyme scheme

    C. Lack of figurative language

    D. Unspecified rhythm

18. Which is the best definition of free verse, or *vers libre*? (Skill 1.2, Average Rigor)

    A. Poetry, which consists of an unaccented syllable followed by an unaccented sound.

    B. Short lyrical poetry written to entertain but with an instructive purpose.

    C. Poetry, which does not have a uniform pattern of rhythm.

    D. A poem which tells the story and has a plot

19. Which term best describes the form of the following poetic excerpt? (Skill 1.2, Rigorous)

> And more to lulle him in his slumber soft,
> A trickling streake from high rock
> tumbling downe,
> And ever-drizzling raine upon the loft.
> Mixt with a murmuring winde, much like a swowne
> No other noyse, nor peoples troubles cryes.
> As still we wont t'annoy the walle'd towne,
> Might there be heard: but careless Quiet lyes,
> Wrapt in eternall silence farre from enemyes.

A. Ballad

B. Elegy

C. Spenserian stanza

D. *Octava rima*

20. In the phrase "The Cabinet conferred with the President," Cabinet is an example of a/an (Skill 1.2, Rigorous)

A. metonym

B. synecdoche

C. metaphor

D. allusion

21. What syntactic device is most evident from Abraham Lincoln's "Gettysburg Address"? (Skill 1.2, Rigorous)

> It is rather for us to be here dedicated to the great task remaining before us -- that from these honored dead we take increased devotion to that cause for which they gave the last full measure of devotion—that we here highly resolve that these dead shall not have died in vain -- that this nation, under God, shall have a new birth of freedom—and that government of the people, by the people, for the people, shall not perish from the earth.

A. Affective connotation

B. Informative denotations

C. Allusion

D. Parallelism

22. A traditional, anonymous story, ostensibly having a historical basis, usually explaining some phenomenon of nature or aspect of creation, defines a/an (Skill 1.3, Easy)

A. proverb.

B. idyll.

C. myth.

D. epic.

23. Which of the following is not a characteristic of a fable? (Skill 1.3, Easy)

    A. Animals that feel and talk like humans.

    B. Happy solutions to human dilemmas.

    C. Teaches a moral or standard for behavior.

    D. Illustrates specific people or groups without directly naming them.

24. Which poem is typified as a villanelle? (Skill 1.3, Rigorous)

    A. "Do not go gentle into that good night"

    B. "Dover Beach"

    C. *Sir Gawain and the Green Knight*

    D. *Pilgrim's Progress*

25. In classic tragedy, a protagonist's defeat is brought about by a tragic flaw which is called (Skill 1.3, Rigorous)

    A. hubris

    B. hamartia

    C. catharsis

    D. the skene

26. Which sonnet form describes the following? (Skill 1.3, Rigorous)

> My galley charg'd with forgetfulness, *A*
> Through sharp seas, in winter night doth pass *B*
> 'Tween rock and rock; and eke mine enemy, alas, *B*
> That is my lord steereth with, cruelness. *A*
> And every oar a thought with readiness, *A*
> As though that death were light in such a case. *B*
> An endless wind doth tear the sail apace *B*
> Or forc'ed sighs and trusty fearfulness. *A*
> A rain of tears, a cloud of dark disdain, *C*
> Hath done the wearied cords great hinderance, *D*
> Wreathed with error and eke with ignorance. *D*
> The stars be hid that led me to this pain *C*
> Drowned is reason that should me consort, *e*
> And I remain despairing of the poet *e*

    A. Petrarchan or Italian sonnet

    B. Shakespearian or Elizabethan sonnet

    C. Romantic sonnet

    D. Spenserian sonnet

27. **What is the salient literary feature of this excerpt from an epic? (Skill 1.3, Rigorous)**

> Hither the heroes and the nymphs resorts,
> To taste awhile the pleasures of a court;
> In various talk th'instructive hours they passed,
> Who gave the ball, or paid the visit last;
> One speaks the glory of the English Queen,
> And another describes a charming Indian screen;
> A third interprets motion, looks, and eyes;
> At every word a reputation dies.

   A. Sprung rhythm

   B. Onomatopoeia

   C. Heroic couplets

   D. Motif

28. **The tendency to emphasize and value the qualities and peculiarities of life in a particular geographic area exemplifies (Skill 1.4, Easy)**

   A. pragmatism.

   B. regionalism.

   C. pantheism.

   D. abstractionism.

29. **Charles Dickens, Robert Browning, and Robert Louis Stevenson were (Skill 1.4, Easy)**

   A. Victorians.

   B. Medievalists.

   C. Elizabethans.

   D. Absurdists.

30. **Among junior-high school students of low-to-average readability levels, which work would most likely stir reading interest? (Skill 1.4, Easy)**

   A. *Elmer Gantry*, Sinclair Lewis

   B. *Smiley's People*, John Le Carre

   C. *The Outsiders*, S.E. Hinton

   D. *And Then There Were None*, Agatha Christie.

31. **What is considered the first work of English literature because it was written in the vernacular of the day? (Skill 1.4, Easy)**

   A. *Beowulf*

   B. *Le Morte d'Arthur*

   C. *The Faerie Queene*

   D. *Canterbury Tales*

32. Considered one of the first feminist plays, this Ibsen drama ends with a door slamming symbolizing the lead character's emancipation from traditional societal norms. (Skill 1.4, Average Rigor)

   A. *The Wild Duck*

   B. *Hedda Gabler*

   C. *Ghosts*

   D. *The Doll's House*

33. Which of the following titles is known for its scathingly condemning tone? (Skill 1.4, Average Rigor)

   A. Boris Pasternak's *Dr Zhivago*

   B. Albert Camus' *The Stranger*

   C. Henry David Thoreau's "On the Duty of Civil Disobedience"

   D. Benjamin Franklin's "Rules by Which a Great Empire May Be Reduced to a Small One"

34. American colonial writers were primarily (Skill 1.4, Average Rigor)

   A. Romanticists.

   B. Naturalists.

   C. Realists.

   D. Neo-classicists.

35. Arthur Miller wrote *The Crucible* as a parallel to what twentieth century event? (Skill 1.4, Average Rigor)

   A. Sen. McCarthy's House un-American Activities Committee Hearing

   B. The Cold War

   C. The fall of the Berlin wall

   D. The Persian Gulf War

36. Which of the writers below is a renowned Black poet? (Skill 1.4, Average Rigor)

   A. Maya Angelou

   B. Sandra Cisneros

   C. Richard Wilbur

   D. Richard Wright

37. Which of the following is not a theme of Native American writing? (Skill 1.4, Average Rigor)

   A. Emphasis on the hardiness of the human body and soul

   B. The strength of multi-cultural assimilation

   C. Contrition for the genocide of native peoples

   D. Remorse for the love of the Indian way of life

38. The writing of Russian naturalists is (Skill 1.4, Average Rigor)

    A. optimistic.

    B. pessimistic.

    C. satirical.

    D. whimsical.

39. Most children's literature prior to the development of popular literature was intended to be didactic. Which of the following would not be considered didactic? (Skill 1.4, Average Rigor)

    A. "A Visit from St. Nicholas" by Clement Moore

    B. *McGuffy's Reader*

    C. Any version of Cinderella

    D. Parables from the Bible

40. Written on the sixth grade reading level, most of S. E. Hinton's novels (for instance, *The Outsiders*) have the greatest reader appeal with (Skill 1.4, Average Rigor)

    A. sixth graders.

    B. ninth graders.

    C. twelfth graders.

    D. adults.

41. Children's literature became established in the (Skill 1.4, Average Rigor)

    A. seventeenth century

    B. eighteenth century

    C. nineteenth century

    D. twentieth century

42. After watching a movie of a train derailment, a child exclaims, "Wow, look how many cars fell off the tracks. There's junk everywhere. The engineer must have really been asleep." Using the facts that the child is impressed by the wreckage and assigns blame to the engineer, a follower of Piaget's theories would estimate the child to be about (Skill 1.4, Rigorous)

    A. ten years old.

    B. twelve years old.

    C. fourteen years old.

    D. sixteen years old.

43. **The most significant drawback to applying learning theory research to classroom practice is that (Skill 1.4, Rigorous)**

   A. today's students do not acquire reading skills with the same alacrity as when greater emphasis was placed on reading classical literature.

   B. development rates are complicated by geographical and cultural In analyzing literature and in looking for ways to bring a work to life for an audience, the use of comparable themes and ideas from other pieces of literature and from one's own life experiences, including from reading the daily newspaper, is very important and useful.

   C. homogeneous grouping has contributed to faster development of some age groups.

   D. social and environmental conditions have contributed to an escalated maturity level than research done twenty of more years ago would seem to indicate.

44. **Which of the following is the best definition of existentialism? (Skill 1.4, Rigorous)**

   A. The philosophical doctrine that matter is the only reality and that everything in the world, including thought, will and feeling, can be explained only in terms of matter.

   B. Philosophy that views things as they should be or as one would wish them to be.

   C. A philosophical and literary movement, variously religious and atheistic, stemming from Kierkegaard and represented by Sartre.

   D. The belief that all events are determined by fate and are hence inevitable.

45. The following lines from Robert Browning's poem "My Last Duchess" come from an example of what form of dramatic literature? (Skill 1.4, Rigorous)

> That's my last Duchess
> painted on the wall,
> Looking as if she were alive. I call
> That piece a wonder
> now: Frà Pandolf's hands
> Worked busily a day
> and there she stands.
> Will 't please you sit and look at her?

A. Tragedy

B. Comic opera

C. Dramatis personae

D. Dramatic monologue

46. "Every one must pass through Vanity Fair to get to the celestial city" is an allusion from a (Skill 1.4, Rigorous)

A. Chinese folk tale.

B. Norse saga.

C. British allegory.

D. German fairy tale.

47. Which author did not write satire? (Skill 1.4, Rigorous)

A. Joseph Addison

B. Richard Steele

C. Alexander Pope

D. John Bunyan

48. What were two major characteristics of the first American literature? (Skill 1.4, Rigorous)

A. Vengefulness and arrogance

B. Bellicosity and derision

C. Oral delivery and reverence for the land

D. Maudlin and self-pitying egocentricism

49. Hoping to take advantage of the popularity of the Harry Potter series, a teacher develops a unit on mythology comparing the story and characters of Greek and Roman myths with the story and characters of the Harry Potter books. Which of these is a commonality that would link classical literature to popular fiction? (Skill 1.4, Rigorous)

A. The characters are gods in human form with human-like characteristics.

B. The settings are realistic places in the world where the characters interact as humans would.

C. The themes center on the universal truths of love and hate and fear.

D. The heroes in the stories are young males and only they can overcome the opposing forces.

50. In the following poem, what literary movement is reflected? (Skill 1.4, Rigorous)

"My Heart Leaps Up" by William Wordsworth

My heart leaps up when I behold
 A rainbow in the sky:
So was it when my life began;
So is it now I am a man;
So be it when I shall grow old,
 Or let me die!
The Child is father of the Man;
And I could wish my days to be
Bound each to each by natural piety

A. Neo-classicism

B. Victorian literature

C. Romanticism

D. Naturalism

51. In preparing a unit on 20th century immigration you prepare a list of books for students to read. Which book would not be appropriate for this topic? (Skill 1.5, Average Rigor)

   A. *The Things They Carried* by Tim O'Brien

   B. *Exodus* by Leon Uris

   C. *The Joy Luck Club* by Amy Tan

   D. *Tortilla Flats* by John Steinbeck

52. To explore the relationship of literature to modern life, which of these activities would not enable students to explore comparable themes? (Skill 1.5, Average Rigor)

   A. After studying various world events, such as the Palestinian-Israeli conflict, students write an updated version of *Romeo and Juliet* using modern characters and settings.

   B. Before studying *Romeo and Juliet*, students watch *West Side Story*.

   C. Students research the major themes of *Romeo and Juliet* by studying news stories and finding modern counterparts for the story.

   D. Students would explore compare the romantic themes of *Romeo and Juliet* and *The Taming of the Shrew*.

53. **Mr. Phillips is creating a unit to study *To Kill a Mockingbird* and wants to familiarize his high school freshmen with the attitudes and issues of the historical period. Which activity would familiarize students with the attitudes and issues of the Depression-era South? (Skill 1.5, Rigorous)**

    A. Create a detailed timeline of 15-20 social, cultural, and political events that focus on race relations in the 1930s.

    B. Research and report on the life of its author Harper Lee. Compare her background with the events in the book.

    C. Watch the movie version and note language and dress.

    D. Write a research report on the stock market crash of 1929 and its effects.

54. **Which choice below best defines naturalism? (Skill 1.5, Rigorous)**

    A. A belief that the writer or artist should apply scientific objectivity in his/her observation and treatment of life without imposing value judgments.

    B. The doctrine that teaches that the existing world is the best to be hoped for.

    C. The doctrine that teaches that God is not a personality, but that all laws, forces and manifestations of the universe are God-related.

    D. A philosophical doctrine that professes that the truth of all knowledge must always be in question.

55. The students in Mrs. Cline's seventh grade language arts class were invited to attend a performance of *Romeo and Juliet* presented by the drama class at the high school. To best prepare, they should (Skill 1.6, Average Rigor)

   A. read the play as a homework exercise.

   B. read a synopsis of the plot and a biographical sketch of the author.

   C. examine a few main selections from the play to become familiar with the language and style of the author.

   D. read a condensed version of the story and practice attentive listening skills.

56. What is the best course of action when a child refuses to complete a reading/ literature assignment on the grounds that it is morally objectionable? (Skill 1.6, Average Rigor)

   A. Speak with the parents and explain the necessity of studying this work

   B. Encourage the child to sample some of the text before making a judgment

   C. Place the child in another teacher's class where they are studying an acceptable work

   D. Provide the student with alternative selections that cover the same performance standards that the rest of the class is learning.

57. The English department is developing strategies to encourage all students to become a community of readers. From the list of suggestions below, which would be the least effective way for teachers to foster independent reading? (Skill 1.6, Average Rigor)

   A. Each teacher will set aside a weekly 30-minute in-class reading session during which the teacher and students read a magazine or book for enjoyment.

   B. Teacher and students develop a list of favorite books to share with each other.

   C. The teacher assigns at least one book report each grading period to ensure that students are reading from the established class list.

   D. The students gather books for a classroom library so that books may be shared with each other.

58. Which of the following responses to literature typically give middle school students the most problems? (Skill 1.6, Average Rigor)

   A. Interpretive

   B. Evaluative

   C. Critical

   D. Emotional

59. Which of the following is a formal reading-level assessment? (Skill 1.6, Average Rigor)

   A. A standardized reading test

   B. A teacher-made reading test

   C. An interview

   D. A reading diary

60. **Which of the following would be the most significant factor in teaching Homer's *Iliad* and *Odyssey* to any particular group of students? (Skill 1.6, Average Rigor)**

   A. Identifying a translation on the appropriate reading level

   B. Determining the students' interest level

   C. Selecting an appropriate evaluative technique

   D. Determining the scope and delivery methods of background study

61. **Which of the following definitions best describes a parable? (Skill 1.6, Average Rigor)**

   A. A short entertaining account of some happening, usually using talking animals as characters.

   B. A slow, sad song or poem, or prose work expressing lamentation.

   C. An extensive narrative work expressing universal truths concerning domestic life.

   D. A short, simple story of an occurrence of a familiar kind, from which a moral or religious lesson may be drawn.

62. **Which teaching method would best engage underachievers in the required senior English class? (Skill 1.6, Average Rigor)**

   A. Assign use of glossary work and extensively footnoted excerpts of great works.

   B. Have students take turns reading aloud the anthology selection

   C. Let students choose which readings they'll study and write about.

   D. Use a chronologically arranged, traditional text, but assigning group work, panel presentations, and portfolio management

63. How will literature help students in a science class understand the following passage? (Skill 1.6, Rigorous)

> Just as was the case more than three decades ago, we are still sailing between the Scylla of deferring surgery for too long and risking irreversible left ventricular damage and sudden death, and the Charibdas of operating too early and subjecting the patient to the early risks of operation and the later risks resulting from prosthetic valves.
> --E. Braunwald, *European Heart Journal,* July 2000

A. They will recognize the allusion to Scylla and Charibdas from Greek mythology and understand that the medical community has to select one of two unfavorable choices.

B. They will recognize the allusion to sailing and understand its analogy to doctors as sailors navigating unknown waters.

C. They will recognize that the allusion to Scylla and Charibdas refers to the two islands in Norse mythology where sailors would find themselves shipwrecked and understand how the doctors feel isolated by their choices.

D. They will recognize the metaphor of the heart and relate it to Eros, the character in Greek mythology who represents love. Eros was the love child of Scylla and Charibdas.

64. Which is not a Biblical allusion? (Skill 1.6, Rigorous)

A. The patience of Job

B. Thirty pieces of silver

C. "Man proposes; God disposes"

D. "Suffer not yourself to be betrayed by a kiss"

65. Before reading a passage, a teacher gives her students an anticipation guide with a list of statements related to the topic they are about to cover in the reading material. She asks the students to indicate their agreement or disagreement with each statement on the guide. This activity is intended to (Skill 1.6, Rigorous)

   A. elicit students' prior knowledge of the topic and set a purpose for reading.

   B. help students to identify the main ideas and supporting details in the text.

   C. help students to synthesize information from the text.

   D. help students to visualize the concepts and terms in the text.

66.
66. Recognizing empathy in literature is mostly a/an (Skill 1.6, Rigorous)

   A. emotional response.

   B. interpretive response.

   C. critical response.

   D. evaluative response.

67. If a student has a poor vocabulary, the teacher should recommend first that (Skill 2.1, Average Rigor)

   A. the student read newspapers, magazines and books on a regular basis.

   B. the student enroll in a Latin class.

   C. the student write the words repetitively after looking them up in the dictionary.

   D. the student use a thesaurus to locate synonyms and incorporate them into his/her vocabulary

68. Which of the following sentences contains a subject-verb agreement error? (Skill 2.1, Average Rigor)

   A. Both mother and her two sisters were married in a triple ceremony.

   B. Neither the hen nor the rooster is likely to be served for dinner.

   C. My boss, as well as the company's two personnel directors, have been to Spain.

   D. Amanda and the twins are late again.

69. The synonyms *gyro, hero,* and *submarine* reflect which influence on language usage? (Skill 2.1, Average Rigor)

   A. Social

   B. Geographical

   C. Historical

   D. Personal

70.

70. Which aspect of language is innate? (Skill 2.1, Rigorous)

   A. Biological capability to articulate sounds understood by other humans

   B. Cognitive ability to create syntactical structures

   C. Capacity for using semantics to convey meaning in a social environment

   D. Ability to vary inflections and accents

71. To understand the origins of a word, one must study the (Skill 2.2, Easy)

   A. synonyms

   B. inflections

   C. phonetics

   D. etymology

72. The Elizabethans wrote in (Skill 2.2 Easy)

   A. Celtic

   B. Old English

   C. Middle English

   D. Modern English

73. Which event triggered the beginning of Modern English? (Skill 2.2, Average Rigor)

    A. Conquest of England by the Normans in 1066

    B. Introduction of the printing press to the British Isles

    C. Publication of Samuel Johnson's lexicon.

    D. American Revolution

74. Which of the following is not true about the English language? (Skill 2.2, Average Rigor)

    A. English is the easiest language to learn.

    B. English is the least inflected language.

    C. English has the most extensive vocabulary of any language.

    D. English originated as a Germanic tongue.

75. Which word in the following sentence is a bound morpheme:

"The quick brown fox jumped over the lazy dog"? (Skill 2.2, Rigorous)

    A. The

    B. fox

    C. lazy

    D. jumped

76. What was responsible for the standardizing of dialects across America in the 20th century? (Skill 2.2, Rigorous)

    A. With the immigrant influx, American became a melting pot of languages and cultures.

    B. Trains enabled people to meet other people of different languages and cultures.

    C. Radio, and later, television, used actors and announcers who spoke without pronounced dialects.

    D. Newspapers and libraries developed programs to teach people to speak English with an agreed-upon common dialect.

77. Latin words that entered the English language during the Elizabethan age include (Skill 2.2, Rigorous)

    A. allusion, education, and esteem

    B. vogue and mustache

    C. canoe and cannibal

    D. alligator, cocoa, and armadillo

78. Which of the following sentences is properly punctuated? (Skill 2.3, Easy)

    A. The more you eat; the more you want.

    B. The authors—John Steinbeck, Ernest Hemingway, and William Faulkner—are staples of modern writing in American literature textbooks.

    C. Handling a wild horse, takes a great deal of skill and patience.

    D. The man, who replaced our teacher, is a comedian.

79. Which sentence below best minimizes the impact of bad news? (Skill 2.3, Rigorous)

    A. We have denied you permission to attend the event.

    B. Although permission to attend the event cannot be given, you are encouraged to buy the video.

    C. Although you cannot attend the event, we encourage you to buy the video.

    D. Although attending the event is not possible, watching the video is an option.

80. The arrangement and relationship of words in sentences or sentence structures best describes (Skill 2.3, Rigorous)

    A. style.

    B. discourse.

    C. thesis.

    D. syntax.

81. The substitution of *went to his rest* for *died* is an example of a/an (Skill 2.4, Easy)

    A. bowdlerism.

    B. jargon.

    C. euphemism.

    D. malapropism.

82. If students use slang and expletives, what is the best course of action to take in order to improve their formal communication skills? (Skill 2.4, Average Rigor)

    A. Ask the students to paraphrase their writing, that is, translate it into language appropriate for the school principal to read.

    B. Refuse to read the students' papers until they conform to a more literate style.

    C. Ask the students to read their work aloud to the class for peer evaluation.

    D. Rewrite the flagrant passages to show the students the right form of expression.

83. Which level of meaning is the hardest aspect of a language to master? (Skill 2.4, Rigorous)

    A. Denotation

    B. Jargon

    C. Connotation

    D. Slang

84. Reading a piece of student writing to assess the overall impression of the product is (Skill 3.1, Easy)

    A. holistic evaluation.

    B. portfolio assessment.

    C. analytical evaluation.

    D. using a performance system.

85. **What is not one of the advantages of collaborative or cooperative learning? (Skill 3.1, Easy)**

   A. Students that work together in groups or teams develop their skills in organizing, leadership, research, communication, and problem solving.

   B. Working in teams can help students overcome anxiety in distance learning courses and contribute a sense of community and belonging for the students.

   C. Students tend to learn more material being taught and retain the information longer than when the same information is taught using different methods.

   D. Teachers reduce their workload and the time spent on individuals the assignments, and grading.

86. **Writing ideas quickly without interruption of the flow of thoughts or attention to conventions is called (Skill 3.1, Easy)**

   A. brainstorming.

   B. mapping.

   C. listing.

   D. free writing.

87. **Which of the following should not be included in the opening paragraph of an informative essay? (Skill 3.1, Easy)**

   A. Thesis sentence

   B. Details and examples supporting the main idea

   C. Broad general introduction to the topic

   D. A style and tone that grabs the reader's attention

88. In the paragraph below, which sentence does not contribute to the overall task of supporting the main idea? (Skill 3.1 Easy)

1) The Springfield City Council met Friday to discuss new zoning restrictions for the land to be developed south of the city. 2) Residents who opposed the new restrictions were granted 15 minutes to present their case. 3) Their argument focused on the dangers that increased traffic would bring to the area. 4) It seemed to me that the Mayor Simpson listened intently. 5) The council agreed to table the new zoning until studies would be performed.

A. Sentence 2

B. Sentence 3

C. Sentence 4

D. Sentence 5

89. In preparing your high school freshmen to write a research paper about a social problem, what recommendation can you make so they can determine the credibility of their information? (Skill 3.1, Average Rigor)

A. Assure them that information on the Internet has been peer-reviewed and verified for accuracy.

B. Find one solid source and use that exclusively.

C. Use only primary sources.

D. Cross check your information with another credible source.

90. Modeling is a practice that requires students to (Skill 3.1, Average Rigor)

A. create a style unique to their own language capabilities.

B. emulate the writing of professionals.

C. paraphrase passages from good literature.

D. peer evaluate the writings of other students.

91. Which of the following are secondary research materials? (Skill 3.1, Average Rigor)

   A. The conclusions and inferences of other historians.

   B. Literature and nonverbal materials, novels, stories, poetry and essays from the period, as well as coins, archaeological artifacts, and art produced during the period.

   C. Interviews and surveys conducted by the researcher.

   D. Statistics gathered as the result of the research's experiments.

92. Which of the following is the least effective procedure for promoting consciousness of audience? (Skill 3.1, Average Rigor)

   A. Pairing students during the writing process

   B. Reading all rough drafts before the students write the final copies

   C. Having students compose stories or articles for publication in school literary magazines or newspapers

   D. Writing letters to friends or relatives

93. In general, the most serious drawback of using a computer in writing is that (Skill 3.1, Average Rigor)

   A. the copy looks so good that students tend to overlook major mistakes.

   B. the spell check and grammar programs discourage students from learning proper spelling and mechanics.

   C. the speed with which corrections can be made detracts from the exploration and contemplation of composing.

   D. the writer loses focus by concentrating on the final product rather than the details.

94. The new teaching intern is developing a unit on creative writing and is trying to encourage her freshman high school students to write poetry. Which of the following would not be an effective technique? (Skill 3.1, Average Rigor)

A. In groups, students will draw pictures to illustrate "The Love Song of J. Alfred Prufrock" by T.S. Eliot.

B. Either individually or in groups, students will compose a song, writing lyrics that try to use poetic devices.

C. Students will bring to class the lyrics of a popular song and discuss the imagery and figurative language.

D. Students will read aloud their favorite poems and share their opinions of and responses to the poems.

95. In this paragraph from a student essay, identify the sentence that provides a detail. (Skill 3.1 Rigorous)

(1) The poem concerns two different personality types and the human relation between them. (2) Their approach to life is totally different. (3) The neighbor is a very conservative person who follows routines. (4) He follows the traditional wisdom of his father and his father's father. (5) The purpose in fixing the wall and keeping their relationship separate is only because it is all he knows.

A. Sentence 1

B. Sentence 3

C. Sentence 4

D. Sentence 5

96. To determine the credibility of information, researchers should do all of the following except (Skill 3.1, Rigorous)

A. establish the authority of the document.

B. disregard documents with bias.

C. evaluate the currency and reputation of the source.

D. use a variety of research sources and methods.

97. Which of the following situations is not an ethical violation of intellectual property? (Skill 3.1, Rigorous)

   A. A student visits ten different websites and writes a report to compare the costs of downloading music. He uses the names of the websites without their permission.

   B. A student copies and pastes a chart verbatim from the Internet but does not document it because it is available on a public site.

   C. From an online article found in a subscription database, a student paraphrases a section on the problems of music piracy. She includes the source in her Works Cited but does not provide an in-text citation.

   D. A student uses a comment from M. Night Shyamalan without attribution claiming the information is common knowledge.

98. Students have been asked to write a research paper on automobiles and have brainstormed a number of questions they will answer based on their research findings. Which of the following is not an interpretive question to guide research? (Skill 3.1, Rigorous)

   A. Who were the first ten automotive manufacturers in the United States?

   B. What types of vehicles will be used fifty years from now?

   C. How do automobiles manufactured in the United States compare and contrast with each other?

   D. What do you think is the best solution for the fuel shortage?

99. In preparing a speech for a contest, your student has encountered problems with gender specific language. Not wishing to offend either women or men, she seeks your guidance. Which of the following is not an effective strategy? (Skill 3.1, Rigorous)

    A. Use the generic "he" and explain that people will understand and accept the male pronoun as all-inclusive.

    B. Switch to plural nouns and use "they" as the gender-neutral pronoun.

    C. Use passive voice so that the subject is not required.

    D. Use male pronouns for one part of the speech and then use female pronouns for the other part of the speech.

100.
100. For their research paper on the effects of the Civil War on American literature, students have brainstormed a list of potential online sources and are seeking your authorization. Which of these represent the strongest source? (Skill 3.1, Rigorous)

    A. http://www.wikipedia.org/

    B. http://www.google.com

    C. http://www.nytimes.com

    D. http://docsouth.unc.edu/ southlit/civilwar.html

101. A formative evaluation of student writing (Skill 3.1, Rigorous)

    A. requires thorough markings of mechanical errors with a pencil or pen.

    B. making comments on the appropriateness of the student's interpretation of the prompt and the degree to which the objective was met.

    C. should require that the student hand in all the materials produced during the process of writing.

    D. several careful readings of the text for content, mechanics, spelling, and usage.

102. In preparing a report about William Shakespeare, students are asked to develop a set of interpretive questions to guide their research. Which of the following would not be classified as an interpretive question? (Skill 3.1, Rigorous)

    A. What would be different today if Shakespeare had not written his plays?

    B. How will the plays of Shakespeare affect future generations?

    C. How does the Shakespeare view nature in *A Midsummer's Night Dream* and *Much Ado About Nothing*?

    D. During the Elizabethan age, what roles did young boys take in dramatizing Shakespeare's plays?

103. In writing a report, Hector has to explain where acid rain comes from and what it has done to the environment. What is the most likely form of organizational structure? (Skill 3.2, Easy)

    A. Cause and effect

    B. Problem and solution

    C. Exposition

    D. Definition

104.

104. Explanatory or informative discourse is (Skill 3.2, Easy)

    A. exposition.

    B. narration.

    C. persuasion.

    D. description.

105. Which of the following is not a technique of prewriting? (Skill 3.2, Easy)

    A. Clustering

    B. Listing

    C. Brainstorming

    D. Proofreading

106. The following passage is written from which point of view? (Skill 3.2, Easy)

As she mused the pitiful vision of her mother's life laid its spell on the very quick of her being —that life of commonplace sacrifices closing in final craziness. She trembled as she heard again her mother's voice saying constantly with foolish insistence: *Dearevaun Seraun! Dearevaun Seraun!**

* "The end of pleasure is pain!" (Gaelic)

A. First person, narrator

B. Second person, direct address

C. Third person, omniscient

D. First person, omniscient

107. Which of the following is most true of expository writing? (Skill 3.2, Easy)

A. It is mutually exclusive of other forms of discourse.

B. It can incorporate other forms of discourse in the process of providing supporting details.

C. It should never employ informal expression.

D. It should only be scored with a summative evaluation.

108. 1Which of the following is not correct? (Skill 3.2, Easy)

A. Because most students have wide access to media, teachers should refrain from using it in their classrooms to diminish the overload.

B. Students can use CD-ROMs to explore information using a virtual reality experience.

C. Teacher can make their instruction more powerful by using educational media.

D. The Internet enables students to connect with people across cultures and to share interests.

109. Which of the following should students use to improve coherence of ideas within an argument? (Skill 3.2, Easy)

A. Transitional words or phrases to show relationship of ideas.

B. Conjunctions like "and" to join ideas together.

C. Use direct quotes extensively to improve credibility.

D. Adjectives and adverbs to provide stronger detail.

110. **Which transition word would show contrast between these two ideas? (Skill 3.2, Average Rigor)**

   We are confident in our skills to teach English. We welcome new ideas on this subject.

   A. We are confident in our skills to teach English, and we welcome new ideas on this subject.

   B. Because we are confident in our skills to teach English, we welcome new ideas on the subject.

   C. When we are confident in our skills to teach English, we welcome new ideas on the subject.

   D. We are confident in our skills to teach English; however, we welcome new ideas on the subject.

111. **In preparing students for their oral presentations, the instructor provided all of these guidelines, except one. Which is not an effective guideline? (Skill 3.2, Average Rigor)**

   A. Even if you are using a lectern, feel free to move about. This will connect you to the audience.

   B. Your posture should be natural, not stiff. Keep your shoulders toward the audience.

   C. Gestures can help communicate as long as you don't overuse them or make them distracting.

   D. You can avoid eye contact if you focus on your notes. This will make you appear more knowledgeable.

112. **Which of the following statements indicates an instructional goal for using multimedia in the classroom? (Skill 3.2, Average Rigor)**

    A. Audio messages invite the listener to form mental images consistent with the topic of the audio.

    B. Print messages appeal almost exclusively to the mind and push students to read with more thought.

    C. Listening to an audio message is more passive than reading a print message.

    D. Teachers who develop activities to foster a critical perspective on audiovisual presentation will decrease passivity.

113. **What is the main form of discourse in this passage? (Skill 3.2, Average Rigor)**

    It would have been hard to find a passer-by more wretched in appearance. He was a man of middle height, stout and hardy, in the strength of maturity; he might have been forty-six or seven. A slouched leather cap hid half his face, bronzed by the sun and wind, and dripping with sweat.

    A. Description

    B. Narration

    C. Exposition

    D. Persuasion

114. **In literature, evoking feelings of pity or compassion is to create (Skill 3.2, Average Rigor)**

    A. colloquy.

    B. irony.

    C. pathos.

    D. paradox

115. Which of the following would not be a major concern in an oral presentation? (Skill 3.2, Average Rigor)

   A. Establishing the purpose of the presentation

   B. Evaluating the audience's demographics and psychographics.

   C. Creating a PowerPoint slide for each point.

   D. Developing the content to fit the occasion.

116. Mr. Ledbetter has instructed his students to prepare a slide presentation that illustrates an event in history. Students are to include pictures, graphics, media clips and links to resources. What competencies will students exhibit at the completion of this project? (Skill 3.2, Rigorous)

   A. Analyze the impact of society on media.

   B. Recognize the media's strategies to inform and persuade.

   C. Demonstrate strategies and creative techniques to prepare presentations using a variety of media.

   D. Identify the aesthetic effects of a media presentation.

117. In the following excerpt from "Civil Disobedience," what type of reasoning does Henry David Thoreau use? (Skill 3.2, Rigorous)

> Unjust laws exist; shall we be content to obey them, or shall we endeavor to amend them, and obey them until we have succeeded, or shall we transgress them at once? Men generally, under such a government as this, think that they ought to wait until they have persuaded the majority to alter them. They think that, if they should resist, the remedy would be worse than the evil. But it is the fault of the government itself that the remedy *is* worse than the evil. … Why does it always crucify Christ, and excommunicate Copernicus and Luther, and pronounce Washington and Franklin rebels?
>
> --"Civil Disobedience" by Henry David Thoreau

   A. Ethical reasoning

   B. Inductive reasoning

   C. Deductive reasoning

   D. Intellectual reasoning

117.

118. Which of the following is not a fallacy in logic? (Skill 3.2, Rigorous)

   A. All students in Ms. Suarez's fourth period class are bilingual.
Beth is in Ms. Suarez's fourth period.
Beth is bilingual.

   B. All bilingual students are in Ms. Suarez's class.
Beth is in Ms. Suarez's fourth period.
Beth is bilingual.

   C. Beth is bilingual.
Beth is in Ms. Suarez's fourth period.
All students in Ms. Suarez's fourth period are bilingual.

   D. If Beth is bilingual, then she speaks Spanish.
Beth speaks French.
Beth is not bilingual.

119. Which of the following is an example of the post hoc fallacy? (Skill 3.2, Rigorous)

   A. When the new principal was hired, student-reading scores improved; therefore, the principal caused the increase in scores.

   B. Why are we spending money on the space program when our students don't have current textbooks?

   C. You can't give your class a 10-minute break. Once you do that, we'll all have to give our students a 10-minute break.

   D. You can never believe anything he says because he's not from the same country as we are.

120. **Identify the type of appeal used by Molly Ivins's in this excerpt from her essay "Get a Knife, Get a Dog, But Get Rid of Guns." (Skill 3.2, Rigorous)**

> As a civil libertarian, I, of course, support the Second Amendment. And I believe it means exactly what it says: *A well regulated militia being necessary to the security of a free state, the right of the people to keep and bear arms shall not be infringed.*

A. Ethical

B. Emotional

C. Rational

D. Literary

121. **What is the common advertising technique used by these advertising slogans? (Skill 3.2, Rigorous)**

> "It's everywhere you want to be." - Visa
> "Have it your way." - Burger King
> "When you care enough to send the very best" - Hallmark
> "Be all you can be" – U.S. Army

A. Peer Approval

B. Rebel

C. Individuality

D. Escape

122.

122. **In presenting a report to peers about the effects of Hurricane Katrina on New Orleans, the students wanted to use various media in their argument to persuade their peers that more needed to be done. Which of these would be the most effective? (Skill 3.2, Rigorous)**

A. A PowerPoint presentation showing the blueprints of the levees before the flood and redesigned now for current construction..

B. A collection of music clips made by the street performers in the French Quarter before and after the flood.

C. A recent video showing the areas devastated by the floods and the current state of rebuilding.

D. A collection of recordings of interviews made by the various government officials and local citizens affected by the flooding.

123. Based on the excerpt below from Kate Chopin's short story "The Story of an Hour," what can students infer about the main character? (Skill 3.2, Rigorous)

She did not stop to ask if it were or were not a monstrous joy that held her. A clear and exalted perception enabled her to dismiss the suggestion as trivial. She knew that she would weep again when she saw the kind, tender hands folded in death; the face that had never looked save with love upon her, fixed and gray and dead. But she saw beyond that bitter moment a long procession of years to come that would belong to her absolutely. And she opened and spread her arms out to . them in welcome.

A. She dreaded her life as a widow.

B. Although she loved her husband, she was glad that he was dead for he had never loved her.

C. She worried that she was too indifferent to her husband's death.

D. Although they had both loved each other, she was beginning to appreciate that opportunities had opened because of his death.

124. Which part of a classical argument is illustrated in this excerpt from the essay "What Should Be Done About Rock Lyrics?" (Skill 3.2, Rigorous)

But violence against women is greeted by silence. It shouldn't be.

This does not mean censorship, or book (or record) burning. In a society that protects free expression, we understand a lot of stuff will float up out of the sewer. Usually, we recognize the ugly stuff that advocates violence against any group as the garbage it is, and we consider its purveyors as moral lepers. We hold our nose and tolerate it, but we speak out against the values it proffers.
"What Should Be Done About Rock Lyrics?" Caryl Rivers

A. Narration

B. Confirmation

C. Refutation and concession

D. Summation

125. **Using the selection below from Edgar Alan Poe's "The Tell-Tale Heart," what form of literary criticism would you introduce to high school students? (Skill 4.1, Average Rigor)**

> And have I not told you that what you mistake for madness is but over-acuteness of the sense? -- now, I say, there came to my ears a low, dull, quick sound, such as a watch makes when enveloped in cotton. I knew that sound well, too. It was the beating of the old man's heart. It increased my fury, as the beating of a drum stimulates the soldier into courage.

A. Marxist

B. Feminist

C. Psychoanalytic

D. Classic

Section III: Answer Key

1	C	26	A	51	A	76	C	101	B
2	C	27	C	52	D	77	A	102	D
3	C	28	B	53	A	78	B	103	A
4	A	29	A	54	A	79	B	104	A
5	D	30	C	55	D	80	D	105	D
6	A	31	D	56	D	81	C	106	C
7	B	32	D	57	C	82	A	107	B
8	D	33	D	58	B	83	C	108	A
9	D	34	D	59	A	84	A	109	B
10	C	35	A	60	A	85	D	110	D
11	D	36	A	61	D	86	D	111	D
12	D	37	B	62	C	87	B	112	D
13	A	38	B	63	A	88	C	113	A
14	A	39	A	64	C	89	D	114	C
15	B	40	B	65	A	90	B	115	C
16	D	41	A	66	C	91	A	116	B
17	A	42	A	67	A	92	C	117	C
18	C	43	D	68	C	93	B	118	A
19	D	44	C	69	B	94	A	119	A
20	B	45	D	70	A	95	C	120	A
21	D	46	B	71	D	96	B	121	C
22	C	47	D	72	D	97	A	122	C
23	D	48	D	73	B	98	A	123	D
24	A	49	C	74	A	99	A	124	C
25	B	50	C	75	D	100	D	125	C

Rigor Table

	Easy 20%	Average Rigor 40%	Rigorous 40%
Question	1, 9, 13, 22, 23, 28, 29, 30, 31, 71, 72, 78, 81, 84, 85, 86, 87, 88, 103, 104, 105, 106, 107, 108, 109,	2, 3, 4, 10, 11, 12, 14, 15, 16, 17, 18, 32, 33, 34, 35, 36, 37, 38, 39, 40, 41, 51, 52, 55, 56, 57, 58, 59, 60, 61, 62, 67, 68, 69, 73, 74, 82, 89, 90, 91, 92, 93, 94, 110, 111, 112, 113, 114, 115, 125	5, 6, 7, 8, 19, 20, 21, 24, 25, 26 17, 42, 43, 44, 45, 46, 47, 48, 49, 50, 53, 54, 63, 64, 65, 66, 70, 75, 76, 77, 79, 80, 83, 95 96, 97, 98, 99, 100, 101, 102, 116, 117, 118, 119, 120, 121, 122, 123, 124

-9

-15   - 25

Rationales with Sample Questions

Explanation of Rigor

Easy: The majority of test takers would get this question correct. It is a simple understanding of the facts and/or the subject matter is part of the basics of an education for teaching English.

Average Rigor: This question represents a test item that most people would pass. It requires a level of analysis or reasoning and/or the subject matter exceeds the basics of an education for teaching English.

Rigorous: The majority of test takers would have difficulty answering this question. It involves critical thinking skills such as a very high level of abstract thought, analysis or reasoning, and it would require a very deep and broad education for teaching English.

Part A

Each underlined portion of sentences 1-10 contains one or more errors in grammar, usage, mechanics, or sentence structure. Circle the choice which best corrects the error without changing the meaning of the original sentence.

1. Joe <u>didn't hardly know his cousin Fred</u> who'd had a rhinoplasty. (Skill 2.3, Easy)

    A. hardly did know his cousin Fred

    B. didn't know his cousin Fred hardly

    C. hardly knew his cousin Fred

    D. didn't know his cousin Fred

    E. didn't hardly know his cousin Fred

The answer is C: using the adverb "hardly" to modify the verb creates a negative, and adding "not" creates the dreaded double negative.

2. **Mixing the batter for cookies**, the cat licked the Crisco from the cookie sheet. (Skill 2.3, Average Rigor)

    A. While mixing the batter for cookies

    B. While the batter for cookies was mixing

    C. While I mixed the batter for cookies

    D. While I mixed the cookies

    E. Mixing the batter for cookies

The answer is C. Answers A and E give the impression that the cat was mixing the batter (it is a dangling modifier.), Answer B that the batter was mixing itself, and Answer D lacks precision: it is the batter that was being mixed, not the cookies themselves.

3. Mr. Smith **respectfully submitted his resignation and had** a new job. (Skill 2.3, Average Rigor)

    A. respectfully submitted his resignation and has

    B. respectfully submitted his resignation before accepting

    C. respectfully submitted his resignation because of

    D. respectfully submitted his resignation and had

The answer is C. Answer A eliminates any relationship of causality between submitting the resignation and having the new job. Answer B just changes the sentence and, by omission, does not indicate the fact that Mr. Smith had a new job before submitting his resignation. Answer D means that Mr. Smith first submitted his resignation, and then got a new job.

4. **Wally <u>groaned</u>, "Why do I have to do an oral interpretation <u>of "The Raven."</u> (Skill 2.3, Average Rigor)**

   A. groaned "Why… of 'The Raven'?"

   B. groaned "Why… of "The Raven"?

   C. groaned ", Why… of "The Raven?"

   D. groaned, "Why… of "The Raven."

The answer is A. The question mark in a quotation that is an interrogation should be within the quotation marks. Also, when quoting a work of literature within another quotation, one should use single quotation marks ('…') for the title of this work, and they should close before the final quotation mark.

5. **<u>The coach offered her assistance but</u> the athletes wanted to practice on their own. (Skill 2.3, Rigorous)**

   A. The coach offered her assistance, however, the athletes wanted to practice on their own.

   B. The coach offered her assistance: furthermore, the athletes wanted to practice on their own.

   C. Having offered her assistance, the athletes wanted to practice on their own.

   D. The coach offered her assistance; however, the athletes wanted to practice on their own.

   E. The coach offered her assistance, and the athletes wanted to practice on their own.

The answer is D. A semicolon precedes a transitional adverb that introduces an independent clause. Answer A is a comma splice. In Answer B, the colon is used incorrectly since the second clause does not explain the first. In Answer C, the opening clause confuses the meaning of the sentence. In Answer E, the conjunction "and" is weak since the two ideas show contrast rather than an additional thought.

6. **The Taj Mahal has been designated one of the Seven Wonders of the World, and people know it for its unique architecture. (Skill 2.3, Rigorous)**

    A. The Taj Mahal has been designated one of the Seven Wonders of the World, and it is known for its unique architecture.

    B. People know the Taj Mahal for its unique architecture, and it has been designated one of the Seven Wonders of the World.

    C. People have known the Taj Mahal for its unique architecture, and it has been designated of the Seven Wonders of the World.

    D. The Taj Mahal has designated itself one of the Seven Wonders of the World.

The answer is A. In the original sentence, the first clause is passive voice and the second clause is active voice, causing a voice shift. Answer B merely switches the clauses but does not correct the voice shift. In Answer C, only the verb tense in the first clause has been changed but it still active voice. Answer D changes the meaning. In Answer A, both clauses are passive voice.

7. **Walt Whitman was famous for his composition, *Leaves* <u>of Grass, serving as a nurse during the Civil War, and a devoted son</u>** (Skill 2.3, Rigorous)

    A. *Leaves of Grass*, his service as a nurse during the Civil War, and a devoted son

    B. composing *Leaves of Grass*, serving as a nurse during the Civil War, and being a devoted son

    C. his composition, *Leaves of Grass*, his nursing during the Civil War, and his devotion as a son

    D. his composition *Leaves of Grass,* serving as a nurse during the Civil War and a devoted son

    E. his composition *Leaves of Grass*, serving as a nurse during the Civil War. and a devoted son

The answer is B: In order to be parallel, the sentence needs three gerunds. The other sentences use both gerunds and nouns, which is a lack of parallelism.

8. **A teacher <u>must know not only her subject matter</u> but also the strategies of content teaching. (Skill 2.3, Rigorous)**

   A. must not only know her subject matter but also the strategies of content teaching

   B. not only must know her subject matter but also the strategies of content teaching

   C. must not know only her subject matter but also the strategies of content teaching

   D. must know not only her subject matter but also the strategies of content teaching

   The answer is D: the correlative conjunction "not only" must come directly after "know" because the intent is to create the clearest meaning link with the "but also" predicate section later in the sentence.

9. **There were <u>fewer pieces</u> of evidence presented during the second trial. (Skill 2.4, Easy)**

   A. fewer peaces

   B. less peaces

   C. less pieces

   D. fewer pieces

   The answer is D. Use "fewer" for countable items; use "less" for amounts and quantities, such as fewer minutes but less time "Peace" is the opposite of war, not a "piece" of evidence.

10. The teacher implied from our angry words that there was conflict between you and me. (Skill 2.4, Average Rigor)

    A. Implied… between you and I

    B. Inferred… between you and I

    C. Inferred… between you and me

    D. Implied… between you and me

The answer is C: the difference between the verb "to imply" and the verb "to infer" is that implying is directing an interpretation toward other people; to infer is to deduce an interpretation from someone else's discourse. Moreover, "between you and I" is grammatically incorrect: after the preposition "between," the object (or 'disjunctive' with this particular preposition) pronoun form, "me," is needed.

Part B

Directions: Select the best answer in each group of multiple choices.

11. **Sometimes readers can be asked to demonstrate their understanding of a text. This might include all of the following except (Skill 1.1, Average Rigor)**

    A. role playing.

    B. paraphrasing.

    C. storyboarding a part of the story with dialogue bubbles.

    D. reading the story aloud

    The answer is D. Reading the text aloud may help readers understand the text but it won't demonstrate their understanding of it. By role playing, paraphrasing, or storyboarding, they will convey their understanding of the purpose and main ideas of the text.

12. **Which of the following reading strategies calls for higher order cognitive skills? (Skill 1.1, Average Rigor)**

    A. Making predictions

    B. Summarizing

    C. Monitoring

    D. Making inferences

    The answer is D. Making inferences from a reading text involves using other reading skills such as making predictions, skimming, scanning, summarizing, then coming to conclusions or making inferences which are not directly stated in the text.

13. **Which definition is the best for defining diction? (Skill 1.2, Easy)**

    A. The specific word choices of an author to create a particular mood or feeling in the reader.

    B. Writing which explains something thoroughly.

    C. The background, or exposition, for a short story or drama.

    D. Word choices that help teach a truth or moral.

The answer is A. Diction refers to an author's choice of words, expressions and style to convey his/her meaning.

14. **In the following quotation, addressing the dead body of Caesar as though he were still a living being is to employ an (Skill 1.2, Average Rigor)**

> O, pardon me, though
> Bleeding piece of earth
> That I am meek and gentle with
> These butchers.
>   -Marc Antony from *Julius Caesar*

    A. apostrophe

    B. allusion

    C. antithesis

    D. anachronism

The answer is A. This rhetorical figure addresses personified things, absent people or gods. An allusion, on the other hand, is a quick reference to a character or event known to the public. An antithesis is a contrast between two opposing viewpoints, ideas, or presentation of characters. An anachronism is the placing of an object or person out of its time with the time of the text. The best-known example is the clock in Shakespeare's *Julius Caesar*.

15. **The literary device of personification is used in which example below? (Skill 1.2, Average Rigor)**

    A. "Beg me no beggary by soul or parents, whining dog!"

    B. "Happiness sped through the halls cajoling as it went."

    C. "O wind thy horn, thou proud fellow."

    D. "And that one talent which is death to hide."

The answer is B. "Happiness," an abstract concept, is described as if it were a person with the words "sped" and "cajoling."

16. **An extended metaphor comparing two very dissimilar things (one lofty one lowly) is a definition of a/an (Skill 1.2, Average Rigor)**

    A. antithesis.

    B. aphorism.

    C. apostrophe.

    D. conceit.

The answer is D. A conceit is an unusually far-fetched metaphor in which an object, person or situation is presented in a parallel and simpler analogue between two apparently very different things or feelings, one very sophisticated and one very ordinary, usually taken either from nature or a well known every day concept, familiar to both reader and author alike. The conceit was first developed by Petrarch and spread to England in the sixteenth century.

17. **Which of the following is a characteristic of blank verse? (Skill 1.2, Average Rigor)**

    A. Meter in iambic pentameter

    B. Clearly specified rhyme scheme

    C. Lack of figurative language

    D. Unspecified rhythm

The answer is A. An iamb is a metrical unit of verse having one unstressed syllable followed by one stressed syllable. This is the most commonly used metrical verse in English and American poetry. An iambic pentameter is a ten-syllable verse made of five of these metrical units, either rhymed as in sonnets, or unrhymed as in free, or blank, verse.

18. **Which is the best definition of free verse, or *vers libre*? (Skill 1.2, Average Rigor)**

    A. Poetry, which consists of an unaccented syllable followed by an unaccented sound.

    B. Short lyrical poetry written to entertain but with an instructive purpose.

    C. Poetry, which does not have a uniform pattern of rhythm.

    D. A poem which tells the story and has a plot

The answer is C. Free verse has lines of irregular length (but it does not run on like prose).

19. Which term best describes the form of the following poetic excerpt? (Skill 1.2, Rigorous)

> And more to lulle him in his
> slumber soft,
> A trickling streake from high rock
> tumbling downe,
> And ever-drizzling raine upon
> the loft.
> Mixt with a murmuring winde,
> much like a swowne
> No other noyse, nor peoples
> troubles cryes.
> As still we wont t'annoy the
> walle'd towne,
> Might there be heard: but
> careless Quiet lyes,
> Wrapt in eternall silence farre
> from enemyes.

A. Ballad

B. Elegy

C. Spenserian stanza

D. *Octava rima*

The answer is D. The *octava rima* is a specific eight-line stanza whose rhyme scheme is abababcc. A ballad is a narrative poem. An elegy is a form of lyric poetry typically used to mourn someone who has died. A form of the English sonnet created by Edmond Spenser combines the English form and the Italian. The Spenserian sonnet follows the English quatrain and couplet pattern but resembles the Italian in its rhyme scheme, which is linked: abab bcbc cdcd ee.

20. **In the phrase "The Cabinet conferred with the President," Cabinet is an example of a/an (Skill 1.2, Rigorous)**

    A. metonym

    B. synecdoche

    C. metaphor

    D. allusion

The answer is B. In a synecdoche, a whole is referred to by naming a part of it. Also, a synecdoche can stand for a whole of which it is a part: for example, the Cabinet for the Government. Metonymy is the substitution of a word for a related word. For example, "hit the books" means "to study." A metaphor is a comparison such as "a cat burglar." An allusion is a reference to someone or something in history. To say that 'she met her Waterloo and was fired" alludes to Napoleon's defeat.

21. **What syntactic device is most evident from Abraham Lincoln's "Gettysburg Address"? (Skill 1.2, Rigorous)**

    > It is rather for us to be here dedicated to the great task remaining before us -- that from these honored dead we take increased devotion to that cause for which they gave the last full measure of devotion—that we here highly resolve that these dead shall not have died in vain -- that this nation, under God, shall have a new birth of freedom—and that government of the people, by the people, for the people, shall not perish from the earth.

    A. Affective connotation

    B. Informative denotations

    C. Allusion

    D. Parallelism

The answer is D. Parallelism is the repetition of grammatical structure. In speeches such as this as well as speeches of Martin Luther King, Jr., parallel structure creates a rhythm and balance of related ideas. Lincoln's repetition of clauses beginning with "that" ties four examples back "to the great task." Connotation is the emotional attachment of words; denotation is the literal meaning of words. Allusion is a reference to a historic event, person, or place.

22. **A traditional, anonymous story, ostensibly having a historical basis, usually explaining some phenomenon of nature or aspect of creation, defines a/an (Skill 1.3, Easy)**

    A. proverb.

    B. idyll.

    C. myth.

    D. epic.

The answer is C. A myth is usually traditional and anonymous and explains natural and supernatural phenomena. Myths are usually about creation, divinity, the significance of life and death, and natural phenomena. A proverb is a saying or adage. An idyll is a short, pastoral poem. In its simplest form, an epic is a narrative poem.

23. **Which of the following is not a characteristic of a fable? (Skill 1.3, Easy)**

    A. Animals that feel and talk like humans.

    B. Happy solutions to human dilemmas.

    C. Teaches a moral or standard for behavior.

    D. Illustrates specific people or groups without directly naming them.

The answer is D. A fable is a short tale with animals, humans, gods, or even inanimate objects as characters. Fables often conclude with a moral, delivered in the form of an epigram (a short, witty, and ingenious statement in verse). Fables are among the oldest forms of writing in human history: it appears in Egyptian papyri of c 1500 BC. The most famous fables are those of Aesop, a Greek slave living in about 600 BC. In India, the *Pantchatantra* appeared in the third century. The most famous modern fables are those of seventeenth century French poet Jean de La Fontaine.

24. Which poem is typified as a villanelle? (Skill 1.3, Rigorous)

   A. "Do not go gentle into that good night"

   B. "Dover Beach"

   C. *Sir Gawain and the Green Knight*

   D. *Pilgrim's Progress*

The answer is A. This poem by Dylan Thomas typifies the villanelle because it was written as such. A villanelle is a form that was invented in France in the sixteenth century, and used mostly for pastoral songs. It has an uneven number (usually five) of tercets rhyming aba, with a final quatrain rhyming abaa. This poem is the most famous villanelle written in English. "Dover Beach" by Matthew Arnold is not a villanelle, while *Sir Gawain and the Green Knight* was written in alliterative verse by an unknown author usually referred to as The Pearl Poet around 1370. *Pilgrim's Progress* is a prose allegory by John Bunyan.

25. In classic tragedy, a protagonist's defeat is brought about by a tragic flaw which is called (Skill 1.3, Rigorous)

   A. hubris

   B. hamartia

   C. catharsis

   D. the skene

The answer is B. Hubris is excessive pride, a type of tragic flaw. Catharsis is an emotional purging the character feels. *Skene* is the Greek word for scene. All of these terms come from Greek drama.

26. Which sonnet form describes the following? (Skill 1.3, Rigorous)

My galley charg'd with
    forgetfulness,
Through sharp seas, in
    winter night doth pass
'Tween rock and rock; and
    eke mine enemy, alas,
That is my lord steereth with,
    cruelness.
And every oar a thought with
    readiness,
As though that death were
    light in such a case.
An endless wind doth tear
    the sail apace
Or forc'ed sighs and trusty
    fearfulness.
A rain of tears, a cloud of dark
    disdain,
Hath done the wearied
    cords great hinderance,
Wreathed with error and eke
    with ignorance.
The stars be hid that led me
    to this pain
Drowned is reason that
    should me consort,
And I remain despairing
    of the poet

A. Petrarchan or Italian sonnet

B. Shakespearian or Elizabethan sonnet

C. Romantic sonnet

D. Spenserian sonnet

The answer is A. The Petrarchan sonnet, also known as Italian sonnet, is named after the Italian poet Petrarch (1304-74). It is divided into an octave rhyming abbaabba and a sestet normally rhyming cdecde.

27. What is the salient literary feature of this excerpt from an epic? (Skill 1.3, Rigorous)

> Hither the heroes and the nymphs resorts,
> To taste awhile the pleasures of a court;
> In various talk th'instructive hours they passed,
> Who gave the ball, or paid the visit last;
> One speaks the glory of the English Queen,
> And another describes a charming Indian screen;
> A third interprets motion, looks, and eyes;
> At every word a reputation dies.

A. Sprung rhythm

B. Onomatopoeia

C. Heroic couplets

D. Motif

The answer is C. A couplet is a pair of rhyming verse lines, usually of the same length. It is one of the most widely used verse-forms in European poetry. Chaucer established the use of couplets in English, notably in the *Canterbury Tales,* using rhymed iambic pentameters (a metrical unit of verse having one unstressed syllable followed by one stressed syllable) later known as heroic couplets. Other authors who used heroic couplets include Ben Jonson, Dryden, and especially Alexander Pope, who became the master of them.

28. **The tendency to emphasize and value the qualities and peculiarities of life in a particular geographic area exemplifies (Skill 1.4, Easy)**

    A. pragmatism.

    B. regionalism.

    C. pantheism.

    D. abstractionism.

The answer is B. Pragmatism is a philosophical doctrine according to which there is no absolute truth. All truths change their trueness as their practical utility increases or decreases. The main representative of this movement is William James who in 1907 published *Pragmatism: A New Way for Some Old Ways of Thinking*. Pantheism is a philosophy according to which God is omnipresent in the world, everything is God and God is everything. The great representative of this sensibility is Spinoza. Also, the works of writers such as Wordsworth, Shelly and Emerson illustrate this doctrine. Abstract Expressionism is one of the most important movements in American art. It began in the 1940's with artists such as Willem de Kooning, Mark Rothko and Arshile Gorky. The paintings are usually large and non-representational.

29. **Charles Dickens, Robert Browning, and Robert Louis Stevenson were (Skill 1.4, Easy)**

    A. Victorians.

    B. Medievalists.

    C. Elizabethans.

    D. Absurdists.

The answer is A. The Victorian Period is remarkable for the diversity and quality of its literature. Robert Browning wrote chilling monologues such as "My Last Duchess," and long poetic narratives such as *The Pied Piper of Hamlin*. Robert Louis Stevenson wrote his works partly for young adults, whose imaginations were quite taken by his *Treasure Island* and *The Case of Dr. Jekyll and Mr. Hyde*. Charles Dickens tells of the misery of the time and the complexities of Victorian society in novels such as *Oliver Twist* or *Great Expectations*.

30. **Among junior-high school students of low-to-average readability levels, which work would most likely stir reading interest? (Skill 1.4, Easy)**

    A. *Elmer Gantry*, Sinclair Lewis

    B. *Smiley's People*, John Le Carre

    C. *The Outsiders*, S.E. Hinton

    D. *And Then There Were None*, Agatha Christie.

The answer is C. The students can easily identify with the characters and the gangs in the book. S.E. Hinton has actually said about this book: "*The Outsiders* is definitely my best-selling book; but what I like most about it is how it has taught a lot of kids to enjoy reading." The other three novels have more mature subject matter, more complex characters, and higher reading levels. Lewis' novel satirizes hypocrisy in the character of a debauched evangelist. Le Carre's novel is the third part of a spy novel trilogy. Christie's mystery has a wide cast of characters who are murdered one by one.

31. **What is considered the first work of English literature because it was written in the vernacular of the day? (Skill 1.4, Easy)**

    A. *Beowulf*

    B. *Le Morte d'Arthur*

    C. *The Faerie Queene*

    D. *Canterbury Tales*

The answer is D. Chaucer wrote the *Canterbury Tales* in the street language of medieval England. *Beowulf* was written during the Anglo-Saxon period and is a Teutonic saga. *Le Morte d'Arthur*, by Thomas Malory was written after Chaucer. Sir Edmund Spencer's *The Faerie Queene* was written during the Renaissance under the reign of Queen Elizabeth I.

32. Considered one of the first feminist plays, this Ibsen drama ends with a door slamming symbolizing the lead character's emancipation from traditional societal norms. (Skill 1.4, Average Rigor)

    A. *The Wild Duck*

    B. *Hedda Gabler*

    C. *Ghosts*

    D. *The Doll's House*

The answer is D. Nora in *The Doll's House* leaves her husband and her children when she realizes her husband is not the man she thought he was. Hedda Gabler, another feminist icon, shoots herself. *The Wild Duck* deals with the conflict between idealism and family secrets. *Ghosts,* considered one of Ibsen's most controversial plays, deals with many social ills, some of which include alcoholism, incest, and religious hypocrisy.

33. Which of the following titles is known for its scathingly condemning tone? (Skill 1.4, Average Rigor)

    A. Boris Pasternak's *Dr Zhivago*

    B. Albert Camus' *The Stranger*

    C. Henry David Thoreau's "On the Duty of Civil Disobedience"

    D. Benjamin Franklin's "Rules by Which a Great Empire May Be Reduced to a Small One"

The answer is D. In this work, Benjamin Franklin adopts a scathingly ironic tone to warn the British about the probable outcome in their colonies if they persist with their policies. These are discussed one by one in the text, and the absurdity of each is condemned.

34. **American colonial writers were primarily (Skill 1.4, Average Rigor)**

   A. Romanticists.

   B. Naturalists.

   C. Realists.

   D. Neo-classicists.

The answer is D. The early colonists had been schooled in England, and even though their writing became quite American in content, their emphasis on clarity and balance in their language remained British. This literature reflects the lives of the early colonists, such as William Bradford's excerpts from "The Mayflower Compact," Anne Bradstreet's poetry and William Byrd's journal, *A History of the Dividing Line*.

35. **Arthur Miller wrote *The Crucible* as a parallel to what twentieth century event? (Skill 1.4, Average Rigor)**

   A. Sen. McCarthy's House un-American Activities Committee Hearing

   B. The Cold War

   C. The fall of the Berlin wall

   D. The Persian Gulf War

The answer is A. The episode of the seventeenth century witch-hunt in Salem, Mass., gave Miller a storyline that was very comparable to what was happening to persons suspected of communist beliefs in the 1950s.

36. **Which of the writers below is a renowned Black poet? (Skill 1.4, Average Rigor)**

    A. Maya Angelou

    B. Sandra Cisneros

    C. Richard Wilbur

    D. Richard Wright

The answer is A. Among her most famous work are *I Know Why the Caged Bird Sings* (1970), *And Still I Rise* (1978), and *All God's Children Need Traveling Shoes* (1986). Richard Wilbur is a poet and a translator of French dramatists Racine and Moliere, but he is not African American. Richard Wright is a very important African American author of novels such as *Native Son* and *Black Boy*. However, he was not a poet. Sandra Cisneros is a Latina author who is very important in developing Latina Women's literature.

37. **Which of the following is not a theme of Native American writing? (Skill 1.4, Average Rigor)**

    A. Emphasis on the hardiness of the human body and soul

    B. The strength of multi-cultural assimilation

    C. Contrition for the genocide of native peoples

    D. Remorse for the love of the Indian way of life

The answer is B. Native American literature was first a vast body of oral traditions from as early as before the fifteenth century. The characteristics include reverence for and awe of nature and the interconnectedness of the elements in the life cycle. The themes often reflect the hardiness of body and soul, remorse for the destruction of the Native American way of life, and the genocide of many tribes by the encroaching settlements of European Americans. These themes are still present in today's contemporary Native American literature, such as in the works of Duane Niatum, Gunn Allen, Louise Erdrich and N. Scott Momaday.

38. The writing of Russian naturalists is (Skill 1.4, Average Rigor)

    A. optimistic.

    B. pessimistic.

    C. satirical.

    D. whimsical.

The answer is B. Although the movement, which originated with the critic Vissarion Belinsky, was particularly strong in the 1840's, it can be said that the works of Dostoevsky, Tolstoy, Chekov, Turgenev and Pushkin owe much to it. These authors' works are among the best in international literature, yet are shrouded in stark pessimism. Tolstoy's *Anna Karenina* or Dostoevsky's *Crime and Punishment* are good examples of this dark outlook.

39. Most children's literature prior to the development of popular literature was intended to be didactic. Which of the following would not be considered didactic? (Skill 1.4, Average Rigor)

    A. "A Visit from St. Nicholas" by Clement Moore

    B. *McGuffy's Reader*

    C. Any version of Cinderella

    D. Parables from the Bible

The answer is A. "A Visit from St. Nicholas" is a cheery, non-threatening child's view of "The Night before Christmas." Didactic means intended to teach some lesson.

40. **Written on the sixth grade reading level, most of S. E. Hinton's novels (for instance, *The Outsiders*) have the greatest reader appeal with (Skill 1.4, Average Rigor)**

    A. sixth graders.

    B. ninth graders.

    C. twelfth graders.

    D. adults.

The answer is B. Adolescents are concerned with their changing bodies, their relationships with each other and adults, and their place in society. Reading *The Outsiders* makes them confront different problems that they are only now beginning to experience as teenagers, such as gangs and social identity. The book is universal in its appeal to adolescents.

41. **Children's literature became established in the (Skill 1.4, Average Rigor)**

    A. seventeenth century

    B. eighteenth century

    C. nineteenth century

    D. twentieth century

The answer is A. In the seventeenth Century, authors such as Jean de La Fontaine and his fables, Pierre Perreault's tales, Mme d'Aulnoye's novels based on old folktales and Mme de Beaumont's *Beauty and the Beast* all created a children's literature genre. In England, Perreault was translated and a work allegedly written by Oliver Smith, *The Renowned History of Little Goody Two Shoes,* also helped to establish children's literature in England.

42. After watching a movie of a train derailment, a child exclaims, "Wow, look how many cars fell off the tracks. There's junk everywhere. The engineer must have really been asleep." Using the facts that the child is impressed by the wreckage and assigns blame to the engineer, a follower of Piaget's theories would estimate the child to be about (Skill 1.4, Rigorous)

    A. ten years old.

    B. twelve years old.

    C. fourteen years old.

    D. sixteen years old.

The answer is A. According to Piaget's theory, children seven-to-eleven years old begin to apply logic to concrete things and experiences. They can combine performance and reasoning to solve problems. They have internalized moral values and are willing to confront rules and adult authority.

43. **The most significant drawback to applying learning theory research to classroom practice is that (Skill 1.4, Rigorous)**

    A. today's students do not acquire reading skills with the same alacrity as when greater emphasis was placed on reading classical literature.

    B. development rates are complicated by geographical and cultural In analyzing literature and in looking for ways to bring a work to life for an audience, the use of comparable themes and ideas from other pieces of literature and from one's own life experiences, including from reading the daily newspaper, is very important and useful.

    C. homogeneous grouping has contributed to faster development of some age groups.

    D. social and environmental conditions have contributed to an escalated maturity level than research done twenty of more years ago would seem to indicate.

The answer is D. Because of the rapid social changes, topics that were not interesting to younger readers are now topics of books for even younger readers. Many books dealing with difficult topics, and it is difficult for the teacher to steer students toward books that they are ready for and to try to keep them away from books whose content, although well written, are not yet appropriate for their level of cognitive and social development. There is a fine line between this and censorship.

44. **Which of the following is the best definition of existentialism? (Skill 1.4, Rigorous)**

    A. The philosophical doctrine that matter is the only reality and that everything in the world, including thought, will and feeling, can be explained only in terms of matter.

    B. Philosophy that views things as they should be or as one would wish them to be.

    C. A philosophical and literary movement, variously religious and atheistic, stemming from Kierkegaard and represented by Sartre.

    D. The belief that all events are determined by fate and are hence inevitable.

The answer is C. Even though there are other very important thinkers in the movement known as Existentialism, such as Camus and Merleau-Ponty, Sartre remains the main figure in this movement.

45. **The following lines from Robert Browning's poem "My Last Duchess" come from an example of what form of dramatic literature? (Skill 1.4, Rigorous)**

> That's my last Duchess painted on the wall,
> Looking as if she were alive. I call
> That piece a wonder
> now: Frà Pandolf's hands
> Worked busily a day
> and there she stands.
> Will 't please you sit and look at her?

A. Tragedy

B. Comic opera

C. Dramatis personae

D. Dramatic monologue

The answer is D. A dramatic monologue is a speech given by a character or narrator that reveals characteristics of the character or narrator. This form was first made popular by Robert Browning, a Victorian poet. Tragedy is a form of literature in which the protagonist is overwhelmed by opposing forces. Comic opera is a form of sung music based on a light or happy plot. Dramatis personae is the Latin phrase for the cast of a play.

46. **"Every one must pass through Vanity Fair to get to the celestial city" is an allusion from a (Skill 1.4, Rigorous)**

A. Chinese folk tale.

B. British allegory.

C. Norse sage.

D. German fairy tale.

The answer is B. This is a reference to John Bunyan's *Pilgrim's Progress* from *This World to That Which Is to Come* (Part I, 1678; Part II, 1684), in which the hero, Christian, flees the City of Destruction and must undergo different trials and tests to get to the Celestial City.

47. **Which author did not write satire? (Skill 1.4, Rigorous)**

    A. Joseph Addison

    B. Richard Steele

    C. Alexander Pope

    D. John Bunyan

The answer is D. John Bunyan was a religious writer, known for his autobiography, *Grace Abounding to the Chief of Sinners,* as well as other books, all religious in their inspiration, such as *The Holy City, or the New Jerusalem* (1665), *A Confession of My Faith,* and *A Reason of My Practice* (1672), or *The Holy War* (1682).

48. **What were two major characteristics of the first American literature? (Skill 1.4, Rigorous)**

    A. Vengefulness and arrogance

    B. Bellicosity and derision

    C. Oral delivery and reverence for the land

    D. Maudlin and self-pitying egocentricism

The answer is D. This characteristic can be seen in Captain John Smith's work, as well as William Bradford's and Michael Wigglesworth's works.

49. Hoping to take advantage of the popularity of the Harry Potter series, a teacher develops a unit on mythology comparing the story and characters of Greek and Roman myths with the story and characters of the Harry Potter books. Which of these is a commonality that would link classical literature to popular fiction? (Skill 1.4, Rigorous)

    A. The characters are gods in human form with human-like characteristics.

    B. The settings are realistic places in the world where the characters interact as humans would.

    C. The themes center on the universal truths of love and hate and fear.

    D. The heroes in the stories are young males and only they can overcome the opposing forces.

The answer is C. Although the gods in Greek and Roman myths take human form, they are immortal as gods must be. The characters in Harry Potter may be wizards, but they are not immortal. Although the settings in these stories have familiar associations, their worlds are vastly different from those inhabited by mortals and Muggles. While male heroes may dominate the action, the females (Hera, Dianna, Hermione) are powerful as well.

50. In the following poem, what literary movement is reflected? (Skill 1.4, Rigorous)

"My Heart Leaps Up" by William Wordsworth

My heart leaps up when I behold
  A rainbow in the sky:
So was it when my life began;
So is it now I am a man;
So be it when I shall grow old,
  Or let me die!
The Child is father of the Man;
And I could wish my days to be
Bound each to each by natural piety

A. Neo-classicism

B. Victorian literature

C. Romanticism

D. Naturalism

The answer is C. The Romantic period of the 19th century is known for its emphasis on feelings, emotions, and passions. William Wordsworth and William Blake were two notable poets from this period. In the neoclassicism of the previous period, the literature echoed the classical ideals of proportion, common sense, and reason over raw emotion and imagination, and the purpose was more didactic than celebratory. The Victorian period of the late 19th century exerted more restraint on emotions and feelings. In naturalistic writing, authors depict the world more harshly and more objectively.

51. In preparing a unit on 20th century immigration you prepare a list of books for students to read. Which book would not be appropriate for this topic? (Skill 1.5, Average Rigor)

    A. The Things They Carried by Tim O'Brien

    B. Exodus by Leon Uris

    C. The Joy Luck Club by Amy Tan

    D. Tortilla Flats by John Steinbeck

The answer is A. O'Brien's book centers on American soldiers serving in Viet Nam. Uris' book details the founding of Israel after World War II. Tan's novel contrasts her family's life in China and in the United States. Steinbeck's novel illustrates the plight of Mexican migrant workers.

52. To explore the relationship of literature to modern life, which of these activities would not enable students to explore comparable themes? (Skill 1.5, Average Rigor)

    A. After studying various world events, such as the Palestinian-Israeli conflict, students write an updated version of *Romeo and Juliet* using modern characters and settings.

    B. Before studying *Romeo and Juliet,* students watch *West Side Story.*

    C. Students research the major themes of *Romeo and Juliet* by studying news stories and finding modern counterparts for the story.

    D. Students would explore compare the romantic themes of *Romeo and Juliet* and *The Taming of the Shrew.*

The answer is D. By comparing the two plays by Shakespeare, students will be focusing on the culture of the period in which the plays were written. In Answer A, students should be able to recognize modern parallels with current culture clashes. By comparing the *Romeo and Juliet* to the 1950's update of *West Side Story,* students can study how themes are similar in two completely different historical periods. In Answer C, students can study local, national, and international news for comparable stories and themes.

53. **Mr. Phillips is creating a unit to study _To Kill a Mockingbird_ and wants to familiarize his high school freshmen with the attitudes and issues of the historical period. Which activity would familiarize students with the attitudes and issues of the Depression-era South? (Skill 1.5, Rigorous)**

    A. Create a detailed timeline of 15-20 social, cultural, and political events that focus on race relations in the 1930s.

    B. Research and report on the life of its author Harper Lee. Compare her background with the events in the book.

    C. Watch the movie version and note language and dress.

    D. Write a research report on the stock market crash of 1929 and its effects.

The answer is A. By identifying the social, cultural, and political events of the 1930s, students will better understand the attitudes and values of America during the time of the novel. While researching the author's life could add depth to their understanding of the novel, it is unnecessary to the appreciation of the novel by itself. The movie version is an accurate depiction of the novel's setting but it focuses on the events in the novel, not the external factors that fostered the conflict. The stock market crash and the subsequent Great Depression would be important to note on the timeline but students would be distracted from themes of the book by narrowing their focus to only these two events.

54. Which choice below best defines naturalism? (Skill 1.5, Rigorous)

    A. A belief that the writer or artist should apply scientific objectivity in his/her observation and treatment of life without imposing value judgments.

    B. The doctrine that teaches that the existing world is the best to be hoped for.

    C. The doctrine that teaches that God is not a personality, but that all laws, forces and manifestations of the universe are God-related.

    D. A philosophical doctrine that professes that the truth of all knowledge must always be in question.

The answer is A. Naturalism is a movement that was started by French writers Jules and Edmond de Goncourt with their novel *Germinie Lacerteux* (1865), but its real leader is Emile Zola, who wanted to bring "a slice of life" to his readers. His saga, *Les Rougon Macquart,* consists in twenty-two novels depicting various aspects of social life. English writing authors representative of this movement include George Moore and George Gissing in England, but the most important naturalist novel in English is Theodore Dreiser's *Sister Carrie*.

55. The students in Mrs. Cline's seventh grade language arts class were invited to attend a performance of *Romeo and Juliet* presented by the drama class at the high school. To best prepare, they should (Skill 1.6, Average Rigor)

    A. read the play as a homework exercise.

    B. read a synopsis of the plot and a biographical sketch of the author.

    C. examine a few main selections from the play to become familiar with the language and style of the author.

    D. read a condensed version of the story and practice attentive listening skills.

The answer is D. By reading a condensed version of the story, students will know the plot and therefore be able to follow the play on stage. It is also important for them to practice listening techniques such as one one-to-one tutoring and peer-assisted reading.

56. **What is the best course of action when a child refuses to complete a reading/ literature assignment on the grounds that it is morally objectionable? (Skill 1.6, Average Rigor)**

   A. Speak with the parents and explain the necessity of studying this work

   B. Encourage the child to sample some of the text before making a judgment

   C. Place the child in another teacher's class where they are studying an acceptable work

   D. Provide the student with alternative selections that cover the same performance standards that the rest of the class is learning.

The answer is D. In the case of a student finding a reading offensive, it is the responsibility of the teacher to assign another title. As a general rule, it is always advisable to notify parents if a particularly sensitive piece is to be studied.

57. **The English department is developing strategies to encourage all students to become a community of readers. From the list of suggestions below, which would be the least effective way for teachers to foster independent reading? (Skill 1.6, Average Rigor)**

   A. Each teacher will set aside a weekly 30-minute in-class reading session during which the teacher and students read a magazine or book for enjoyment.

   B. Teacher and students develop a list of favorite books to share with each other.

   C. The teacher assigns at least one book report each grading period to ensure that students are reading from the established class list.

   D. The students gather books for a classroom library so that books may be shared with each other.

The answer is C. Teacher-directed assignments such as book reports appear routine and unexciting. Students will be more excited about reading when they can actively participate. In Answer A, the teacher is modeling reading behavior and providing students with a dedicated time during which time they can read independently and still be surrounded by a community of readers. In Answers B and D, students share and make available their reading choices.

58. Which of the following responses to literature typically give middle school students the most problems? (Skill 1.6, Average Rigor)

    A. Interpretive

    B. Evaluative

    C. Critical

    D. Emotional

The answer is B. Middle school readers will exhibit both emotional and interpretive responses. In middle/junior high school, organized study models enable students to identify main ideas and supporting details, to recognize sequential order, to distinguish fact from opinion, and to determine cause/effect relationships. Also, a child's being able to say why a particular book was boring or why a particular poem made him/her sad evidences critical reactions on a fundamental level. It is a bit early for evaluative responses, however. These depend on the reader's consideration of how the piece represents its genre, how well it reflects the social/ethical mores of a given society, and how well the author has approached the subject for freshness and slant. Evaluative responses are made only by a few advanced high school students.

59. Which of the following is a formal reading-level assessment? (Skill 1.6, Average Rigor)

    A. A standardized reading test

    B. A teacher-made reading test

    C. An interview

    D. A reading diary

The answer is A. If assessment is standardized, it has to be objective whereas Answers B, C and D are all subjective assessments.

60. **Which of the following would be the most significant factor in teaching Homer's *Iliad* and *Odyssey* to any particular group of students? (Skill 1.6, Average Rigor)**

    A. Identifying a translation on the appropriate reading level

    B. Determining the students' interest level

    C. Selecting an appropriate evaluative technique

    D. Determining the scope and delivery methods of background study

The answer is A. Students will learn the importance of these two works if the translation reflects both the vocabulary that they know and their reading level. Greece will always be foremost in literary assessments due to Homer's works. Homer is the most often cited author, next to Shakespeare. Greece is the cradle of both democracy and literature. This is why it is so crucial that Homer be included in the works assigned.

61. **Which of the following definitions best describes a parable? (Skill 1.6, Average Rigor)**

    A. A short entertaining account of some happening, usually using talking animals as characters.

    B. A slow, sad song or poem, or prose work expressing lamentation.

    C. An extensive narrative work expressing universal truths concerning domestic life.

    D. A short, simple story of an occurrence of a familiar kind, from which a moral or religious lesson may be drawn.

The answer is D. A parable is usually brief, and should be interpreted as an allegory teaching a moral lesson. Jesus' forty parables are the model of the genre, but modern, secular examples exist such as Wilfred Owen's "The Parable of The Young Man" and "The Young" (1920), or John Steinbeck's prose work *The Pearl* (1948).

62. Which teaching method would best engage underachievers in the required senior English class? (Skill 1.6, Average Rigor)

  A. Assign use of glossary work and extensively footnoted excerpts of great works.

  B. Have students take turns reading aloud the anthology selection

  C. Let students choose which readings they'll study and write about.

  D. Use a chronologically arranged, traditional text, but assigning group work, panel presentations, and portfolio management

The answer is C. It will encourage students to react honestly to literature. Students should take notes on what they're reading so they will be able to discuss the material. They should not only react to literature, but also experience it. Small-group work is a good way to encourage them. The other answers are not fit for junior-high or high school students. They should be encouraged, however, to read critics of works in order to understand criteria work.

63. How will literature help students in a science class able understand the following passage? (Skill 1.6, Rigorous)

> Just as was the case more than three decades ago, we are still sailing between the Scylla of deferring surgery for too long and risking irreversible left ventricular damage and sudden death, and the Charibdas of operating too early and subjecting the patient to the early risks of operation and the later risks resulting from prosthetic valves.
> --E. Braunwald, *European Heart Journal,* July 2000

A. They will recognize the allusion to Scylla and Charibdas from Greek mythology and understand that the medical community has to select one of two unfavorable choices.

B. They will recognize the allusion to sailing and understand its analogy to doctors as sailors navigating unknown waters.

C. They will recognize that the allusion to Scylla and Charibdas refers to the two islands in Norse mythology where sailors would find themselves shipwrecked and understand how the doctors feel isolated by their choices.

D. They will recognize the metaphor of the heart and relate it to Eros, the character in Greek mythology who represents love. Eros was the love child of Scylla and Charibdas.

The answer is A. Scylla and Charibdas were two sea monsters guarding a narrow channel of water. Sailors trying to elude one side would face danger by sailing too close to the other side. The allusion indicates two equally undesirable choices.

64. Which is not a Biblical allusion? (Skill 1.6, Rigorous)

  A. The patience of Job

  B. Thirty pieces of silver

  C. "Man proposes; God disposes"

  D. "Suffer not yourself to be betrayed by a kiss"

The answer is C. This saying is attributed to Thomas à Kempis (1379-1471) in his *Imitation of Christ,* Book 1, chapter 19. Anyone who exhibits the patience of Job is being compared to the Old Testament biblical figure who retained his faith despite being beset by a series of misfortunes. "Thirty pieces of silver" refers to the amount of money paid to Judas to identify Jesus. Used by Patrick Henry, the quote in D is a biblical reference to Judas' betrayal of Judas by a kiss.

65. Before reading a passage, a teacher gives her students an anticipation guide with a list of statements related to the topic they are about to cover in the reading material. She asks the students to indicate their agreement or disagreement with each statement on the guide. This activity is intended to (Skill 1.6, Rigorous)

  A. elicit students' prior knowledge of the topic and set a purpose for reading.

  B. help students to identify the main ideas and supporting details in the text.

  C. help students to synthesize information from the text.

  D. help students to visualize the concepts and terms in the text.

The correct answer is A. Establishing a purpose for reading, the foundation for a reading unit or activity, is intimately connected to activating the students' prior knowledge in strategic ways. When the reason for reading is developed in the context of the students' experiences, they are far better prepared to succeed because they can make connections from a base they thoroughly understand. This influences motivation, and with proper motivation, students are more enthused and put forward more effort to understand the text. The other choices are only indirectly supported by this activity and are more specific in focus.

66. **Recognizing empathy in literature is mostly a/an (Skill 1.6, Rigorous)**

    A. emotional response.

    B. interpretive response.

    C. critical response.

    D. evaluative response.

The answer is C. In critical responses, students make value judgments about the quality and atmosphere of a text. Through class discussion and written assignments, students react to and assimilate a writer's style and language.

67. **If a student has a poor vocabulary, the teacher should recommend first that (Skill 2.1, Average Rigor)**

    A. the student read newspapers, magazines and books on a regular basis.

    B. the student enroll in a Latin class.

    C. the student write the words repetitively after looking them up in the dictionary.

    D. the student use a thesaurus to locate synonyms and incorporate them into his/her vocabulary

The answer is A. The teacher can personally influence what the student chooses as reading material, but the student must be able to choose independently where to search for the reading pleasure indispensable for enriching vocabulary.

68. Which of the following sentences contains a subject-verb agreement error? (Skill 2.1, Average Rigor)

    A. Both mother and her two sisters were married in a triple ceremony.

    B. Neither the hen nor the rooster is likely to be served for dinner.

    C. My boss, as well as the company's two personnel directors, have been to Spain.

    D. Amanda and the twins are late again.

The answer is C. The reason for this is that the true subject of the verb is "My boss," not "two personnel directors."

69. The synonyms *gyro, hero,* and *submarine* reflect which influence on language usage? (Skill 2.1, Average Rigor)

    A. Social

    B. Geographical

    C. Historical

    D. Personal

The answer is B. They are interchangeable but their use depends on the region of the United States, not on the social class of the speaker. Nor is there any historical context around any of them. The usage can be personal but will most often vary with the region.

70. Which aspect of language is innate? (Skill 2.1, Rigorous)

    A. Biological capability to articulate sounds understood by other humans

    B. Cognitive ability to create syntactical structures

    C. Capacity for using semantics to convey meaning in a social environment

    D. Ability to vary inflections and accents

The answer is A. Language ability is innate and the biological capability to produce sounds lets children learn semantics and syntactical structures through trial and error. Linguists agree that language is first a vocal system of word symbols that enable a human to communicate his/her feelings, thoughts, and desires to other human beings.

71. To understand the origins of a word, one must study the (Skill 2.2, Easy)

    A. synonyms

    B. inflections

    C. phonetics

    D. etymology

The answer is D. Etymology is the study of word origins. A synonym is an equivalent of another word and can substitute for it in certain contexts. Inflection is a modification of words according to their grammatical functions, usually by employing variant word-endings to indicate such qualities as tense, gender, case, and number. Phonetics is the science devoted to the physical analysis of the sounds of human speech, including their production, transmission, and perception.

72. The Elizabethans wrote in (Skill 2.2 Easy)

    A. Celtic

    B. Old English

    C. Middle English

    D. Modern English

The answer is D. There is no document written in Celtic in England, and a work such as Beowulf is representative of Old English in the eighth century. It is also the earliest Teutonic written document. Before the fourteenth century, little literature is known to have appeared in Middle English, which had absorbed many words from the Norman French spoken by the ruling class, but at the end of the fourteenth century there appeared the works of Chaucer, John Gower, and the novel *Sir Gawain and the Green Knight*. The Elizabethans wrote in modern English and their legacy is very important: they imported the Petrarchan, or Italian, sonnet, which Sir Thomas Wyatt and Sir Philip Sydney illustrated in their works. Sir Edmund Spencer invented his own version of the Italian sonnet and wrote *The Faerie Queene*. Other literature of the time includes the hugely important works of Shakespeare and Marlowe.

73. Which event triggered the beginning of Modern English? (Skill 2.2, Average Rigor)

    A. Conquest of England by the Normans in 1066

    B. Introduction of the printing press to the British Isles

    C. Publication of Samuel Johnson's lexicon.

    D. American Revolution

The answer is B. With the arrival of the written word, reading matter became mass-produced, so the public tended to adopt the speech and writing habits printed in books and the language became more stable.

74. **Which of the following is not true about the English language? (Skill 2.2, Average Rigor)**

   A. English is the easiest language to learn.

   B. English is the least inflected language.

   C. English has the most extensive vocabulary of any language.

   D. English originated as a Germanic tongue.

The answer is A. Just like any other language, English has inherent difficulties which make it difficult to learn, even though English has no declensions such as those found in Latin, Greek, or contemporary Russian, or a tonal system such Chinese.

75. **Which word in the following sentence is a bound morpheme: "The quick brown fox jumped over the lazy dog"? (Skill 2.2, Rigorous)**

   A. The

   B. fox

   C. lazy

   D. jumped

The answer is D. The suffix "-ed" is an affix that cannot stand alone as a unit of meaning. Thus it is bound to the free morpheme "jump." "The" is always an unbound morpheme since no suffix or prefix can alter its meaning. As written, "fox" and "lazy" are unbound but their meaning is changed with affixes, such as "foxes" or "laziness."

76. **What was responsible for the standardizing of dialects across America in the 20th century? (Skill 2.2, Rigorous)**

    A. With the immigrant influx, American became a melting pot of languages and cultures.

    B. Trains enabled people to meet other people of different languages and cultures.

    C. Radio, and later, television, used actors and announcers who spoke without pronounced dialects.

    D. Newspapers and libraries developed programs to teach people to speak English with an agreed-upon common dialect.

The answer is C. The growth of immigration in the early part of the 20th century created pockets of language throughout the country. Coupled with regional differences already in place, the number of dialects grew. Transportation enabled people to move to different regions where languages and dialects continued to merge. With the growth of radio and television, however, people were introduced to a standardized dialect through actors and announcers who spoke so that anyone across American could understand them. Newspapers and libraries never developed programs to standardize spoken English.

77. **Latin words that entered the English language during the Elizabethan age include (Skill 2.2, Rigorous)**

    A. allusion, education, and esteem

    B. vogue and mustache

    C. canoe and cannibal

    D. alligator, cocoa, and armadillo

The answer is A. These words reflect the Renaissance interest in the classical world and the study of ideas. The words in Answer B are French derivation, and the words in Answers C and D are more modern with younger etymologies.

78. Which of the following sentences is properly punctuated? (Skill 2.3, Easy)

   A. The more you eat; the more you want.

   B. The authors—John Steinbeck, Ernest Hemingway, and William Faulkner—are staples of modern writing in American literature textbooks.

   C. Handling a wild horse, takes a great deal of skill and patience.

   D. The man, who replaced our teacher, is a comedian.

The answer is B. Dashes should be used instead of commas when commas are used elsewhere in the sentence for amplification or explanation —here within the dashes.

79. Which sentence below best minimizes the impact of bad news? (Skill 2.3, Rigorous)

   A. We have denied you permission to attend the event.

   B. Although permission to attend the event cannot be given, you are encouraged to buy the video.

   C. Although you cannot attend the event, we encourage you to buy the video.

   D. Although attending the event is not possible, watching the video is an option.

The answer is B. Subordinating the bad news and using passive voice minimizes the impact of the bad news. In Answer A, the sentence is active voice and thus too direct. The word *denied* sets a negative tone. In Answer C, the bad news is subordinated but it is still active voice with negative wording. In Answer D, the sentence is too unclear.

80. The arrangement and relationship of words in sentences or sentence structures best describes (Skill 2.3, Rigorous)

    A. style.

    B. discourse.

    C. thesis.

    D. syntax.

The answer is D. Syntax is the grammatical structure of sentences. Style is the manner of expression of writing or speaking. Discourse is an extended expression of thought through either oral or written communication. A thesis is the unifying main idea that can be either explicit or implicit.

81. The substitution of *went to his rest* for *died* is an example of a/an (Skill 2.4, Easy)

    A. bowdlerism.

    B. jargon.

    C. euphemism.

    D. malapropism.

The answer is C. A euphemism replaces an unpleasant or offensive word or expression by a more agreeable one. It also alludes to distasteful things in a pleasant manner, and it can even paraphrase offensive texts. Bowdlerism is named after Thomas Bowdler who excised from Shakespeare what he considered vulgar and offensive. Jargon is a specialized language used by a particular group. What was groovy to one generation has become awesome to another. Named after Mrs. Malaprop, a character in a play by Richard Sheridan, a malapropism is a misuse of words, often to comical effect. Mrs. Malaprop once said "...she's as headstrong as an allegory on the banks of Nile" misusing allegory for alligator.

82. **If students use slang and expletives, what is the best course of action to take in order to improve their formal communication skills? (Skill 2.4, Average Rigor)**

   A. Ask the students to paraphrase their writing, that is, translate it into language appropriate for the school principal to read.

   B. Refuse to read the students' papers until they conform to a more literate style.

   C. Ask the students to read their work aloud to the class for peer evaluation.

   D. Rewrite the flagrant passages to show the students the right form of expression.

The answer is A. Asking the students to write for a specific audience will help them become more involved in their writing. If they continue writing to the same audience—the teacher—they will continue seeing writing as just another assignment, and they will not apply grammar, vocabulary and syntax the way they should be. By rephrasing their own writing, they will learn to write for a different public.

83. **Which level of meaning is the hardest aspect of a language to master? (Skill 2.4, Rigorous)**

   A. Denotation

   B. Jargon

   C. Connotation

   D. Slang

The answer is C. Connotation refers to the meanings suggested by a word, rather than the dictionary definition. For example, the word "slim" means thin, and it is usually used with a positive connotation, to compliment of admire someone's figure. The word "skinny" also means thin, but its connotations are not as flattering as those of the word "slim." The connotative aspect of language is more difficult to master than the denotation (dictionary definition), as the former requires a mastery of the social aspect of language, not just the linguistic rules.

84. **Reading a piece of student writing to assess the overall impression of the product is (Skill 3.1, Easy)**

    A. holistic evaluation.

    B. portfolio assessment.

    C. analytical evaluation.

    D. using a performance system.

The answer is A. Holistic scoring assesses a piece of writing as a whole. Usually a paper is read quickly through once to get a general impression. The writing is graded according to the impression of the whole work rather than the sum of its parts. Often holistic scoring uses a rubric that establishes the overall criteria for a certain score to evaluate each paper.

85. **What is not one of the advantages of collaborative or cooperative learning? (Skill 3.1, Easy)**

    A. Students that work together in groups or teams develop their skills in organizing, leadership, research, communication, and problem solving.

    B. Working in teams can help students overcome anxiety in distance learning courses and contribute a sense of community and belonging for the students.

    C. Students tend to learn more material being taught and retain the information longer than when the same information is taught using different methods.

    D. Teachers reduce their workload and the time spent on individuals the assignments, and grading.

The answer is D. Teacher continue to expend time in planning, monitoring and evaluating the students, their groups, and their activities.

86. **Writing ideas quickly without interruption of the flow of thoughts or attention to conventions is called (Skill 3.1, Easy)**

    A. brainstorming.

    B. mapping.

    C. listing.

    D. free writing.

The answer is D. Free writing for ten or fifteen minutes allows students to write out their thoughts about a subject. This technique allows the students to develop ideas that they are conscious of, but it also helps them to develop ideas that are lurking in the subconscious. It is important to let the flow of ideas run through the hand. If the students get stuck, they can write the last sentence over again until inspiration returns.

87. **Which of the following should not be included in the opening paragraph of an informative essay? (Skill 3.1, Easy)**

    A. Thesis sentence

    B. Details and examples supporting the main idea

    C. Broad general introduction to the topic

    D. A style and tone that grabs the reader's attention

The answer is B. The introductory paragraph should introduce the topic, capture the reader's interest, state the thesis and prepare the reader for the main points in the essay. Details and examples, however, should be given in the second part of the essay, so as to help develop the thesis presented at the end of the introductory paragraph, following the inverted triangle method consisting of a broad general statement followed by some information, and then the thesis at the end of the paragraph.

88. **In the paragraph below, which sentence does not contribute to the overall task of supporting the main idea? (Skill 3.1 Easy)**

> 1) The Springfield City Council met Friday to discuss new zoning restrictions for the land to be developed south of the city. 2) Residents who opposed the new restrictions were granted 15 minutes to present their case. 3) Their argument focused on the dangers that increased traffic would bring to the area. 4) It seemed to me that the Mayor Simpson listened intently. 5) The council agreed to table the new zoning until studies would be performed.

   A. Sentence 2

   B. Sentence 3

   C. Sentence 4

   D. Sentence 5

The answer is C. The other sentences provide detail to the main idea of the new zoning restrictions. Because sentence 4 provides no example or relevant detail, it should be omitted.

89. **In preparing your high school freshmen to write a research paper about a social problem, what recommendation can you make so they can determine the credibility of their information? (Skill 3.1, Average Rigor)**

   A. Assure them that information on the Internet has been peer-reviewed and verified for accuracy.

   B. Find one solid source and use that exclusively.

   C. Use only primary sources.

   D. Cross check your information with another credible source.

The answer is D. When researchers find the same information in multiple reputable sources, the information is considered credible. Using the Internet for research requires strong critical evaluation of the source. Nothing from the Internet should be taken without careful scrutiny of the source. To rely on only one source is dangerous and short-sighted. Most high school freshmen would have limited skills to conduct primary research for a paper about a social problem.

90. **Modeling is a practice that requires students to (Skill 3.1, Average Rigor)**

    A. create a style unique to their own language capabilities.

    B. emulate the writing of professionals.

    C. paraphrase passages from good literature.

    D. peer evaluate the writings of other students.

The answer is B. Modeling has students analyze the writing of a professional writer and try to reach the same level of syntactical, grammatical and stylistic mastery as the author whom they are studying.

91. **Which of the following are secondary research materials? (Skill 3.1, Average Rigor)**

    A. The conclusions and inferences of other historians.

    B. Literature and nonverbal materials, novels, stories, poetry and essays from the period, as well as coins, archaeological artifacts, and art produced during the period.

    C. Interviews and surveys conducted by the researcher.

    D. Statistics gathered as the result of the research's experiments.

The answer is A. Secondary sources are works written significantly after the period being studied and based upon primary sources. In this case, historians have studied artifacts of the time and drawn their conclusion and inferences. Primary sources are the basic materials that provide raw data and information. Students or researchers may use literature and other data they have collected to draw their own conclusions or inferences.

92. **In general, the most serious drawback of using a computer in writing is that (Skill 3.1, Average Rigor)**

    A. the copy looks so good that students tend to overlook major mistakes.

    B. the spell check and grammar programs discourage students from learning proper spelling and mechanics.

    C. the speed with which corrections can be made detracts from the exploration and contemplation of composing.

    D. the writer loses focus by concentrating on the final product rather than the details.

The answer is C. Because the process of revising is very quick with the computer, it can discourage contemplation, exploring, and examination, which are very important in the writing process.

93. **Which of the following is the least effective procedure for promoting consciousness of audience? (Skill 3.1, Average Rigor)**

    A. Pairing students during the writing process

    B. Reading all rough drafts before the students write the final copies

    C. Having students compose stories or articles for publication in school literary magazines or newspapers

    D. Writing letters to friends or relatives

The answer is B. Reading all rough drafts will not encourage the students to take control of their text and might even inhibit their creativity. On the contrary, pairing students will foster their sense of responsibility, and having them compose stories for literary magazines will boost their self-esteem as well as their organization skills.

94. **The new teaching intern is developing a unit on creative writing and is trying to encourage her freshman high school students to write poetry. Which of the following would not be an effective technique? (Skill 3.1, Average Rigor)**

   A. In groups, students will draw pictures to illustrate "The Love Song of J. Alfred Prufrock" by T.S. Eliot.

   B. Either individually or in groups, students will compose a song, writing lyrics that try to use poetic devices.

   C. Students will bring to class the lyrics of a popular song and discuss the imagery and figurative language.

   D. Students will read aloud their favorite poems and share their opinions of and responses to the poems.

The answer is A. While drawing is creative, it will not accomplish as much as the other activities to encourage students to write their own poetry. Furthermore, "The Love Song of J. Alfred Prufrock" is not a freshman-level poem. The other activities involve students in music and their own favorites, which will be more appealing.

95. **In this paragraph from a student essay, identify the sentence that provides a detail. (Skill 3.1 Rigorous)**

   (1) The poem concerns two different personality types and the human relation between them. (2) Their approach to life is totally different. (3) The neighbor is a very conservative person who follows routines. (4) He follows the traditional wisdom of his father and his father's father. (5) The purpose in fixing the wall and keeping their relationship separate is only because it is all he knows.

   A. Sentence 1

   B. Sentence 3

   C. Sentence 4

   D. Sentence 5

The answer is C. Sentence 4 provides a detail to sentence 3 by explaining how the neighbor follows routine. Sentence 1 is the thesis sentence, which is the main idea of the paragraph. Sentence 3 provides an example to develop that thesis. Sentence 4 is a reason that explains why.

96. To determine the credibility of information, researchers should do all of the following except (Skill 3.1, Rigorous)

    A. establish the authority of the document.

    B. disregard documents with bias.

    C. evaluate the currency and reputation of the source.

    D. use a variety of research sources and methods.

The answer is B. Keep an open mind. Researchers should examine the assertions, facts, and reliability of the information.

97. Which of the following situations is not an ethical violation of intellectual property? (Skill 3.1, Rigorous)

    A. A student visits ten different websites and writes a report to compare the costs of downloading music. He uses the names of the websites without their permission.

    B. A student copies and pastes a chart verbatim from the Internet but does not document it because it is available on a public site.

    C. From an online article found in a subscription database, a student paraphrases a section on the problems of music piracy. She includes the source in her Works Cited but does not provide an in-text citation.

    D. A student uses a comment from M. Night Shyamalan without attribution claiming the information is common knowledge.

The answer is A. In this scenario, the student is conducting primary research by gathering the data and using it for his own purposes. He is not violating any principle by using the names of the websites. In Answer B, students who copy and paste from the Internet without documenting the sources of their information are committing plagiarism, a serious violation of intellectual property. Even when a student puts information in her own words by paraphrasing or summarizing as in Answer C, the information is still secondary and must be documented. While dedicated movie buffs might consider anything that M. Night Shyamalan says to be common knowledge in Answer D, his comments are not necessarily known in numerous places or known by a lot of people.

98. Students have been asked to write a research paper on automobiles and have brainstormed a number of questions they will answer based on their research findings. Which of the following is not an interpretive question to guide research? (Skill 3.1, Rigorous)

   A. Who were the first ten automotive manufacturers in the United States?

   B. What types of vehicles will be used fifty years from now?

   C. How do automobiles manufactured in the United States compare and contrast with each other?

   D. What do you think is the best solution for the fuel shortage?

The answer is A. The question asks for objective facts. Answer B is a prediction that asks how something will look or be in the future, based on the way it is now. Answer C asks for similarities and differences, which is a higher-level research activity that requires analysis. Answer D is a judgment question that requires informed opinion.

99. In preparing a speech for a contest, your student has encountered problems with gender specific language. Not wishing to offend either women or men, she seeks your guidance. Which of the following is not an effective strategy? (Skill 3.1, Rigorous)

   A. Use the generic "he" and explain that people will understand and accept the male pronoun as all-inclusive.

   B. Switch to plural nouns and use "they" as the gender-neutral pronoun.

   C. Use passive voice so that the subject is not required.

   D. Use male pronouns for one part of the speech and then use female pronouns for the other part of the speech.

The answer is A. No longer is the male pronoun considered the universal pronoun. Speakers and writers should choose gender-neutral words and avoid nouns and pronouns that inaccurately exclude one gender or another.

100. For their research paper on the effects of the Civil War on American literature, students have brainstormed a list of potential online sources and are seeking your authorization. Which of these represent the strongest source? (Skill 3.1, Rigorous)

   A. http://www.wikipedia.org/

   B. http://www.google.com

   C. http://www.nytimes.com

   D. http://docsouth.unc.edu/southlit/civilwar.html

The answer is D. Sites with an "edu" domain are associated with educational institutions and tend to be more trustworthy for research information. Wikipedia has an "org" domain, which means it is a nonprofit. While Wikipedia may be appropriate for background reading, its credibility as a research site is questionable. Both Google and the New York Times are "com" sites, which are for profit. Even though this does not discredit their information, each site is problematic for researchers. With Google, students will get overwhelmed with hits and may not choose the most reputable sites for their information. As a newspaper, the New York Times would not be a strong source for historical information.

101. A formative evaluation of student writing (Skill 3.1, Rigorous)

   A. requires thorough markings of mechanical errors with a pencil or pen.

   B. making comments on the appropriateness of the student's interpretation of the prompt and the degree to which the objective was met.

   C. should require that the student hand in all the materials produced during the process of writing.

   D. several careful readings of the text for content, mechanics, spelling, and usage.

The answer is B. It is important to give students numerous experiences with formative evaluation (evaluation as the student writes the piece). Formative evaluation will assign points to every step of the writing process, even though it is not graded. The criteria for the writing task should be very clear, and the teacher should read each step twice. Responses should be non critical and supportive, and the teacher should involve students in the process of defining criteria, and make it clear that formative and summative evaluations are two distinct processes.

102. In preparing a report about William Shakespeare, students are asked to develop a set of interpretive questions to guide their research. Which of the following would not be classified as an interpretive question? (Skill 3.1, Rigorous)

    A. What would be different today if Shakespeare had not written his plays?

    B. How will the plays of Shakespeare affect future generations?

    C. How does the Shakespeare view nature in *A Midsummer's Night Dream* and *Much Ado About Nothing*?

    D. During the Elizabethan age, what roles did young boys take in dramatizing Shakespeare's plays?

The answer is D. This question requires research into the historical facts; Shakespeare in Love notwithstanding, women did not act In Shakespeare's plays, and their parts were taken by young boys. Answers A and B are hypothetical questions requiring students to provide original thinking and interpretation. Answer C requires comparison and contrast, which are interpretive skills.

103. In writing a report, Hector has to explain where acid rain comes from and what it has done to the environment. What is the most likely form of organizational structure? (Skill 3.2, Easy)

    A. Cause and effect

    B. Problem and solution

    C. Exposition

    D. Definition

The answer is A. This report would discuss what has caused acid rain and what effects acid rain has had on the environment. Although it could offer a solution, the report questions do not focus on that. Most report writing is expository because it provided information and an explanation. While a definition might be an important detail, it would not be the major organizational structure.

104. Explanatory or informative discourse is (Skill 3.2, Easy)

    A. exposition.

    B. narration.

    C. persuasion.

    D. description.

The answer is A. Exposition sets forth a systematic explanation of any subject. It can also introduce the characters of a literary work, and their situations in the story. Narration relates a sequence of events (the story) told through a process of narration (discourse), in which events are recounted in a certain order (the plot). Persuasion strives to convince either a character in the story or the reader.

105. Which of the following is not a technique of prewriting? (Skill 3.2, Easy)

    A. Clustering

    B. Listing

    C. Brainstorming

    D. Proofreading

The answer is D. Proofreading cannot be a method of prewriting, since it is done on already written texts only. Clustering, listing, and brainstorming are all prewriting strategies.

106. The following passage is written from which point of view? (Skill 3.2, Easy)

> As she mused the pitiful vision of her mother's life laid its spell on the very quick of her being —that life of commonplace sacrifices closing in final craziness. She trembled as she heard again her mother's voice saying constantly with foolish insistence: *Dearevaun Seraun! Dearevaun Seraun!**
>
> * "The end of pleasure is pain!" (Gaelic)

A. First person, narrator

B. Second person, direct address

C. Third person, omniscient

D. First person, omniscient

The answer is C. The passage is clearly in the third person (the subject is "she"), and it is omniscient since it gives the characters' inner thoughts.

107. Which of the following is most true of expository writing? (Skill 3.2, Easy)

A. It is mutually exclusive of other forms of discourse.

B. It can incorporate other forms of discourse in the process of providing supporting details.

C. It should never employ informal expression.

D. It should only be scored with a summative evaluation.

The answer is B. Expository writing sets forth an explanation or an argument about any subject and can use distinct or combined forms of discourse, a sign of academic literacy. This directly contradicts Answer A. Writing can use formal and informal language and can be evaluated in many subjective and objective ways.

108. Which of the following is not correct? (Skill 3.2, Easy)

    A. Because most students have wide access to media, teachers should refrain from using it in their classrooms to diminish the overload.

    B. Students can use CD-ROMs to explore information using a virtual reality experience.

    C. Teacher can make their instruction more powerful by using educational media.

    D. The Internet enables students to connect with people across cultures and to share interests.

The answer is A. Teachers can use media in productive ways to enrich instruction. Rather than ignoring it, educators should use a wide assortment of media for the benefit of their students.

109. Which of the following should students use to improve coherence of ideas within an argument? (Skill 3.2, Easy)

    A. Transitional words or phrases to show relationship of ideas.

    B. Conjunctions like "and" to join ideas together.

    C. Use direct quotes extensively to improve credibility.

    D. Adjectives and adverbs to provide stronger detail.

The answer is B. Transitional words and phrases are two-way indicators that connect the previous idea to the following idea. Sophisticated writers use transitional devices to clarify text (for example), to show contrast (despite), to show sequence (first, next), to show cause (because).

110. Which transition word would show contrast between these two ideas? (Skill 3.2, Average Rigor)

> We are confident in our skills to teach English. We welcome new ideas on this subject.

   A. We are confident in our skills to teach English, and we welcome new ideas on this subject.

   B. Because we are confident in our skills to teach English, we welcome new ideas on the subject.

   C. When we are confident in our skills to teach English, we welcome new ideas on the subject.

   D. We are confident in our skills to teach English; however, we welcome new ideas on the subject.

The answer is D. Transitional words, phrases and sentences help clarify meanings. In A, the transition word "and" introduces another equal idea. In Answer B, the transition word "because" indicates cause and effect. In Answer C, the transition word "when" indicates order or chronology. In Answer D, "however," shows that these two ideas contrast with each other.

111. In preparing students for their oral presentations, the instructor provided all of these guidelines, except one. Which is not an effective guideline? (Skill 3.2, Average Rigor)

   A. Even if you are using a lectern, feel free to move about. This will connect you to the audience.

   B. Your posture should be natural, not stiff. Keep your shoulders toward the audience.

   C. Gestures can help communicate as long as you don't overuse them or make them distracting.

   D. You can avoid eye contact if you focus on your notes. This will make you appear more knowledgeable.

The answer is D. Although many people are nervous about making eye contact, they should focus on two or three people at a time. Body language, such as movement, posture, and gestures, helps the speaker connect to the audience.

112. Which of the following statements indicates an instructional goal for using multimedia in the classroom? (Skill 3.2, Average Rigor)

    A. Audio messages invite the listener to form mental images consistent with the topic of the audio.

    B. Print messages appeal almost exclusively to the mind and push students to read with more thought.

    C. Listening to an audio message is more passive than reading a print message.

    D. Teachers who develop activities to foster a critical perspective on audiovisual presentation will decrease passivity.

The answer is D. Each of the statements is true but only the last one establishes a goal for using multimedia in the classroom.

113. What is the main form of discourse in this passage? (Skill 3.2, Average Rigor)

> It would have been hard to find a passer-by more wretched in appearance. He was a man of middle height, stout and hardy, in the strength of maturity; he might have been forty-six or seven. A slouched leather cap hid half his face, bronzed by the sun and wind, and dripping with sweat.

    A. Description

    B. Narration

    C. Exposition

    D. Persuasion

The answer is A. A description presents a thing or a person in detail, and tells the reader about the appearance of whatever it is presenting. Narration relates a sequence of events (the story) told through a process of narration (discourse), in which events are recounted in a certain order (the plot). Exposition is an explanation or an argument within the narration. It can also be the introduction to a play or a story. Persuasion strives to convince either a character in the story or the reader.

114. In literature, evoking feelings of pity or compassion is to create (Skill 3.2, Average Rigor)

   A. colloquy.

   B. irony.

   C. pathos.

   D. paradox

The answer is C. A very well known example of pathos is Desdemona's death in *Othello*, but there are many other examples of pathos. In *King Lear*, Cordelia accepts defeat with this line: "We are not the first / Who with best meaning have incurred the worst." A colloquy is a formal conversation. Irony is a discrepancy between what is expected and what occurs. A paradox is a contradictory statement.

115. Which of the following would not be a major concern in an oral presentation? (Skill 3.2, Average Rigor)

   A. Establishing the purpose of the presentation

   B. Evaluating the audience's demographics and psychographics.

   C. Creating a PowerPoint slide for each point.

   D. Developing the content to fit the occasion.

The answer is C. PowerPoint slides should be kept to a minimum of one slide per minute and should not overwhelm the presentation. The slides should be a supplement so that the speaker can accomplish the purpose. To reach that goal, the speaker should understand the makeup of the audience: demographics, such as age, education level or other quantifiable characteristic; and, psychographics, such as attitudes or values. Knowing the purpose and the audience will enable the speaker to develop the content to fit the occasion.

116. **Mr. Ledbetter has instructed his students to prepare a slide presentation that illustrates an event in history. Students are to include pictures, graphics, media clips and links to resources. What competencies will students exhibit at the completion of this project? (Skill 3.2, Rigorous)**

   A. Analyze the impact of society on media.

   B. Recognize the media's strategies to inform and persuade.

   C. Demonstrate strategies and creative techniques to prepare presentations using a variety of media.

   D. Identify the aesthetic effects of a media presentation.

The answer is B. Students will have learned how to use various media to convey a unified message.

117. **In the following excerpt from "Civil Disobedience," what type of reasoning does Henry David Thoreau use? (Skill 3.2, Rigorous)**

   Unjust laws exist; shall we be content to obey them, or shall we endeavor to amend them, and obey them until we have succeeded, or shall we transgress them at once? Men generally, under such a government as this, think that they ought to wait until they have persuaded the majority to alter them. They think that, if they should resist, the remedy would be worse than the evil. But it is the fault of the government itself that the remedy *is* worse than the evil. ... Why does it always crucify Christ, and excommunicate Copernicus and Luther, and pronounce Washington and Franklin rebels?

   --"Civil Disobedience" by Henry David Thoreau

   A. Ethical reasoning

   B. Inductive reasoning

   C. Deductive reasoning

   D. Intellectual reasoning

The answer is C. Deductive reasoning begins with a general statement that leads to the particulars. In this essay, Thoreau begins with the general question about what should be done about unjust laws. His argument leads to the government's role in suppressing dissent.

118. Which of the following is not a fallacy in logic? (Skill 3.2, Rigorous)

    A. All students in Ms. Suarez's fourth period class are bilingual.
       Beth is in Ms. Suarez's fourth period.
       Beth is bilingual.

    B. All bilingual students are in Ms. Suarez's class.
       Beth is in Ms. Suarez's fourth period.
       Beth is bilingual.

    C. Beth is bilingual.
       Beth is in Ms. Suarez's fourth period.
       All students in Ms. Suarez's fourth period are bilingual.

    D. If Beth is bilingual, then she speaks Spanish.
       Beth speaks French.
       Beth is not bilingual.

The correct answer is A. The second statement, or premise, is tested against the first premise. Both premises are valid and the conclusion is logical. In Answer B, the conclusion is invalid because the first premise does not exclude other students. In Answer C, the conclusion cannot be logically drawn from the preceding premises—you cannot conclude that all students are bilingual based on one example. In Answer D, the conclusion is invalid because the first premise is faulty.

119. Which of the following is an example of the post hoc fallacy? (Skill 3.2, Rigorous)

A. When the new principal was hired, student-reading scores improved; therefore, the principal caused the increase in scores.

B. Why are we spending money on the space program when our students don't have current textbooks?

C. You can't give your class a 10-minute break. Once you do that, we'll all have to give our students a 10-minute break.

D. You can never believe anything he says because he's not from the same country as we are.

The correct answer is A. A post hoc fallacy assumes that because one event preceded another, the first event caused the second event. In this case, student scores could have increased for other reasons. Answer B is a red herring fallacy in which one raises an irrelevant topic to side track from the first topic. In this case, the space budget and the textbook budget have little effect on each other. Answer C is an example of a slippery slope, in which one event is followed precipitously by another event. Answer D is an ad hominem ("to the man") fallacy in which a person is attacked rather than the concept or interpretation.

120. Identify the type of appeal used by Molly Ivins's in this excerpt from her essay "Get a Knife, Get a Dog, But Get Rid of Guns." (Skill 3.2, Rigorous)

As a civil libertarian, I, of course, support the Second Amendment. And I believe it means exactly what it says:
A well regulated militia being necessary to the security of a free state, the right of the people to keep and bear arms shall not be infringed.

A. Ethical

B. Emotional

C. Rational

D. Literary

The answer is A. An ethical appeal is using the credentials of a reliable and trustworthy authority. In this case, Ivins cites the Constitution. Pathos is an emotional appeal and logos is a rational appeal. Literature might appeal to you but it's not a rhetorical appeal.

121. **What is the common advertising technique used by these advertising slogans? (Skill 3.2, Rigorous)**

> "It's everywhere you want to be." - Visa
> "Have it your way." - Burger King
> "When you care enough to send the very best" - Hallmark
> "Be all you can be" – U.S. Army

A. Peer Approval

B. Rebel

C. Individuality

D. Escape

The answer is C. All of these ads associate products with people who can think and act for themselves. Products are linked to individual decision making. With peer approval, the ads would associate their products with friends and acceptance. For rebelling, the ads would associates products with behaviors or lifestyles that oppose society's norms. Escape would suggest the appeal of getting away from it all.

122. **In presenting a report to peers about the effects of Hurricane Katrina on New Orleans, the students wanted to use various media in their argument to persuade their peers that more needed to be done. Which of these would be the most effective? (Skill 3.2, Rigorous)**

    A. A PowerPoint presentation showing the blueprints of the levees before the flood and redesigned now for current construction..

    B. A collection of music clips made by the street performers in the French Quarter before and after the flood.

    C. A recent video showing the areas devastated by the floods and the current state of rebuilding.

    D. A collection of recordings of interviews made by the various government officials and local citizens affected by the flooding.

The answer is C. For maximum impact, a video would offer dramatic scenes of the devastated areas. A video by its very nature is more dynamic than a static PowerPoint presentation. Further, the condition of the levees would not provide as much impetus for change as seeing the devastated areas. Oral messages such as music clips and interviews provide another way of supplementing the message but, again, they are not as dynamic as video.

123. **Based on the excerpt below from Kate Chopin's short story "The Story of an Hour," what can students infer about the main character? (Skill 3.2, Rigorous)**

> She did not stop to ask if it were or were not a monstrous joy that held her. A clear and exalted perception enabled her to dismiss the suggestion as trivial. She knew that she would weep again when she saw the kind, tender hands folded in death; the face that had never looked save with love upon her, fixed and gray and dead. But she saw beyond that bitter moment a long procession of years to come that would belong to her absolutely. And she opened and spread her arms out to them in welcome.

A. She dreaded her life as a widow.

B. Although she loved her husband, she was glad that he was dead for he had never loved her.

C. She worried that she was too indifferent to her husband's death.

D. Although they had both loved each other, she was beginning to appreciate that opportunities had opened because of his death.

The answer is D. Dismissing her feeling of "monstrous joy" as insignificant, the young woman realizes that she will mourn her husband who had been good to her and had loved her. But that "long procession of years" does not frighten her; instead she recognizes that this new life belongs to her alone and she welcomes it with open arms.

124. Which part of a classical argument is illustrated in this excerpt from the essay "What Should Be Done About Rock Lyrics?" (Skill 3.2, Rigorous)

But violence against women is greeted by silence. It shouldn't be.

This does not mean censorship, or book (or record) burning. In a society that protects free expression, we understand a lot of stuff will float up out of the sewer. Usually, we recognize the ugly stuff that advocates violence against any group as the garbage it is, and we consider its purveyors as moral lepers. We hold our nose and tolerate it, but we speak out against the values it proffers.
--"What Should Be Done About Rock Lyrics?" Caryl Rivers

A. Narration

B. Confirmation

C. Refutation and concession

D. Summation

The answer is C. The author acknowledges refutes the idea of censorship and concedes that society tolerates offensive lyrics as part of our freedom of speech. Narration provides background material to produce an argument. In confirmation, the author details the argument with claims that support the thesis. In summation, the author concludes the argument by offering the strongest solution.

125. Using the selection below from Edgar Alan Poe's "The Tell-Tale Heart," what form of literary criticism would you introduce to high school students? (Skill 4.1, Average Rigor)

> And have I not told you that what you mistake for madness is but over-acuteness of the sense? --now, I say, there came to my ears a low, dull, quick sound, such as a watch makes when enveloped in cotton. I knew that sound well, too. It was the beating of the old man's heart. It increased my fury, as the beating of a drum stimulates the soldier into courage.

A. Marxist

B. Feminist

C. Psychoanalytic

D. Classic

The answer is C. Poe's writings focus on the workings of the human mind and would provide a clear introduction of Freudian literary analysis. Marxist criticism focuses on class conflict and the exploitation of the workers, which is not evident in this short story. Feminist criticism focuses on gender roles, which is also not obvious in this short story. Classic criticism is not a recognized type of literary criticism; however, this story could be analyzed according to the New Criticism where the story would be studied as a work of literature.

XAMonline, INC. 21 Orient Ave. Melrose, MA 02176

Toll Free number 800-509-4128

TO ORDER Fax 781-662-9268 OR www.XAMonline.com

WEST SERIES

PO#   Store/School:

Address 1:

Address 2 (Ship to other):

City, State Zip

Credit card number_____-_____-_____-_____   expiration_____

EMAIL _____

PHONE   FAX

ISBN	TITLE	Qty	Retail	Total
978-1-58197-638-0	WEST-B Basic Skills			
978-1-58197-609-0	WEST-E Biology 0235			
978-1-58197-693-9	WEST-E Chemistry 0245			
978-1-58197-566-6	WEST-E Designated World Language: French Sample Test 0173			
978-1-58197-557-4	WEST-E Designated World Language: Spanish 0191			
978-1-58197-614-4	WEST-E Elementary Education 0014			
978-1-58197-636-6	WEST-E English Language Arts 0041			
978-1-58197-634-2	WEST-E General Science 0435			
978-1-58197-637-3	WEST-E Health & Fitness 0856			
978-1-58197-635-9	WEST-E Library Media 0310			
978-1-58197-674-8	WEST-E Mathematics 0061			
978-1-58197-556-7	WEST-E Middle Level Humanities 0049, 0089			
978-1-58197-568-0	WEST-E Physics 0265			
978-1-58197-563-5	WEST-E Reading/Literacy 0300			
978-1-58197-552-9	WEST-E Social Studies 0081			
978-1-58197-639-7	WEST-E Special Education 0353			
978-1-58197-633-5	WEST-E Visual Arts Sample Test 0133			
	SUBTOTAL		**Ship**	$8.25
	FOR PRODUCT PRICES VISIT WWW.XAMONLINE.COM		**TOTAL**	

CPSIA information can be obtained at www.ICGtesting.com
Printed in the USA
BVOW050244140513

320655BV00004B/207/P

9 781607 871392